NOTHING PERSONAL
IT'S ONLY BUSINESS

ISBN: 978-0-615-76979-0

Interior print layout by Booknook.biz.

NOTHING PERSONAL
IT'S ONLY BUSINESS

MICHAEL J. MC MAHON

Acknowledgements

A special thanks to my wife, Elva, for all the encouragement and help. She was always there, every step of the way. Without her love and care, there would never have been a book.

To Rhianette, thanks for all the help and time that you gave to me.

To Vionette, thanks for your help and encouragement.

To Coco, many thanks for all the help and ideas that you gave me.

To Deanna, with all your bright ideas and great writing skills.

Rhianette, Deanna and Olivia. Cover design.

Preface

Here I am, nearly at the end of my career and my life, where did all the time go? It went by so fast. As I look back on my life, it's like watching a movie picture. All the things that happened along the way are kind of hard to believe. I guess I could say that I'm a product of the streets. When I was a young guy I used to run around with the guys in my neighborhood. We grew up thinking that the wise guys were our hero's and we all wanted to be just like them. The neighborhood was mostly Italian immigrants and many of them were related and they all knew each other, which made us all very closely knit. It was a very crowded and lively neighborhood with shops and restaurants and festivals and feasts going on most of the time.

When the war broke out, most of us young guys in the neighborhood joined up and a lot of the older and married guys got drafted. I was sent to Fort Dix in New Jersey for basic training. After basic, I wound up in the Infantry and was sent to Europe. I was promoted to Corporal and I received the bronze star and some other medals. That was something. I never got anything in my life and now I was somebody. When the war was over, I was sent home.

I was treated like a hero by everyone in the neighborhood. They threw a parade for me and everyone was yelling, that's the Pellagrino boy and look, he's a Corporal and look at all those ribbons he's got on his chest. Everywhere I went, people wouldn't let me spend a dime and everyone started calling me Corporal and it stuck to this day. I was respected by all our neighbors and friends everywhere I went.

I started working in the city and the best job I could find was pushing a rack of clothes around the garment center. There wasn't much money to be made in those days, but it paid the rent.

While I was working downtown, I met a few guys that were hooked up in the numbers racket. After getting to know them a little better, they asked me if I would be interested in meeting a few of the bosses involved in the rackets. I said sure, that's when I got started on my long road to having my own family.

I finally got in with a family up in the Bronx, and I was made in a few years. Now I was a man of respect. I really felt I had arrived. The money started rolling in. I got myself a nice car and a few suits. I was getting known around town as a stand up guy and I was introduced to all the big bosses.

One day while I was visiting my mother up in the Bronx, a few of my mothers friends stopped by and I was introduced to their daughter. She was the most beautiful girl I had ever seen. Her name was Josephine Latronica.

When Josephine and her parents left, I asked my mother all about her. My mother told me that she was nineteen and was going to college and she asked if I liked Josephine?

Yeah, Mom, I like her.

Would you like to take her out to a movie sometime?

Yeah, I sure would.

Well, I'll see what I can do.

So, the next time I went to see my mother, she told me that Josephine would like to go to the movie with me.

Josephine and me went out on our first date that following Saturday. We started seeing each other steady. I never told Josephine that I was involved with the rackets. I told her that I worked for a rich businessman and I was his chauffeur. Being with her was wonderful and we were getting hot and heavy.

One day her mother told my mother that they were moving and that Josephine wouldn't be seeing me again.

I was moving right along in the Family and I got promoted to Captain and then I started to make more money that I ever dreamed of.

I had my own crew and was given control of some of the family numbers and sports and other operations. Whenever I would go to Little Italy or Harlem or to Brooklyn or to the Zerega Club in the Bronx, men and woman would point me out and say, that's Corporal.

A turf war broke out between our Family and another Family down in the south Bronx and I got shot in the back. After I got out of the hospital my back started giving me a lot of pain. The doctor's told me there was nothing that could be done about it.

The boss of my Family called me one day and asked if I could step up and take over our Family. He was told he had cancer and that he had about a year or two to live. I told him that I could handle it. He gave me his blessing and I was made the Boss of the Family.

During those early years my back pain got so bad that I could hardly walk and I had to resort to getting around in a wheelchair.

One of the best things that ever happened to me was Sally. We got married and she's always been there through thick and thin. Sally would always encourage me, she got me through my tough years. She never complained and she never interfered with my business. When I couldn't walk much anymore and had to use a wheelchair she took care of me. I don't think that I could have ever made it without Sally.

Yeah, I look back on all those years and it's nearly over. Was it all worth it? Well, I made a lot of money but so did a lot of people but most of them are dead and buried. I sometimes wonder if I had gone another way, how would things have turned out?

If I were to give advice to anyone, I would tell them to forget about getting into this business. Once you're in, you can never get out. No sense complaining, it's the life that I chose.

Chapter 1

It's Tuesday night. Chris, Tony, Lou, Jimmy and Al meet at the Allerton Steak House up in the Bronx. Carl, the manager is there and he takes them to their regular table. There's the usual bunch sitting at the bar and a few in the dining room. They all wave to each other and a few come by the table to say hello. It's a friendly place where a lot of the wise guys come to have a bite to eat or drink and have some fun. Carl brings a bottle of wine over and has a drink with them. The waiter suggests the veal Parmesan or the steaks and it's a must for the pasta va sou. Everyone orders and they go on with their small talk.

Did you hear about Ernie, asks Lou? He's getting out next week after 8 years, great guy. I hear that he'll be stopping by next Tuesday and Corporal will be throwing a bash for him, don't want to miss that one.

Corporal is the Underboss under Carlino and this is really his place. He has to use a wheelchair most of the time because he was shot in the back years ago in a turf war. But, when he comes into the restaurant all the made guys go to him and pay their respects and also everyone else that knows him. He runs a lot of the operations in Las Vegas and when all these well known entertainers that work out there come to New York, they make sure they come up here to pay their respects to Corporal. They don't want to get on the wrong side of him.

Everybody is laughing and kidding around and having a good time and the dinner was very good.

Al asks, how about going over to this new place that just opened? It's called Conrad's Cloud Room and it's right over the Whitestone Bridge across from La Guardia Airport.

Hey, that's a good idea, lets go, yells Tony.

They get their coats and take care of the bill. Everyone gets into Tony's car and they get there in about 20 minutes.

Tony gives the keys to the parking lot attendant and they go in.

Conrad's Cloud Room looks like a place right out of Las Vegas. The place is packed.

Al takes care of the maitre d' and they get a table right up front. The band is great and the place is jumping. The broads are all over the place and they're beauties.

A cocktail waitress comes to the table.

Hi, what can I get you fellas?

Boy, she's a knockout with curly red hair and a face like an angel. She's wearing a little cocktail costume and it's all the way up to her ass. Right away, everyone is trying to hit on her, but she's heard all the bullshit before.

She takes their order and serves the drinks and tells them that she'll be back to see how they're doing.

Al and Lou are out on the dance floor dancing with a couple of bimbos and Tony is talking to Chris about what a beauty the cocktail waitress is.

Conrad, the owner is making the rounds and shaking hands with everyone. Conrad is a black guy and everyone seems to like him. He stops by their table to say hello.

They compliment Conrad on his place and wish him luck.

After a few more drinks Tony takes care of the check and they all tip the waitress. Tony hands her a 50 dollar bill and she smiles at him.

My name is Amy, Amy Collins. I work nights, Tuesday to Saturday, and I hope to see you again.

I'm Anthony Graco, and I'll be back to see you.

They all get into Tony's car and he drives back to the Bronx and stops at Gino's Italian Restaurant for a drink. When they finish, Tony drops them off at their cars.

Everyone gets into their cars and go home except Lou. He heads up to the Club Paddock in Yonkers. It's near the Yonkers race track where a lot of the Yonkers and Bronx wise guys hang out. It's owned by Moe Silverman, he's an associate in the Corporal family.

Lou parks his car and goes in and he spots Moe and they have a drink.

Moe asks, how do you like the blue girl that's dancing up there on the stage? I'm trying her out for a few days. The reason that he calls her a blue girl is that they don't like black people up in Yonkers.

Lou answers, she's OK.

So whats happening, Lou?

I got a little problem with a guy down in the city and I was wondering if you could help me out.

Sure, what's the problem?

The guy owes me some money.

Chapter 2

Chris arrives at his Funeral Home about 9:30 in the morning and he looks around and everything seems OK. He checks his messages, nothing important, so he picks up the newspaper to see what's happening. There's a knock on his office door.

Hey, Chris. how you doing? It's his friend Sal.

What brings you around so early in the morning.

Sal's a very wealthy guy and a very shrewd investor.

Do you have a few minutes? I just want to talk to you about something.

Sure, Sal. Let me close the door so we can talk.

Chris, I just found out about a piece of property over in the Pelham section that's up for sale at a great price and it's going to be rezoned for commercial use. I've had my eye on that property for awhile. The guy that told me about it is in the Bronx Borough Presidents Office and I have an in with Stanley Shaffer, the only problem is, somebody else is interested in it too and Stanley Shaffer is into this guy for plenty.

Chris asks, what do you want with that property?

Chris, I got a bunch of doctors that are looking to open a Hospital in the Bronx and they're really serious about this and since Medicare started, everybody and their brothers are looking to get into the act. The guy that's interested in that property don't know about the rezoning yet. If he's out of the picture, you and I can make a fortune.

Are you interested, Chris?

Sounds pretty good to me, tell me more.

OK, but we have to act fast on this one. If this guy is out of the picture, there's no problem. We buy the property before it's rezoned, get the doctors in and have Shaffer give us the approval to build the hospital. Sal asks, what do you think?

You've always been right in the past, lets do it.

How about some lunch over at City Island and then we can talk more on my boat?

OK, lets go.

Have you ever been here, Sal?

No, I haven't.

Well, you're going to like this place. They go into the City Island Clam House and get a table up front overlooking the water. The waiter comes over and hands them a menu and tells them that the snapper just got delivered.

OK, we'll have the snapper. Would you like a bottle of white wine to go with your meals?

Yeah, that will be fine, thank you.

I'll get in touch with Sonny Falco down in Harlem and see what I can come up with, maybe have a couple of his guys go over and talk to that guy that wants that property. What do you think, Sal?

Maybe, Shaffer owes him a lot and this guy might want everything that's owed to him before he pulls out.

How much does Shaffer owe this guy?

I don't know, but I heard that it's more than 100,000.

Wow, I was thinking that we could take care of it by offering him something just to get rid of him, but that's way too much.

Yeah, maybe they could scare him and he'll back out of this deal, but Shaffer still owes him and Shaffer could be pressured into going into a different deal and if it gets out about rezoning, the price goes up. Then this guy will buy the property no matter how much it costs. Once this property goes commercial it'll be worth 10 times more than it is now.

The waiter arrives and serves the snapper and pours the wine. Will there be anything else, gentlemen?

No, thank you.

When they finish their meal, Sal asks, how about a little espresso?

Yeah, that's a good idea.

Hey, waiter, bring us some espresso and give me the check.

Chris, it might be a bad idea to have someone talk to this guy, then the cat's out of the bag.

Let me ask you, Sal. How sure are you about Shaffer, will he make sure that we get the permit to build?

Yeah, if that guy is out of way and we take care of Shaffer, then it's a done deal.

Lets get out of here and go over to my boat.

Sal takes care of the check and they go over to Ray's Boat Yard.

They go on board and down into the cabin.

Hey, you want a drink?

Yeah, sure.

Chris pours a couple of drinks and they continue to talk. Well, Sal. The only way I see it, we'll have to go all the way with this. If we don't, we'll have all sorts of problems.

What do you mean, all the way, Chris?

Just what I said, we'll have to have this guy whacked.

Sal thinks for a minute, well, if there's no other way, then we'll have to have him whacked.

OK, I'll set up a meeting with Sonny. Lets finish our drinks and get going.

Chapter 3

Chris gets home about 6 o'clock and his wife is there and she's cooking supper. Hi, honey, how was your day?

He kisses her, pretty good, how was your day?

Well, Eddie isn't doing too well in school. The principal called and wants to see one of us about him. It seems that he skipped classes a couple of times and his grades have fallen off.

Where is he right now?

He just called and said he's on his way home. Now don't get angry, lets see what he has to say first. I'm certain that we can work this out with him.

Yeah, OK, honey. How about Francine, is everything alright with her?

She's fine, she's studying for her finals and getting ready to go to college.

Did she decide on which college she's going to?

Not yet, she's still checking a few things out, but don't worry about her, she'll be fine.

Eddie walks in. Hi, Mom. Hi, Dad.

Everyone sits down at the table and Eileen serves supper.

Mom. Those pork chops and spaghetti were great. What's for desert?

Eileen brings out apple pie and ice cream.

Eddie, Mom tells me that your principal called and would like to see your mother or me to have a talk with him. Seems that your grades are not so good and you've skipped some classes, what's happening?

Well, Dad. I was having a little problem with one of the guys at school but we straightened everything out. I didn't want to worry you or Mom about it.

Chris asks, are you sure everything's all right? You know you can come to us with anything.

Yeah, everything's fine now.

Do you want to talk to us about anything?

Naw, everything's OK.

Alright, but your mother or me still have to go and see your principal.

OK, Dad.

It's about 3 am and Chris and his wife are sound asleep and the phone rings. Chris picks up the phone.

Hello, Chris. It's Carmine. Sorry to call you at this time of the morning but something happened and I need your help.

Hold on a moment until I get the other phone. OK, Carmine. I'm back, what's going on?

I'm at my brother in laws home over in Kew Gardens and my brother in law died and his doctor is going to sign the death certificate in the morning. The medical examiner said for you to go ahead and move the body and you can pick up the death certificate from his doctor in the morning.

OK, what's your brother in laws address and what's the medical examiners name and phone number? OK, I got it. I'll send Bob over and he'll take care of everything. He should be there in about an hour. Give me the phone number where you are.

Chris calls Bob and gives him the information and tells Bob to pick up the death certificate in the morning and that Dr. Brodsky, the Medical Examiner, gave us permission to move the body.

Bob gets to the house at about 4:15 am and Carmine takes him and his assistant down to the recreation room in the basement. The body is on a small sofa with his feet hanging over one end of the sofa and his head hanging over the other end. The body's eyes are popping out of their sockets and his tongue is swollen and bulging out of his mouth. Bob opens the stretcher and starts to put a sheet around the body when he notices what appears to be a rope mark around the body's neck. Bob then wraps the body up and he and his assistant put the body into the stretcher.

OK, Carmine, we're leaving now.

Everything alright?

Yep, everything's fine, good night.

When they're gone. Carmine tells his cousin. Call John in the morning and tell him everything is taken care of and I'll be over to see him tomorrow.

Chapter 4

Chris parks in front of the Funeral Home in Harlem and goes inside. Hi, Kenny, he's the manager of the Funeral home. Is everything OK? Did anyone go for that death certificate yet?

Yeah, and the family will be here soon with Carmine to pick out the casket and finish the arrangements.

OK, I have to make a few phone calls, let me know when Carmine gets here. Chris goes into his office and calls Sonny.

Hey, Sonny. It's Chris. That thing we were talking about, there's been a change. Are you going to be at your place this afternoon about 2 o'clock?

Yeah, I'll be here.

OK, Sonny. I'll see you.

There's a knock on the door. Carmine is here.

Hey, Carmine. Come in and have a seat.

I have all the papers and I'm going to make the arrangements for the family.

OK, let's see the papers that you have.

He hands them over to Chris and he looks at them. Yep, everything's here except the death certificate and I have somebody picking that up now.

Fine, but first I have to tell you something. My brother in law met with a little accident and we got it all cleared with the medical examiner so it appears he died naturally. And the doctor was told to go ahead and sign the death certificate.

As long as the doctor signs the death certificate, there's no problem. How about his family?

No problem, everything's OK.

They finish making the arrangements and Chris tells him, the body will be ready for viewing this evening.

About 10 minutes later Bob arrives with the death certificate.

Hey, Chris. got a minute? I have to talk to you.

Yeah, sure. Come in, Bob. Chris closes the office door. What's up?

When I got to the house in Kew Gardens there was something strange. The body was on a small sofa down in the recreation room, but his head was hanging over the arm rest and his eyes were popping out of their sockets and the guys tongue was swollen and bulging out of his mouth. And Chris, there was a rope mark around his neck. I didn't say anything. I just wrapped him up and put him in the stretcher and left. Now, when I got to the doctor's office this morning for the death certificate, he told me that he never saw this guy and that the medical examiner told him to sign the Death Certificate. Then he asked me what to put down as the cause of death. I told him to write Coronary Heart Disease and ASHD. (arterio sclerotic heart disease).

You did well, as long as the medical examiner told the doctor to sign the death certificate and he did, that's the end of that. How about some lunch, Bob?

Chapter 5

Chris drives down to Pleasant Avenue and parks outside Sonny Falco's place. Sonny is the boss of the family and they run all the action in Harlem. There's no one there except an old guy behind the bar.

Hi, is Sonny here?

Are you Chris?

Yeah, I'm Chris.

Have a seat, Sonny will be back in a few minutes. I'm Benny, he's expecting you. Would you like to have a drink while your waiting?

No thanks, but I'll have a glass of water. Boy, this place has been here for a long time.

Yeah, says Benny, this was quite a place.

Hey, here comes Sonny.

How you doin, Chris? You been waiting very long?

No, I just got here.

Lets go into my office. We'll be in the back for awhile, Benny.

Would you like a drink?

No thanks, Sonny.

OK, Chris, what's up?

I had this little thing come up and it started to come apart because of this guy that we were talking about. Well, yesterday, this guys luck turned sour and he's got some big trouble with the government. He was arrested on tax fraud and income tax evasion and the IRS put a freeze on all his assets. We won't have to do anything now, Sonny, but I want to thank you for being there for me.

Hey, Chris. No problem. I'm glad that I could have been of help to you.

Sonny, if there's anything I can ever do for you, just say the word. How about we have dinner some evening?

Yeah, that would be nice, answers Sonny.

OK, I'll call you next week and we'll set up an evening for us. I'll be going now. Thanks a million, Sonny.

Nice meeting you, Benny.

Chris goes back to his office and Kenny tells him that Sal called and to call him at this number.

Sal answers.

Hey, Sal. this is Chris. How did you make out?

Everything's fine. How about meeting me at the Boston Road Diner in the morning about 9:30.

OK, Sal. By the way, l saw our friend Sonny, everything is fine, see you in the morning.

Kenny tells him that Carmine and his family will be coming in about 5 pm and everything's set. It's nearly 5 o'clock now and here they come.

Hi, Carmine. We're upstairs in the Big Chapel, follow me please.

They follow Chris upstairs and they all start to crowd around the casket. The women start to cry like a bunch of banshees and then all of them start in and some of them start touching the body and then one of the men pulls on the shirt collar and he yells out that there are rope marks on his neck.

All hell breaks loose and they're shouting and screaming that they know who killed him and that they're going to kill whoever did this.

All of a sudden, this small heavy set guy steps into the doorway and two big guys are standing on either side of him. They have enormous bodies with small heads, just like gumba's and the small guy is smoking a cigarette.

Everyone in the room becomes very quiet and he goes over to the widow who is sitting on the sofa and he stares at her for a few moments. He's still smoking his cigarette and then he asks the widow. "Everything alright?"

She's terror stricken.

She trembling as she answers, yes.

He drops his cigarette in front of the widow and grinds it out on the carpet, turns and walks out followed by his two gumba's.

He is well known. He is the Godfather. There was no more trouble at the Funeral Home.

Chapter 6

Lou, have a seat and tell me more about this guy, asks Moe.

He owns Wilson Meats and the meat plant is down on 125th street under the highway. Could you send a couple of guys to him and get the money he owes me?

Lou, let me ask you a few things. Did you try to get the money?

Yeah, a couple of times, but he keeps giving me this bullshit that business is bad and the last time I went to see him he said not to bother him anymore and that he'll get in touch with me when he has the money and don't call him, he'll call me.

Lou, how much does he owe you?

He owes me 75,000.

How did he get so far into the hole?

He's a heavy gambler and he likes the ponies.

OK, Lou. Where can we get hold of him?

He stays late at his place every Friday night.

They all work until about 9 o'clock and then he leaves after they're all gone.

OK, Lou. we'll pay him a visit this Friday night.

Thanks Moe, is there anything you need?

Not right now. I'll call and let you know what's happening.

Lou leaves and drives home, relieved that Moe is taking care of things.

Moe calls Timmy, his enforcer, and asks him to stop by.

OK, I'll be there in a little while.

Things are starting to pick up at the club and Moe goes over to the bar and has a drink. People are really starting to come in now and Moe is greeting everyone.

Timmy shows up and they go into Moe's office.

How's everything, Timmy?

Not bad, the wife came down with the flu but the Doctor said she'll be back to normal in about a week.

I'm glad to hear that she'll be OK.

Timmy, we have to pay somebody a visit on Friday night, so get hold of one of the guys and we'll meet here about 6 o'clock. Make sure there's no drinking before we go. One more thing, make sure you guys are packing, just in case.

On Friday, Moe gets to the club around 4 pm and checks on things. Friday is usually a busy night and he wants to make sure things are ready before he leaves. About 6 o'clock, Timmy and Gingy walk into the club.

Lets go into the office. Sit down, boys, here's what's happening. We're going to see this guy about some money that he owes a friend of mine. We talk to him and if he doesn't give us the money right away we'll rough him up a little bit so that he gets the message. Are the two of you packing?

Yep, we're all set.

I want to collect the money tonight and he's not expecting anything to happen. Also, there's going to be a lot of money there, it's pay day and the money from sales is there too. The guy might have a piece on him, so lets pat him down so there's no trouble, understand? OK, lets get going.

They get on the Westside Highway and get off at 125th street and park across the street away from the trucks.

They get out and go into the meat plant. Everybody's gone. The place is empty except for Wilson sitting in his office. They go straight to his office and barge in.

Wilson is startled and caught off guard.

What are you guys doing in here?

We're here to collect the money you owe Lou and we want it right now.

Hey, wait a minute, you can't bust in here like this.

Shut up, and just get the money.

There's no money here right now.

Don't give me any of that bullshit, tell us where the money is.

I told you, I don't have the money now.

OK, boys. Refresh his memory.

Timmy and Gingy pat him down.

Hey, look at this. He's got a piece.

Gingy gives it to Moe and they go to work on Wilson.

That's enough for now. Where's the money?

Screw you and he spits in Moe's face.

Son of a bitch, teach him a lesson.

Timmy and Gingy go to work on him again.

Hold up, we don't want to kill him.

Now, you ready to give us the money?

Please, please, no more. The money's in a strong box over there under the floor boards.

OK, boys, go get the money.

They pull up the floor boards and there's the strong box. They hand it to Moe and he opens it up and takes the money out and counts it. There's over 200,000 in the box.

I thought you said you didn't have any money here.

What kind of a machine is that over there?

Timmy looks, it's a hamburger grinder.

Spit in my face, will ya. OK. boys, turn that hamburger machine on and feed him to it feet first. It starts with a loud roar and it sounds like it's grinding rocks.

No, no, please don't, he keeps pleading. He's screaming and yelling and crying as Timmy and Gingy pick him up and put him in the grinder feet first.

Chapter 7

Hey, Sally. Are you ready yet? Corporal yells out in his gravely voice, we gotta get down to the club. I gotta take care of some business, so hurry up.

OK, Sweetie Pie, I'll be ready in a minute. Sally brings his wheelchair into the living room and helps him into it.

OK, lets get going.

Sally pushes the wheelchair to the elevator and they get on.

Be careful getting off this thing, I don't wanna fall like the last time.

Sally is very careful handling him and his wheelchair this time. She doesn't want to have him going ballistic again.

Hi, Boss. Hi, Sally. Vito helps Corporal and Sally into the car. Vito is Corporal's driver and he's a made man and a Captain in Corporal's family. They've been together for years. Vito folds up the wheelchair and puts it into the trunk and he gets into the car.

Where to Corporal?

Take us to the club.

OK, Boss. Vito starts the car and off they go. They drive cross town to Arthur Avenue, the little Italy of the Bronx. He parks in front of the Zerega Fish and Hunt Club and he opens the car door and helps Sally out and he goes back to help Corporal into the wheelchair.

Hey, Sally. Go open the door, Vito's gonna wheel me into the club.

OK, Honey.

They go inside and everyone comes over to Corporal and hug and kiss him. Great to see you, Boss. You look great, we missed you. Then they all say hello to Sally and hug Vito.

Corporal is pleased and happy to see everyone and Vito wheels him to his table.

Tiny comes over and asks if he would like to have anything?

Yeah, Tiny, how about a little espresso with a slice of lemon peel and some anisette on the side?

Sure, anything else, Corporal?

Naw, thanks, that's fine.

Vito, take Sally over to Bronxville so she can do a little shopping. Call me before you start back, I have to take care of some business, kabich?

OK. Boss.

Sally, Vito's gonna drive you over to Bronxville so you can do some shopping, take your time, I gotta take care of a few things, so I'm gonna be a little while.

OK, Honey.

Sally takes off to do a little shopping.

Tiny comes back with the espresso. Thanks, Tiny.

Hey, Jimmy. Come over here.

Jimmy comes over and sits down.

Corporal begins to hold court. Everyone drifts into the other room without being told.

How's things going with the number's over at Boston Post Road?

Fine, answers Jimmy.

Well, why are you guys coming up short the past two weeks?

I don't know, seems like we're losing a lot of the regular's.

Anything unusual going on around there?

I heard there's a couple of molyams doing business out of the projects, but no one seems to know exactly where, or maybe things are just a little tight and they don't have the money to play.

OK, Jimmy, keep your eyes and ears open and keep me posted. By the way, Ernie is out and he'll be around in a couple of days. I'm sending him over to you, so show him around. I'm moving you up, but I want you to keep this to yourself, got it?

Now, send Al in here on your way out, and remember, mums the word about everything we spoke about.

Hey, Al. Corporal wants to see you.

Hi, Corporal. How you doing?

Good. Have a seat. How's everything with the sports action?

Fine, no problems. We picked up a few heavy hitters, and business is picking up. Al hands Corporal a fat envelope and he looks inside. Looks good. Do you need anything?

Naw, everything is going nice.

I'm throwing a little bash for Ernie next week at the Allerton and I'll let you know when a few days ahead of time. Bring your crew along, I'd like them to meet Ernie and give him a big welcome home.

Swell, Corporal. I know they'll like that.

Keep up the good work. Send Moe in.

Hi, Corporal. Good to see you.

I heard that you took care of that little matter downtown.

Yeah, all taken care of as Moe hands Corporal a big envelope.

Corporal puts it in the inside pocket of his suit coat.

How's business at the Paddock?

It seems to be picking up.

Anything I can help you with, Moe?

Well, maybe Corporal. I was thinking about a little shylock action. There's some opportunities right now, if it's alright with you.

Let me talk to some people and make sure we're not stepping on anybody's toes.

OK, Corporal, thanks.

Moe, don't forget, I'm throwing a bash for Ernie at the Allerton and I'll let you know when a few days before. It's a welcome home party and I expect to see you there.

You bet, Corporal, I wouldn't miss that for anything.

Moe, on your way out, send Lou in here.

Sure Corporal, see ya.

Hey, Lou. Corporal wants to see you.

How you doin, Lou? Have a seat.

Lou hands Corporal an envelope.

How's that window contract coming along, Lou?

Everything's right on track, we'll be signing all the contracts with the city, the unions and the sub contractors.

Sounds good, everything else alright?

So far, so good, Corporal.

Don't forget the bash I'm throwing for Ernie at the Allerton. He's home now and I'll let you know when a few days ahead of time. I'll expect you there.

I'll be there with bell's on.

Lou, do me a favor and wheel me out to the front room. I want to talk to the rest of the guys for awhile.

Corporal is talking to the guys and having a good time and everyone seems to be in a great mood.

Vito calls and asks Corporal if he and Sally should come back to the club now.

Yeah, Vito. Come on back now, how's Sally?

She's very happy and she did a lot of shopping.

Good, see you in a little while.

Chapter 8

Chris is up and the kids are getting ready to go to school and Eileen is going to the hairdresser. See you later and Eileen kisses Chris. Have a good day, and they all run out the door. The phone rings and it's Sal.

Hey, Chris. It's me Sal. Can we get together later on today?

Sure, how about 2 o'clock at the Boston Road Diner? I gotta take care of a funeral downtown first.

OK, Chris, see you at 2 o'clock.

He has a fast cup of coffee and heads to Harlem. He parks his car across the street from the Funeral Home and goes in.

Hi, Kenny. Is everything alright?

Yep, the driver's and the pallbearers are all here. Here's all the papers and checks and the petty cash.

Is Carmine upstairs?

Yeah, he's here too.

Chris goes upstairs and spots Carmine talking to the widow. He goes over and says hello to her and he asks Carmine if he could speak to him for a moment. Lets go downstairs to the office. They go into the office and Chris closes the door. Is everything alright, Carmine?

Yeah, so far, so good.

OK, we'll start in a few minutes and head for the church. Now, Carmine. Stay with the widow and I'll be right next to you all the way.

They go back upstairs and the Priest arrives and he starts saying prayers. When he's finished, he goes over to the widow and he speaks to her for a minute.

Chris helps her to get up from the sofa and walks her to the casket to say a last goodbye to her husband.

She starts sobbing quietly as he's leading her away, then all the family members start screaming and crying. That lasts for a few minutes and the pallbearers start leading everyone out to the waiting limousines. When everyone's in the limousine's, they start taking out all the flowers and putting them into the flower cars.

Chris closes the casket and the pallbearers come over and pick up the casket. Chris leads them out onto the street and the pallbearers take the casket off their shoulders and put it into the hearse.

The streets are lined with people from all over Harlem. There's police cars up and down the street and all the way over to the church.

The hearse starts moving and all the flower cars, limousines and private cars follow. There must be over 50 cars in the funeral procession. They arrive at the church and the pallbearers take the casket out and lift it onto their shoulders.

Everyone follows Chris up the stairs and into the church.

After the church service is over, Chris assists the widow and everyone follows them out. The pallbearers put the casket into the hearse and everyone goes to their limousines and cars and follow the hearse to the cemetery.

They arrive at the cemetery and the drivers help everyone out of the cars and direct them to the grave.

The casket is already on the lowering device over the open grave. A lot of the mourners are standing close to the edge of the grave and the priest starts saying the last prayers. Then the cemetery workers start lowering the casket into the grave. The widow and some of the relatives start crying and carrying on and some of them start pushing closer to the grave.

There's an old guy standing at the edge of the grave and he's making a big racket and screaming that he wants to jump into the grave and he's yelling, let me go, let me jump into the grave so I can go with him.

Suddenly, the old guy yells out. HEY, DON'T PUSH.

Chapter 9

It's 9 am and Corporal is already up and on the phone.

Vito, it's Corporal, are you up yet?

Yeah, good morning, Corporal.

Vito, pick me up. How long will it take you?

About 30 minutes.

Good, I'll be downstairs waiting for you.

Sally, bring the wheelchair here.

OK, Sweetie, I'll be right there. Sally pushes the wheelchair over to the sofa where Corporal is sitting and helps him into the wheelchair.

OK, Sally, take me downstairs. Vito's going to pick me up in a few minutes.

They get on the elevator and get off at the lobby and Sally wheels him into the lobby.

Hi, Corporal. Hi, Sally.

Good morning, Vito. Lets get going, see you later Sally.

Vito wheels Corporal out of the building while Sally holds the door open.

I want to sit up front.

Where to, Boss?

Over to Ernie's place, he'll be waiting for us.

OK, Boss. They drive over to Sherman Avenue and there's Ernie waiting in front of his building. Vito parks in front of the building and Ernie gets into the rear seat.

Hi, Corporal. It's been a long time. It's great seeing you again.

Yeah, it's good to see you again, Ernie, we all missed you.

Vito, great to see you.

Ernie, it's good to have you back.

Ernie is Corporal's right hand man and he's a Captain and Corporal is really happy to have him back.

Vito, go over to the Allerton Steak House.

Vito drives there and parks in front of the restaurant and Ernie helps Corporal while Vito gets the wheelchair. They get Corporal into the wheelchair and go inside.

Carl is waiting for them.

Hi, Corporal and he hugs and kisses Corporal and hugs Ernie and Vito. it's been a long time, you look great and it's good to have you back, we all missed you.

Thanks, it's great to be back, I missed all you guys.

OK, boys. Lets sit down. Carl prepared something special in honor of Ernie coming home.

Carl brings over a bottle of the best wine in the house and pours for everyone and he offers a toast to everyone. They all tap each others glass and drink.

The waiter brings a big platter of ante pasta and serves them all. Next comes baked shrimps and lobster tails. Then comes spaghetti with clam sauce and if that wasn't enough, WA-LAH, here comes Carl with broiled T- bone steaks done to a turn. Everyone is really enjoying themselves and Carl makes sure they all have enough to drink. After they've eaten to their heart's content, Carl brings out cake and espresso along with anisette. Life is good. Ernie is overwhelmed, what a great meal, everything was out of this world. After that great meal they enjoy desert and each others company.

Ernie, lets sit over there. I wanna talk a little bit with you.

OK, Corporal. He wheels Corporal over to the end table and Ernie pulls up a seat.

Ernie, I hope you enjoyed the spread that we had for you, it was from our hearts. Corporal reaches into his inside coat pocket and pulls out a fat envelope and hands it to Ernie.

Thanks, Corporal.

Now, lets get down to business. I told Jimmy that you're going to be with him for a couple of weeks so that you can be brought up to speed. A few things are going on that I don't like, so just keep your eyes and ears open and let me know what you think is happening. I told Jimmy that I'm moving him up, but I think he's up to something. Don't mention this to anyone. Starting Monday morning, go over to the Boston Post Road store and let Jimmy fill you in about the numbers. In the meantime, take the rest of the week off and do what you have to do and say hello to the wife for me. Don't forget the bash that we're throwing for you. I'll let you know when.

OK, Corporal and thanks for everything.

Ernie, wheel me back to the front and we'll have a couple of drinks with Vito and Carl before we leave.

Carl, that was a great spread that you prepared for us, you outdid yourself again.

Thanks, Corporal. I'm glad you all enjoyed everything. Can I get any of you something else?

Sure, bring a nice bottle of red wine and some more espresso.

OK, Corporal, coming right up. Everyone's talking about how wonderful the feast was and they're all full and content.

Well, Carl. We have to go now.

Chapter 10

The phone rings. It's John. Meet me over at the Boulevard Club. How long will it take you to get here?

About an hour. Carmine hangs up and gets into to his car and drives over to Queens. John's one of the big Bosses in Manhattan and Queens. I hope nothing is goin on about my brother in law. He sounded alright. I'm just about there and I'll find out soon enough. He parks in front of the Boulevard and goes into the club.

John is waiting there. Carmine, come in and have a seat. You guys wait out here, he tells his two gumbas, Casper and Doug.

The reason I asked you over is, we got a little problem. The cop's are asking some questions about your brother in law and how come he wound up dead. He was told not to get involved with dope and now I find out there's some other guys mixed up with the dope business. Carmine, tell me the truth, are you mixed up with that crap?

On my mother's grave, I swear to you, I'm not involved with any of that dope business.

OK, Carmine, I believe you. It came up and that's why I asked you. Now I was told to take care of it and we have to find out who's doing this and clean it up. Find out who your brother in law was dealing with and do it quietly. Don't let on that anything is going on. When we find out, we'll leave a message for the cop's that's it's all taken care of and they'll back off and it'll be business as usual. Now, keep in touch with me. John hands him a slip of paper, call me only at this number, memorize it and give it back to me before you leave.

Everything has to be cleared through me and I don't have to remind you, nobody is to know about this, only you and me. A lotta people are gonna be upset about the thing's that are going to happen. Now, you're going to Ernie's bash up at Corporal's, right?

Yeah, John.

Good, keep your eye's and ear's open. I'd like to know what's going on up there and keep an eye on Sonny's guys down in Harlem.

Do you know anything about this Conrad's Cloud Room over by La Guardia Airport.

Yeah, I was over there with a couple of guys last week. Nice place, it's owned by a black guy and he's doing pretty good.

Who was there with you? Well, there was Chris, the Funeral Director, Tony Graco, the Contractor, Lou, Jimmy and Al. It seems like it's getting to be a regular hangout with them and Tony's got his eye on a little redhead cocktail waitress.

Carmine, everything else OK?

Yeah.

Anything else said about your brother in law?

Naw.

Well, you had to take care of him, you're the only one that could get close to him, you did a good job.

Thanks, and John, when you showed up with your two guy's at the Funeral Home, they all shit in their pants. You won't hear a peep from any of them.

OK, I'll let you know when I want you to take care of this thing. Don't forget, keep me posted and mums the word.

Holy shit, I thought he was going to point the finger at me. I better be careful, it was a good thing that I took care of my brother in law or he might have started wondering about me. So far nobody knows anything about my involvement with him. He drives up to the Bronx and stop's at Gino's on Boston Road.

Carmine, how you been? Good.

And how about you, Gino? Fine.

The bartender comes over. Beer for the two of us. Gino's brother in law is a big shot in the Republican Party and he's also Chairman of the New York State Liquor Authority. The bartender serves them their beers and they both toast each other.

How's your brother in law making out?

He's doing great, he's thinking of running for Congress, answers Gino.

Wow, that's something, let me know and I'll make a contribution.

Excuse me, Carmine, I gotta take a look in the kitchen, we got a big party coming in later.

OK, Gino. Nice seeing ya.

He has another beer and then goes to the pay phone and call's Chris.

Hey, Chris. It's me, Carmine. What are you up to?

Nothing much, I'm going to meet Tony and the guy's, you want to come along?

Sure, what time you going to meet them?

Eight o'clock at the Allerton Steak House.

OK, I'll go home and get ready, see you then. Carmine finishes his drink and leave's a tip for the bartender. He gets into his car and goes home.

This is great, I'll go with them and see what's happening and they won't think anything of it, just another night on the town with the boys. He gets home and turn's on the TV. Same old thing, he switches channels and finds an old movie starring George Raft and James Cagney. He likes those old movies.

The phone rings and it's John. Carmine, meet me at the Boulevard tomorrow about 1 o'clock. I have to go over a few thing's with you.

OK, see you then. I guess thing's are happening faster that I thought they would. Well, might as well get this stuff out of the way fast. After the movie, I'll take a shower and get ready. I got plenty of time.

Chapter 11

Jimmy is up and ready to go over to the Boston Post Road store and the phone rings.

Hey, Jimmy. It's Sammy, you got a minute?

Yeah, what's up?

The Mount Vernon guys want to know how things are coming along?

Things are moving right along. Suppose we meet up at the diner in Mount Vernon. How about 11 this morning?

OK. I'll see you then.

Jimmy drives to the Boston Post Road store and goes in. He asks the old guy at the counter. Everything alright?

Yeah, but it's a little slow so far this morning.

OK, I'll be in the back.

A couple of people come in. A black guy says 10 on 152 straight, 10 on 451 boxed, gimme 20 on 000 and 10 on 679 combo.

OK, you got it, says the old man. Here's your slip.

How you doing? Millie.

Good. 15 on 583 combo, 3 on 639 straight and 5 on 444.

OK, here's your slip, good luck.

It goes on like this for a while. People come in, make their bets and leave.

A police car comes by and a cop comes in and asks, is Jimmy in?

Yeah, I'll get him for you.

Hey, Jimmy. Your buddy, Mac the cop, is here to see you.

OK, send him in.

Hey, Jimmy. How you doing?

Great. And you, Mac?

Good.

Jimmy pulls out a envelope from the desk drawer and gives it to Mac.

Thanks, Jimmy. See you next week. The cop leaves and goes on his way to make the rest of his collections and deliver the envelopes to the Precinct Captain.

Well, it seems like things are starting to pick up this morning.

Jimmy tells the old guy that he has to take care of a few things and he'll be back later on. He gets into his car and drives to Mount Vernon.

A thought crosses his mind. Corporal believes that the blacks in Mount Vernon are making a move on his operation. Meanwhile, me and Sammy are going to take over the numbers in the Bronx and I'll hook up with the Yonkers and Mount Vernon bunch. Corporal don't have the muscle to do anything about it. Before you know it, he'll be out altogether. Who knows, I might be running everything some day.

Jimmy pulls into the diner parking lot and goes in.

Sammy calls out, Jimmy. I'm over here.

The waitress comes by. Hi, guys. What will it be?

Tuna on white toast and coffee. Egg salad on white with a pickle and coffee for me.

I'll be back in a minute, guys.

Well, things should be happening in a week or so explains Jimmy. Corporal is sold on the idea that the blacks in Mount Vernon are making a move on his numbers.

This guy Ernie is back and Corporal wants me to bring him up to speed and keep an eye on him. He don't know shit, he's been away for so long he can't even remember his own name, and get this.

Corporal said he's moving me up, you know what that means. I'll be in line to be second in command. I'll be needing you to be my assistant. It's about time for these old jerks to retire. We're the new blood and it's time for a change. I got a lot of ideas.

The waitress comes with the sandwiches and coffee.

Jimmy and Sammy are enjoying their lunch and talking about their future and how promising things are looking.

Sammy. I'll let you know what's happening and when it's time to move.

Hey, waitress. Let me have the check. Jimmy takes care of the check and tip.

They leave the diner and Jimmy tells Sammy, I'll call you tomorrow and he drives back down to the store on Boston Post Road .

Is everything alright, he asks the old man?

Yeah, business picked up today, a lot of people playing 444 and 000. You better call the office and tell them.

Yeah, I'd better do it now. Jimmy calls the office and tells them about all the action on 000 and 444.

You should have called a little earlier when you saw this kind of action. Didn't you notice this happening, yells Abe?

I had to step out for a little while.

What do you mean you had to step out for a little while?

Well, the old guy was here and he should have called you.

Who's in charge, you or the old guy? You stay there unless you let us know, understand?

Yeah, I understand.

I want you to come over here after you close the store tonight.

OK, I'll be there.

It's time to close up. Jimmy puts the money and receipts into a canvas bag and locks up the store and he gets into his car and drives over to the office on Bainbridge avenue.

Abe is busy counting the money from the days numbers and the sports action will be coming in later.

Jimmy knocks on the door and Abe tells him to come into the office.

Jimmy, what's going on with you? Do you know what could happen if we don't layoff some of those heavy bets and they hit? You better straighten your ass out now or you're going to be in deep shit. Corporal wants to see you tomorrow at the Zerega club. He'll call you tomorrow morning. Did you bring today's money and receipts with you?

Yeah, here it is.

OK, go home and have a good night's sleep.

Jimmy leaves and heads home. I screwed up today, bad move. Now I got Corporal on my ass. I better not go out with the guys tonight, I better be ready for tomorrow. The shit's going to hit the fan and Corporal can see right through you. I better get my story right because he'll check it out. It's better not to talk to anyone about this, you never know who'll turn on you and I'd better be careful with Sammy. He seemed a little too anxious about all this, maybe he's got ideas of his own. Well, gotta keep my cool and get some sleep.

Chapter 12

All the guy's meet at the Allerton Steak House except Jimmy. Carl greets them and leads them to their table. He takes their orders and brings them a bottle of wine and fills their glasses.

Hey, where's Jimmy? I thought he was going to be here tonight, asks Tony?

I don't know, something must have come up. I hope he's alright.

The waiter's come out with their orders and they start digging in.

Carl comes over and asks if everything was alright. Oh, it was swell, remarks Carmine.

How about a little desert and espresso? Yeah, sounds good. After they finish desert, they all start getting ready to leave.

Tony gets the check and takes care of the tip. OK, lets all get into my car and go over to the Cloud Room. So long Carl, see you next week.

They all go into the Cloud Room and Conrad, the owner, comes over and greets them. He escorts them to a front table and has Amy, the waitress, come over and take their order.

Hi, guys. Nice to see you fellas back here again. And she gives Tony a big hug and kiss.

She takes their order and tells them she'll be right back.

The Cloud Room is packed and the place is jumping. Looks like everybody's having a great time. Amy, the waitress comes back with the drinks and serves them. The guys start moving around and meeting some of the loose women and dancing with them. A couple of the guys invite a few of the women over to the table for drinks and they're all having a great time. Amy, the waitress, is working the table and serving drinks to everyone.

Tony starts talking to her and he's hooking up with her for when she get's off. He tells Chris that she's spending the night with him and would he mind taking the guys back to the Bronx.

Sure, Tony. No problem. Have a good time, you lucky dog.

Amy comes over to the table and tells Tony that she's getting off early and they can leave as soon as she changes. He takes care of the check and the guys take care of the tips.

The guys going back with Chris get into a taxi and they go back to the Bronx. The other guys that are hooked up get cabs and head to the nearest passion pits.

Amy comes over to Tony and they leave arm in arm and get into Tony's car and drive to Manhattan and pull up in front of the Plaza Hotel. The doorman open's the car door and they get out. Tony hands him the keys and tells him that they'll be checking in. Then Tony and Amy go to the front desk.

Good evening. Will you folks be checking in?

Yes, and we would like a king size bed.

Yes, sir. Cash or credit card.

Cash.

That will be 125 dollars.

Send a bottle of champagne up to our room.

Yes, sir. Bell boy, Room 2159. Have a nice stay at the Plaza.

What a night that was. Carmine picked up this broad at Conrad's and she turned out to be a nonstop nympho. I gotta make sure I don't lose her number. What was her name? Oh, yeah. Margie.

Well, I better get going over to Queens and meet John, I don't wanna be late. He goes down to the garage and gets into his car. Nice day, I hope it stays this way. After I finish with

John, I better get in touch with Chris and give him the insurance check for the funeral. OK, I'm nearly there, just be cool and see what's up with John. He parks in front of the Boulevard Night Club and goes in.

John's gumba's are waiting outside his office.

Is John in?

Yeah, he's waiting for you. One of them knocks on John's door. Hey, John. Carmine's here.

Send him in.

Close the door and have a seat. Well, here's what's happening. Sonny's son in law is in this shit up to his eyeball's and there's a few other guys in this with him. The word came down to get rid of this, no matter who it is and that means his son in law and all the rest of them. Nobody knows about this yet, just you and me, so make sure you keep this to yourself and I don't have to remind you, anything else pops up, don't talk to anyone but me. I'll let you know who, when and where, understand?

Carmine nods his head.

I'll be in touch with you tomorrow, so go on with business just like usual.

OK, John. I'll be talking to you tomorrow. He says goodbye to John's gumba's and leaves.

He heads to the Bronx and stops on the other side of the Whitestone Bridge and goes to one of the pay phones.

Hey, Chris. I'm glad I got a hold of you. How about meeting me at the German Stadium for a drink. I got the insurance check for the funeral and I'd like to give it to you.

Sure, I should be there in about 20 minutes.

Good, see you then.

Carmine parks in front of the German Stadium and goes in and has a seat at the bar.

What'll you have?

A bottle of beer.

In walks Chris.

Hi, Chris. Have a seat.

The bartender serves Carmine.

How about you, Chris?

Bottle of beer.

Take it out of here, says Carmine. Here's to good times. Before I forget, here's the insurance check for my brother in laws funeral and thanks for everything. I don't know what I would have done without your help.

I'm glad I could help, replies Chris.

That was a great time at Conrad's last night. How did you make out, Carmine?

Like a fat rat, that broad I picked up was like a wild animal, she must be a nymphomaniac.

Yeah, you're kidding.

No, she was nuts, she nearly screwed me to death.

Wow, that's really something. I'm glad you scored.

How did you make out, Chris?

News and Mirror. (that's a New York term used by a guy that doesn't score, he goes home with the News and Mirror newspapers.)

Too bad, there was a lot of foxes there. Better luck next time. Did you notice Tony and that little red head? Looked like they were as hot as firecrackers.

Yeah, he's gonna call me later on today and give me all the details. Well, it was good to see you, I gotta get back to the office and thanks again for the check. I'll give you the balance as soon as the check clears.

OK, Chris. Thanks for everything.

Chris gets into his car and goes back to his office and Carmine gets into his car and drives home.

Carmine is thinking, everything seems alright with Chris and John. Otherwise, they'd be acting differently. John seemed a little uptight about everything, but I guess anybody in his position would be. He has to whack Sonny's son in law and some of his close friends and their relatives. Man, if he knew anything about me, I'd be on that hit list too. It was a lucky thing I kept everything quiet about my brother in law and me. Good thing that I took care of him and not somebody else. I better never get involved with any of that shit again. It never dawned on me how easy that kind of talk could get out. Well, I'll know who's getting hit pretty soon. Sonny's a boss and he has to go along with it, he has no choice. Oh, brother. There could be a blood bath. Well, have to take care of number one, it could be a big step up for me. I'll get a bite to eat and watch a little TV and hit the sack early tonight and recuperate from that wild woman, she nearly killed me.

Chapter 13

Jimmy is up at 6 o'clock in the morning, he shaves and showers and gets dressed. Let's see what's on TV. Nothing new, just weather and traffic reports. He boils a few eggs and makes coffee and toast. It seems like forever waiting for Corporal to call.

Corporal is just getting up and he calls Vito to pick him up about 9 o'clock. Sally, run a bath for me and make some breakfast for us.

Corporal is really bothered about Jimmy. I don't like what's happening. He been getting greedy ever since he started hanging out with that schmuck, Sammy. Well, we just kill two birds with one stone and at the same time straighten out those assholes in Yonkers and Mount Vernon.

Honey, your bath is ready, do you want to eat or take your bath first?

Aw, I'll take my bath first.

OK, Sweetie. She helps him get into the bathtub. Let me know when you're finished.

Corporal calls out, Sally, I'm done.

I'll be right there, Honey. She comes into the bathroom with a big oversize towel and helps him out of the bathtub. She dries him off and helps him put on his bathrobe. Then she wheels him into the kitchen and helps him get seated at the table.

They both start having their breakfast and he tells her he's going to be busy today.

OK, I have some cleaning to do around the apartment, so don't worry, if I need anything, I'll let you know.

That was a good breakfast, Sally.

She helps him into the wheelchair and they go into the bedroom where she has his clothes laid out for him. She helps him get dressed and when he's finished dressing, she tells him.

Oh, Honey, you look so handsome and dapper. I love that suit and tie on you, they make your eyes sparkle.

Aw, cut the bullshit, but I love to hear you say that.

With that she gives him a great big kiss. Yep, Corporal loves his Sally and she's the apple of his eye.

The buzzer rings. Sally asks, who is it?

It's me, Vito.

OK, we'll be down in a minute.

She wheels Corporal onto the elevator and presses lobby. The door opens and Vito helps him out.

Good morning to you and Sally.

Good morning, Vito.

See you later, Sally.

Love you, honey. Drive carefully, Vito

Vito wheels Corporal out as Sally holds the door open.

I'll sit up front with you.

OK, Boss. He helps Corporal into the front seat and puts the wheelchair into the trunk.

Lets go to the Zerega club.

OK, Boss. He starts the car and they head to the club. When they get there Vito gets out and gets the wheelchair. He helps Corporal out and they go into the club as Tiny holds the door open.

Good morning, Corporal. Tiny hugs and kisses him. How about something to eat and drink?

Yeah, espresso with some lemon peels.

OK, coming right up.

Vito, call Jimmy and tell him to come over here right away and to make it snappy.

The phone rings and Jimmy picks it up.

It's Vito. Corporal wants you to come to the club right away and make it snappy.

OK, I'll be right there.

Jimmy is a nervous wreck. What took him so long to call? He's about ready to crap in his pants. I need something to calm me down, but I better not or he'll know that I'm ready to fall apart. I'll get a hold of myself and show him I'm not afraid of him. Jimmy runs down to his car. He gets to the Zerega in no time flat and parks in front of the club.

Tiny opens the door and Jimmy goes over to Corporal and hugs and kisses him.

Have a seat. You want some espresso?

No, thanks.

Vito is standing right next to Corporal and Tiny is standing right behind Jimmy.

Tell me Jimmy, what's going on? Something bothering you? You can tell me.

No, nothing is going on and nothing is bothering me.

Something tells me something's not right. How come the other day you left the store and made a few mistakes that could have cost us a lot of money and before that you came up short a couple of times. Where did you go that day?

I had to see somebody?

That's no kind of an answer. What do you take us for, a bunch of idiots? Who did you have to go see?

I had to see somebody about something personal.

Well, I want to know who it was and what was so personal. I told you last week about coming up short and I want you to make up the short count and I want answers by tomorrow. You make sure that you show up and see Abe with the money and the answers and I don't wanna hear any excuses. You're off for the next two weeks and off the books too. And you're paying for the guy that's filling in for you. Understand? Any questions?

No, Corporal.

OK. Now get out of here before I lose my temper.

Jimmy leaves and gets into his car and drives home.

Holy shit, I was lucky to get out of there alive. He suspects everything that's going on and if I don't show up tomorrow with the money and some answers, my goose is cooked. I gotta go home and figure out something to get this straightened out.

Chapter 14

Tonight's going to be the welcome home party for Ernie and everybody that's been invited should show up. Carl has some extra people to help him out and it should be a great time for Ernie and all the invited guests. Corporal is really excited and he wants this party to be special because Ernie is his favorite and he's a real stand up guy. He took the hit and kept quiet about everything and did his time without squawking. Now it's Ernie's time to get rewarded for his loyalty. There's also going to be some entertainers from Hollywood and Las Vegas showing up.

The phone rings. It's me, Sal. We got the permit and everything's moving right along and I'm meeting with the Doctor's and we'll have them get the money up, then we can go and see my friends and take care of them. Meet me at the diner on Boston Road in about 30 minutes.

Chris is already dressed and he drives to the diner.

Hey, Chris. Over here.

The waitress comes over and asks, what can I get you fellas?

Coffee and bagels for the both of us.

So tell me, Sal.

As I said, we got the permit and I'll be meeting with the Doctors.

How much are you getting up front from them?

Fifty thousand up front from each one of them. Then we have to go see our friends and take care of them. Now, we should get together with Tony and find out how soon he can get going on construction, and this way we'll have a timetable for everything.

Good, I'll see Tony tonight at the Allerton and I'll set up a date for us to meet. Don't forget, you're going too, right Sal?

Oh, yeah. I'll be there.

The waitress serves the coffee and bagels.

Don't mention anything about this to anyone tonight, and by the way Sal, bring an envelope for Ernie.

Thanks for reminding me, Chris.

They leave and Chris drives to his office. Is everything alright, Andy?

Yeah, everything's fine.

Chris picks up the newspaper and flips through it and spots an article about an impending investigation by the District Attorney's Office about corruption in the Bronx involving some elected officials. When contacted, the District Attorney's Office refused comment. Chris wonders what this is all about. I better get in touch with Sal about this.

Sal, did you see page five in the Daily News?

No, what's it about?

Take a look and let me know what you think.

Wow, this is the first I've heard of anything like this.

Chris thinks it could be nothing or you just never know. I hope this has nothing to do with us. There's always some sort of investigation about something going on in this city, just the same we got to keep our eyes and ears open. Aw, I'll go home and relax for awhile and then I'll get ready to go to Ernie's affair. This should be some bash. All the big wigs will be there. Corporal is something. They all respect him and he don't take shit from anyone. For a guy stuck in a wheelchair, he does pretty good for himself and he's got connections all over the country.

As soon as he opens the door the phone rings and it's Sal.

Hey, Chris. I just made a few calls and no one seems to know anything about that article. Lets just keep on doing what we have to and keep tabs on things.

OK, Sal. Thanks for calling me back. See you at the party.

Down at the Bronx District Attorney's Office, DA Gallo is talking to his assistants. Seems like we shook some cages with that press release, lets see what kind of reaction we get. Remember, when asked by the press or anyone, tell them you cannot comment about anything at this time. That ought to make a lot of people feel pretty uneasy. We'll give another press release about a week from now. Until then, lets see what happens.

Chapter 15

Jimmy isn't feeling so good today, I gotta see Abe and I gotta have some answers for him besides getting up the money for them.

Let me see, I'll call Liz and ask her if she can do me a favor. She can say she thought she was pregnant and called me because she didn't know what to do. But it turned out alright, she finally got her period. I better call her now before she goes to work. He dials her number and she answers.

Hi, Liz. It's me, Jimmy.

Hi, what's up?

Liz, could you do me a small favor? I skipped work for a few hours the other day and the boss wants to know why. I gotta come up with a good excuse, so I was thinking that if you could cover me by saying that you missed your time of the month and that you called me because you didn't know what to do and you asked me to come to see you and I did. I met you at the Mount Vernon Diner and was with you for about two hours. But the next day you got your period, so everything is alright now. Could you do that for me, Liz?

Sure, Jimmy. No problem.

Thanks, Liz. How about we meet tomorrow night? I can pick you up about eight.

OK, Jimmy. See you then.

He hangs up the phone and lets out a sigh of relief. That should take care of that.

Liz came through for me, what a gal. I'll get ready and go see Abe and that should cool everyone down. I better forget my big ideas, it's too dangerous. I'll get a hold of Sammy in a couple of days and tell him everything is off and forget that we ever talked about anything. I better pick up the money and get over to Abe.

Jimmy drives to the bar and says hello to Charlie the bartender. Is Abe in the office?

The bartender picks up the phone. Abe, Jimmy is here.

OK, Jimmy. Go ahead, he's waiting for you up in the office.

Jimmy goes upstairs and opens the door to the office and goes in.

Have a seat. Did you bring the money?

Yeah, Abe. Here it is. Jimmy puts an envelope on Abe's desk.

Is it all here?

Yep, all there.

What's going on, you got a little problem? Corporal want's to know.

Yeah, my girl missed her time of the month and she got real worried about it and she asked me to go and see her. That's why I left the store the other day.

So, what's going to happen now?

Well, she finally got her period and everything seems to be alright now.

OK, good. Why didn't you tell Corporal that yesterday?

Are you kidding, He was boiling. I just sat there and listened. He was right, there was no excuse. I just wasn't thinking right.

You gotta understand, this is a very serious business and there's no room for mistakes. Corporal has no choice but to take action very fast when it comes to things like this. OK, Jimmy. I'll talk to Corporal, but the action against you still stands and you know he's going to check everything out, so that's it. You better forget about going to Ernie's bash tonight, but make sure that you give an envelope to Ernie.

Yeah, Abe. Could I leave it with you?

Sure, I'll make sure he gets it. Just stay put until this blows over and if there's anything bothering you, give me a call.

Jimmy leaves and gets into his car. Oh, brother. I was sweating bullets. Abe's a tough cookie and if he thought there was anything fishy about my story, I'd be a dead duck. I'll see Liz tomorrow night and get everything straightened out with her. She's a sweetheart, she saved my ass. I'll just stop by the grocery store and pick up a few things and go home and collect my thoughts. I gotta be real careful from here on out, they'll be watching me like a hawk, this is only the beginning. I have to stay away from those guys in Yonkers and Mount Vernon. I can feel it, things are going to get very hot. They must be on to something. They really over reacted about this whole thing. I need a few days off. I know, Liz and me can fly down to Sanibel Island and stay there for a week or so. She'll like that. Maybe stay down there for the rest of our lives. Yeah, I'll check out the airlines and make reservations when I get home.

Chapter 16

It's starting to rain, I hope that it doesn't keep up all night, Chris says to himself. This is a big shindig that Corporal is throwing for Ernie and now that Ernie is back from prison, I'll bet that Corporal is planning a big move. All the bosses are going to be there. Yep, Corporal is letting everybody know that he is in firm control and that they had better tow the mark and tighten up their act. Well, I better get ready.

Meanwhile, Corporal is getting ready and Sally is helping him get dressed. Sally, I'm going to be late getting home tonight, so don't wait up for me and don't you forget to have something nice for dinner.

OK, honey, you have a nice time with the guys and don't forget to take your umbrella.

Yeah, Vito has one in the car, he should be here pretty soon.

The phone rings and Sally answers it.

Hi, Sally. It's Vito, I'll be there in ten minutes, you want me to meet you and Corporal downstairs?

Hold on, I'll ask Corporal.

Honey, it's Vito. He'll be here in ten minutes. Do you want him to wait downstairs?

Yeah, tell him we're coming down.

Tony is getting ready to go to the banquet and he's all decked out. He wants to make a good appearance. All the big shots will be there.

I better call Amy and tell her I won't be seeing her tonight. Oh, boy. I really enjoy being with her, I haven't had such a good time with a woman in such a long time. All these one night stands can drain a guy. Well, we'll get together tomorrow night.

Ernie is just about ready and he tells his wife not to wait up for him, I have to go to a meeting with some people and I'll be home late.

OK, Babe. I love you. Be careful and take your umbrella with you.

Ernie kisses her. I love you, see you later.

He goes downstairs and gets into his car and drives to the Allerton Steak House. This is a big night for Corporal and me and I know that he wants to let everyone know that he can depend on me and besides that, he's going to spread out and take over Yonkers and Mount Vernon. Good move, he's right on the money. I always knew he was the smartest Boss in the business. Well, he can count on me.

Everyone is arriving at the Allerton Steak House and Carl and his waiters are ready. He makes sure that everyone is seated correctly and that there's no confusion about seating. The band starts playing and Corporal arrives with Vito. Carl makes sure that they're seated nicely. Ernie arrives and Carl seats him right next to Corporal.

The waiters start serving drinks and appetizers. Carl announces that the main courses will be arriving soon and to enjoy themselves. This is going to be the best feast ever. The waiters start with roast beefs, steaks, hams, turkeys, seafood and pasta There's all sorts of fruits and desserts and everything else that their hearts desire. This is truly a feast fit for a king and it's in honor of Corporal's best friend, Ernie. After everyone has eaten and had their fill, coffee and desserts are served and Cuban cigars are offered to everyone.

Corporal taps his glass and he gets everyone's attention. Thank you all for joining us at this wonderful feast in honor of my great friend Ernie. He's joined us again after a long absence and he's here to stay. Ernie has been one of us for many, many years and he's a man of honor. Please join me in a toast to Ernie. Here's to you Ernie, my Friend. May you have a long and healthy life. Ernie leans over and kisses Corporal on both cheeks and Corporal kisses him on both cheeks also. Everyone cheers and claps and hug and kiss Corporal and they all hug Ernie and he is given an envelope by everyone.

Corporal taps his glass. Again, thanks for attending this wonderful banquet in honor of Ernie and a special thanks to Carl and his waiters for preparing and serving this great feast. Carl, you outdid yourself and I hope that everyone here enjoyed themselves. There are cheers and clapping that last for minutes.

It's starting to get late and people are leaving and thanking Corporal for inviting them to this great feast.

Corporal leans over to Ernie and asks him to leave with him and Vito.

After everyone leaves, Corporal tells them, we can go now. Vito helps Corporal into his wheelchair and they leave and get into the car.

Where to boss?

Go to the Spanish Steps. I wanna say hello to Angelo.

Ernie, I'm happy your back, and I want Vito and you to work together. We're gonna make some changes and some moves. We'll talk some more about everything tomorrow. Now, is there anything you guys want to tell me?

Boss, I think your going to have to do something about that problem in Mount Vernon.

Your right, Vito. We'll take care of that.

Ernie, got anything?

Not right now, Boss. Maybe after tomorrow.

They get to the Spanish Steps and Vito parks right in front of the club. Vito gets the wheelchair and they help Corporal out. They go in and Angelo spots Corporal and hugs him and he takes them to a front table. The waiter comes to the table and Angelo tells him to bring the best bottle of wine in the house and anything else that they want.

Corporal asks Angelo, how's business?

It's very good.

I want to see you tomorrow about 1 o'clock at the club.

Sure Corporal, 1 o'clock. I'll be there.

Angelo, you know Ernie and Vito.

Oh, sure. How you guys been?

They say fine, nice to see you again.

The waiter arrives with the wine and fills their glasses. Well, here's to us and they all toast each other.

Corporal, would you like to have some of the girls come over to the table for a drink?

No, thanks. We have to be leaving now, we just stopped by to say hello. We'll see you tomorrow. They all leave and get into the car and go back to the Bronx.

OK, I guess you guys are wondering about what that was all about. We'll talk about all that tomorrow. In the meantime lets all go home and have a good night's sleep.

Chapter 17

There's Sal's car. Chris goes in to his Funeral Home and Sal is sitting in his office.

Hey, Sal. How you doing?

Hi, Chris.

Andy. anything doing?

No, just Sal is here.

Chris closes the office door. Is everything OK, Sal?

It's just that everybody is running around like a chicken without it's head. Nobody seems to know what's going on. I think the Bronx D.A. is just trying to rattle everybody's cage and he's trying to get some publicity for himself. We just have to keep our eyes open. I spoke to Tony last night and he said he would stop by today and I'm going to see our friends in the Bronx Burough President's Office this morning and take care of them. I'll find out if anything is going on.

OK, Sal. How much are you going to give them?

Ten to my friend and 25 to Stanley Shaffer.

Where are you going to meet them?

At the Concourse Plaza Hotel.

OK, but be very careful.

OK, Chris. I better get going. I'll call when I'm finished.

Hey, Chris. Tony's on the phone.

I'm at a meeting right now. When I'm finished I'll be over to see you.

OK, Tony. I'll be here.

Carmine is still at home when the phone rings. This is John. Come on over about 2 o'clock.

OK, John, see you then. It's show time. I know that Sonny wants me to hit his son in law. No sense thinking about it. I'll get the facts from John and get it done. I wonder who else is going to get it?

Corporal tells Ernie and Vito, we're going into the night club business and that's only part of it. We're taking over Mount Vernon and Yonkers. Those guys up there were planning on making a move on us for quite awhile. Jimmy and that guy Sammy thought they had it all worked out and that we were going to be eaten up by those idiots in Yonkers. Well, that's all changed now. During the next couple of days, we'll layout all the details of this operation. I want the two of you to line up your crews and have them standby. Don't let on that anything is going on. Remember, business as usual.

Now, Ernie. You are the Underboss in this family. Vito, you are now my top Captain and nobody but you goes anywhere with me.

Get me a list of all our guys and Associates. I want to know everything about all of them.

Ernie, I understand that Jimmy is going to Florida with his girlfriend. Let them go for now and make him think everything is alright, understand? And keep tabs on Sammy.

Tiny comes over, Angelo is on the phone.

Hi, Corporal. I'll be there at 1 o'clock.

Sal is having a bite to eat with Stanley Shaffer and Edward at the Concourse Plaza. He slips an envelope under each of their napkins and they both put them into their vest pockets.

I hear that the Bronx D.A. is stirring up a little noise down at the court house. Anything to it, Stanley?

No, he's just trying to get a little free publicity. He's coming up for reelection. Nothing to worry about.

Well, I got to get going, it was nice seeing you again. Sal goes to a pay phone in the lobby and calls Chris. Hey, it's Sal. I just got finished. I'll be there in about 20 minutes.

Carmine is on his way to Queens and he'll be seeing John in a few minutes. Hope everything is going alright. I just have to remain calm and let this thing play out. He parks his car in front of the club and goes in. The two gumba's are standing outside John's office and one of them knocks on John's door.

Who?

It's Carmine.

Send him in.

Have a seat. OK, lets get down to business. You're going to take Sonny's son in law out. I want you to set it up and get it over with as soon as possible. He's hiding out all over Harlem, but there's no place to go. I want you to get in touch with him and tell him that Sonny is fixing everything up, but he's got to get out of New York for awhile until this thing blows over. Tell him that you're going to arrange for him to stay with some friends of yours in Florida and when things cool down you'll let him know. Then he can come back to New York. Let him know that he can't be hiding out in basements like a rat. Tell him Sonny is taking care of everything and you'll get him out of here. Now, here's where you're going to send him and after a few weeks you go down to Florida and take care of him. Got it?

OK, John.

Call me as soon as you find him, start on this right away.

OK, I'll call you as soon as I get in touch with him.

Wow, John laid a load on me. I was starting to think he could read my mind. I gotta calm down and get this thing out of the way. This whole thing came down from the top and the bosses are on John's ass to clean up this mess. I should never have gotten involved with this shit. I'm lucky nobody can connect me with it, just my brother in law and he's dead.

Chapter 18

Tony is on his way to meet Chris and Sal and he's just about there. These guys are going to make a fortune off this thing, I should have been in on this thing instead of just building it for them. Oh, well. I'll mention that I wouldn't mind getting involved in some of the next opportunities that might come up. OK, here we are. Tony parks right in front of the Funeral Home and goes in.

They all have a seat and get down to business.

OK, first we need to have blueprints and plans drawn up to submit to the building department. Sal, do you have the building permits yet, asks Tony?

I'm going to get them this morning.

Good. I'll have the architects go to the site and have them start drawing up the plans for the hospital. We'll start clearing and preparing the site and breaking ground. Next, we'll put in the foundation and then we'll start building. Now, I'll figure out how much this whole thing will cost, and we'll need to have some money up front.

How much do you need to get started, asks Chris?

A rough estimate, about 500,000. Are you guys able to handle that?

That's a lot, I was thinking we could finance the whole thing.

Tony says, in order to start, we better get the financing worked out. Did you close the deal with the owner and transfer ownership of the property?

Yeah, that's taken care of.

OK, are you going to work with a bank or a private party?

We don't know yet.

Well, it would be better to work with a private party, it'll move faster. These banks work pretty slow.

How soon would you like to get started, asks Tony?

As soon as possible, replies Sal.

OK, how much can the two of you get up now?

I can put up 100,000. And I can do the same, answers Chris.

Alright, I'll make a few calls and see what I can do.

Come on, Sal, lets take a walk. We'll be back in a few minutes. Go ahead and make your calls.

Sal and Chris close the office door and Chris tells Andy. Tony is making some calls, don't let anyone into the office. We'll be back in a few minutes.

What do you think, Chris?

Well, lets see what Tony can come up with. He deals with these things all the time. We have to think about what this might cost us and what kind of deals we might have to make. We're already in for 300,000 on the cost of the property, but it's free and clear. We can use that as collateral.

Yeah, you're right.

Aw, don't worry, Sal, you know that Tony will come up with something. Lets go back and see what's happening.

They go in and Tony is off the phone.

OK, I just talked with a few people and here's a few things that we can do. There's a couple of investors and a few others that might be willing to lend that kind of money. Here's what I was thinking, this isn't the biggest deal in the world. My company builds the Hospital and does the financing and you guys cut me in for a third and the Hospital pays my company for the work and financing.

Chris asks, let me understand. We cut you in for a third and your company does all the work and financing. The Hospital pays back everything out of profits, is that right?

Yeah. How does that sound?

What do you think, Sal?

Tony, give us a minute.

Tony walks outside.

Sounds OK to me. How about you, Chris?
OK by me, then it's a deal.
Chris opens the door and brings Tony in.
OK, partner. We got a deal.

Chapter 19

Carmine goes over to Harlem to find Sonny's son in law. Let me see, I'll go over to the Delight Diner, he hangs out there a lot, maybe they know where he is. He goes in and sits at the counter.

The waitress comes over. What would you like?

Coffee and a corn muffin.

OK, I'll be right back. She comes back with the coffee and corn muffin.

Have you seen Charlie around lately, asks Carmine?

Charlie who?

You know, Sonny Falco's son in law.

Oh, that Charlie. Naw, I haven't seen him in a couple of weeks. You might try Patsy's, he hangs out there a lot.

OK, if you see him, tell him Carmine was asking for him. He finishes his coffee and muffin and pays the tab and leaves a tip.

He walks over to Patsy's Clam House and goes in.

Hey, Carmine. How ya doing? Haven't seen you in quite a while.

Yeah, I've been kinda busy. Hey, have you seen Charlie, you know, Sonny Falco's son in law?

Naw, not recently, you might try the Tuxedo place over on Third avenue.

OK, thanks. He goes back to his car and drives over to Third avenue and parks in front of Mario's Tuxedo and goes in.

Hey, Mario. I gotta see Charlie, Sonny Falco's son in law, it's very important.

Mario looks a little frightened. Look, I don't want any trouble. He's sleeping in the back room.

OK, Mario. Everything's alright. I just wanna talk to him.

OK, come with me. Mario taps on the door and opens it. Charlie, it's me, Mario. Carmine is here and wants to talk to you.

Oh, alright. Come in Carmine.

Hi, Charlie. I'm glad to see you. Look, don't be worried. Sonny sent me to tell you that everything is going to be alright. He had to pull some strings and get you off the hook. He told me to get you out of town for awhile till things cool down.

Really, things are going to be alright?

Yeah, I got some relatives down in Florida and you can stay with them until this blows over.

That's great, I'll go over and see Sonny now.

No, not yet. He'll let you know when the coast is clear and then you can come back. He don't want anyone to see you around Harlem right now.

OK, but I'm tapped out right now.

Look, I understand, here's some money to tide you over for awhile. Get yourself cleaned up and I'll get you down to Florida. You want to fly down?

Naw, I don't like flying.

How about the train?

OK.

While you're getting ready, I'll call and find out when the train is leaving for Florida.

Hey, Mario. Get a nice suit and shirt ready for Charlie and some underwear and socks.

Sure, Carmine. I'll have everything ready in about 20 minutes.

Mario, can I use your phone to make a call?

Sure. Carmine.

I'll call Florida now and let them know when you'll arrive and I'll have them pick you up. Now, don't call anybody while you're in Florida. I'll keep in touch with you and let you know what's going on. Sonny will take care of your family while your gone, so don't worry about nothin and I'll send you more money when you're down there.

He calls Penn Station and makes a reservation for the trip to Fort Lauderdale, leaving at 5:15 today. Then he calls Florida and lets them know when Charlie will get there.

OK, Charlie. Everything's all set. We'll pick up the ticket and you'll be on you way to sunny Florida.

Mario comes in with the suit and clothes and Charlie puts them on.

Hey, you look like a million bucks, says Carmine.

Thanks, Mario. How much do I owe you?

That's OK, Carmine. I'm glad that I could help.

Mario, I appreciate everything you've done. Take this.

OK, Charlie. Lets go.

They arrive at Penn Station and Carmine gets the ticket. OK, Charlie. The train is leaving in fifteen minutes, lets get you on board and off to Florida. They go over to track 29 and get on the train. Here we are, seat 31. Remember, this is a sleeper. Here's your ticket.

Thanks for everything, Carmine.

Don't mention it. Have a nice trip and I'll be talking to you.

All aboard, the conductor calls out.

OK, Charlie. Have a nice trip

He goes to the main floor and finds a pay phone and calls John. It's me, Carmine, he's on his way and they'll be waiting for him.

Good job. Come by tomorrow. Call before you come.

Chapter 20

Ernie is up and his wife is still sleeping. Aw, let her sleep, she's had it tough. Me being away all that time, but I'll make it up to her. He goes to the phone and calls Jimmy.

Hey, Jimmy. Are you and your girlfriend up and ready to go to the airport?

Yeah, we're ready.

OK, I'll be there in about 20 minutes.

We'll be downstairs waiting for you.

Ernie tip toes into the bedroom and kisses his wife on the cheek and leaves.

It looks like it's going to be a nice sunny day as he drives to pick up Jimmy and his girlfriend. It turned out good that Jimmy asked Abe if it was alright to go to Florida for a few weeks. If we had told him not to go he would have suspected something was up. This way him and his girlfriend will have a nice time and we'll know where they are and we won't have to look for them. OK, there they are, all smiles. Just like their going on a honeymoon. Ernie pulls up in front of them and opens the trunk.

How are you two lovebirds? What a nice day to start a vacation. He helps them put their bags into the trunk.

You didn't forget anything, did you?

Nope, we got everything.

They get into the car and off they go. Ernie goes over the Whitestone Bridge towards La Guardia airport. He pays the toll for the bridge.

What a bunch of thieves, before I went away the toll was 50 cents and now it's 4 bucks. I can't believe it, they're robbing us blind.

We're nearly there. You got the plane tickets?

Yep, I got them.

Ernie stops in front of the terminal and they all get out and the baggage handlers take the bags and ticket them.

Jimmy gives the baggage guys a few bucks and then he and Liz say goodbye to Ernie.

Ernie drives back to the Bronx. He goes back over the Whitestone Bridge and pays the 4 bucks. He mumbles to himself. Rotten thieves, they should all be locked up. He gets to the club and parks in front.

All the shop keepers on Arthur Avenue are getting their stands ready for business. There's a lot of hustle and bustle going on. Trucks delivering meats, fish, vegetables, fruits and food.

Amy Collins is getting her kids ready to go shopping. Her husband works as a mechanic at Kennedy airport so she has to take the kids with her. Anyway, her son needs a haircut and her daughter needs a trim too. She'll do a little shopping and say hello to some of her boyfriends.

She hails a cab. Take us up to the market on Arthur Avenue in the Bronx. You know where it is?

Yeah, up by the Bronx Zoo.

The cabbie heads for the Bronx and he gets there in about 25 minutes.

OK, stop right here by the fish market. She gives the cab driver a twenty dollar bill and tells him to keep the change.

Thank you very much. You and your kid's have a very nice day.

You're welcome, and you have a nice day too.

OK, kids. Be careful getting out of the taxi.

They head for the barber shop.

Hey, Amy. I got some nice fish for you today.

OK, I'll be there in a few minutes.

Hey, Amy. Don't forget me, I got some sausage just for you, yells out the butcher.

OK, I won't forget you.

Now all the guys are getting excited. Amy's here.

She goes into the barber shop and the two barbers say hello to her.

Everybody's been asking for you, Amy.

I've been very busy lately. Come on kids, get up on the chairs.

You start cutting the kids hair, the boss tells the younger barber. I'll be back.

Amy, come in the back with me. I've been waiting for you to stop by.

Did you miss me, asks Amy?

Yeah, I sure did.

OK, kids. You look good, they did a nice job.

And you did a nice job too, Amy. The barber hands her a twenty as she's leaving.

Amy starts her shopping and taking care of her boyfriend's. She has meat and fish and all kinds of goodies. She and her husband and kids wont be able to eat it all. She'll have to give a lot of it away. Amy just loves shopping on Arthur Avenue and taking care of her boyfriends.

Chapter 21

Brian Collins is working on a plane engine at Kennedy Airport and his mind is running wild. Amy is having one of her boy friends over tonight and she thinks I don't know anything about all the guys she has over when I'm working. She locks the kids in their room and she's in our bedroom screwing them. Well, I'm going home early tonight and I'm going to surprise her and whoever she's screwing. This can't keep going on, the kids are starting to ask me who's in the bedroom at night with Mommy and they can't sleep because of all the noise going on. About eleven o'clock, he tells his boss he's not feeling good and he's going home. He clocks out and gets in his car and drives home.

When he gets there, he parks the car and he sees a light on in the bedroom. He sits there in his car and watches the bedroom window for awhile. All of a sudden, he see's two figures in the bedroom and then the lights go out. I'll bet she's got a guy in there. I'll give them a few minutes and then go down to the cellar and listen to them going at it. He gets out of the car and goes down to the cellar and goes over to just under his bedroom. Sure enough, he can hear the bed springs making noise and her and the guy moaning and groaning away while he's screwing the ass off her. That's it, I'm going up there and give that guy the beating of his life.

He goes upstairs and opens the door quietly and then barges into the bedroom and turns on the light. They're caught in the act and they jump out of the bed. Brian grabs the guy and starts beating the hell out of him. She's screaming at the top of her lungs and the guy breaks away and jumps right through the plate glass window.

Lucky for him it was only the first floor. He lands on the ground and starts running for his life down the street bare ass naked.

Brian start's slapping her around and calling her all sorts of names and he picks up the guys clothes and tosses them out the window. By now all the neighbors have their lights on and are looking out their windows.

He tells her to get dressed. The kids are crying and screaming. Brian gets the keys and opens the kids bedroom door and tries to calm them down and he tells them a bad man was there and he's gone now.

Everything is alright, kids. Daddy is here and Mommy is alright. Lets get back to bed and go to sleep. I'll be right here with you.

Amy is dressed and he tells her to go into the kids room and tell them everything is alright. Just tell them a bad man was here and he's gone now and he'll never come back again.

She goes in and talks to the kids and they finally go to sleep. When she comes out of the kids room he tells her, don't bother talking now, we'll talk tomorrow. But if I ever catch another guy in this house I'll kill him.

He goes to the living room, turns off the light and lays down on the sofa and try's to go to sleep.

She goes to her bedroom and fixes up the bed and lays down. What a night, I never thought anything like this would ever happen. I never saw Brian act the way he did. If that guy didn't get out of here, Brian would have killed him. I'd better be careful around here or the next time he might kill me. The poor kids, I'm sorry this had to happen to them.

The next day Amy calls Tony at his office.

Hey, Amy. What's up?

Can we meet later on today?

Sure, where would you like me to meet you?

How about Conrad's Cloud Room in the hotel lobby at about 2 o'clock?

Sure, I'll see you then.

Tony wonders, she never calls me at my office. What's going on? Well, she probably needs some money.

Aw, we'll get a room at the hotel, have a nice little dinner and then go to the room and have some fun. That's nice for a change, a chick chasing me instead of me chasing her. Well, I'll call home and tell Marie I'm going to meet some people about a building project and I might have to stay over.

OK, that's taken care of. I'll make a few calls and see if everything is alright with the business.

That was nice to be cut in for a third of the business with that hospital. They couldn't have handled that by themselves. They had a tiger by the tail, but they needed me to put it together. That was one of the sweetest and fastest deals that I ever made. Well, who knows? They might come up with some more nice deals like this one.

Chapter 22

Lou is on his way to the club this morning. Corporal is already at the club and so is Vito and Ernie.

Tiny, could you bring some more coffee for me and the boys?

Sure, boss. Would you like anything else?

No thanks.

How about you fellas?

Yeah, how about some bagels.

OK, Ernie. Coming right up.

Corporal tells Ernie and Vito that Lou will be here soon and Al will be stopping by later on. Now, I want you two guys to sit here and just listen, understand?

Yep, says Ernie and Vito.

From now on, when I have a meeting with the guys I want both of you sitting next to me. Everybody has to know how you guys stand in the family without me getting up there announcing anything. When the meetings are over, we'll discuss things and see if we have to do anything else about business.

There's a knock on the door and Tiny looks.

It's Lou.

OK, let him in.

Have a seat, Lou. How about some coffee?

No, thanks.

How's business, Lou?

It's going real smooth and the first major money came in and it'll be coming in on a monthly basis. Lou hands Corporal a big brown envelope stuffed with money.

Hmm, nice, as Corporal opens it and looks inside the envelope.

Any bitching or moaning on that job?

No, it seems like everybody is real happy.

OK, good. How many no show jobs do you have? I got a few guys that I have to put on the payroll.

I have 5 slots open. When do you want me to fill them?

Ernie or Vito will stop by tomorrow or the next day and let you know. Now, what else are you working on?

We got the incinerator contract coming up with the city and I'm sure that everyone is very happy with the windows and that everybody will be on board. I got a meeting with Sweeney about some other big projects that he wants to talk to me about and they got a big event coming up to raise money for the upcoming elections.

Sure, put us down for two tables and take out a full page ad in their journal, compliments of the Construction Workers Local 54 and that we support our Mayor.

Lou. You're doing a good job, keep me informed. You'll be seeing more of Vito and Ernie on all of your projects. Anything else you want to talk to me about?

No, everything is fine. Lou gets up and hugs and kisses Corporal and then hugs Ernie and Vito and leaves.

Well, Al should be here soon.

Ernie and Vito, let me know who you think should be given those no show jobs. I'd like to get that list over to Lou by tomorrow.

Tiny comes over. Al just got here.

OK, Tiny. Show him in.

Hey, Corporal.

Hi, Al, and he comes over and kisses and hugs Corporal and then hugs Ernie and Vito.

Sit down Al. How about some coffee?

No, thanks.

How's business, Al?

Good, we've been picking up some heavy hitters. We put on a couple of new guys and they're doing great. They were working downtown and business got bad and they asked if we had a spot for them. We put them on and they've been bringing in a lot of action. We checked them out and they're OK.

Al hands Corporal a big envelope.

He looks inside it. Looks alright.

Al, we'll be branching out and I'm going to move you up. You'll be running some more places and you'll be getting some new help and I want you to train them the right way. We're gonna clean house and get rid of all the dead wood. I want you to get some people that know how to run the numbers up in Mount Vernon and Yonkers. Can you handle it?

Yeah, I can handle it.

You and Abe still run the Sports action and don't let this get out, got it? I'll get in touch with Abe and let him know about everything.

OK, Corporal.

Al hugs and kisses Corporal and then hugs Ernie and Vito and leaves.

Getting hungry, guys? How about some Chinese?

Yeah, that sounds good.

Chapter 23

Tony gets to the Sheridan Hotel where Conrad's Cloud Room is located. He parks his car and goes into the lobby and sees Amy sitting there.

Amy, what happened to you?

Brian and me got into little argument and he slapped me around.

That son of a bitch, I'll have him taken care of.

No, don't touch him, it was my fault.

Are you sure? You look like you got hit by a truck.

It looks worse than it is. Lets go into the lounge and have a drink.

Yeah, that's a good idea. They sit in a booth and order a couple of drinks.

Tell me, Amy, what happened? Tell me the truth.

We were arguing over him working nights and not making enough money. The kids are going into school pretty soon and it's going to be to much for me working and taking care of the kids and by the time I get finished, it will be time for them to get to school and kindergarten. I'll be lucky to get a few hours of sleep and pick them up and then it's time to go to work again. Then he's bellyaching about the kids, he wants to get a divorce and take them with him. I just don't know what to do, I'm so confused.

Take it easy, lets see what can be done. Lets have another drink and a bite to eat. Waiter, bring us another drink and a menu.

The waiter is back in a few minutes with the drinks and two menus. I'll check back in a few minutes and see if your ready to order.

Where's the kids now?

They're with my mother. She said she would take them for a few days until things calm down.

That was nice of her to do that.

Yeah, she's a great mom. I'm feeling better now that you're here.

Good, I don't like to see you like this, all banged up and down in the dumps.

The waiter comes by and takes their order.

Tony, I have to go to the ladies room and I'll be back in a few minutes.

She goes to a phone booth and dials a number.

It's me, Amy. How you doing, Joey?

Are you kidding? It's lucky for me that I jumped out the window. I thought your husband was going to kill me. I had to run through all the back alleys to get home. Good thing I had a key under the floor mat or I would have had to break a window to get in. Man, that was a close call.

Yeah, I called to find out how you are and let you know I can't meet you tonight.

OK, Amy. I'll call you at Conrad's tomorrow and maybe we can see each other after you get off and then we can finish what we started last night.

OK, I'd like that. I can't wait until I see you tomorrow.

She goes into the ladies room and looks into the mirror. I did a very convincing makeup job, enough to fool Tony. We'll eat and go up to the room and I'll give him a good ride.

After they finish eating and have a few more drinks they go up to the hotel room. They start talking about what a bad a situation she has.

Yeah, she tells him, I wish we had met a long time ago and then it would be just you and me.

Yeah, I know, he tells her, but I'm married with kids and you're married with two kids. If you didn't have two little kids I'd get divorced and you could get divorced and I would marry you.

She kisses him. Do you really mean it?
Yeah, just you and me.
She's all over him.

Chapter 24

The plane lands in Tampa and Jimmy and his girl get off the plane and get their bags. Then they go over to the car rental counter.

Can I help you?

Yes, we would like to rent a car.

The attendant fills out the papers and tells him the car will be outside in a few minutes and before you return the car, please fill the gas tank.

They walk outside and the car is waiting for them. Jimmy gives the driver a tip and he helps them put the bags into the trunk and they get into the car and drive off.

They get on I-75 and cross over the bridge into Sanibel and over to the Holiday Inn right on the Gulf of Mexico. Just in time to see the sunset.

Oh, Jimmy. I never saw a sunset like this in my whole life, it's beautiful.

Yeah, you're right, it sure is.

The clerk asks his name.

James Di Napoli.

We've been expecting you. Welcome to the Sanibel Holiday Inn. We have your room ready and it overlooks the Gulf of Mexico. I hope that you both enjoy your stay. The bellhop gets the bags. Follow me, please. He opens the door and turns on the lights. Jimmy puts a tip into the bellhops hand.

The view is wonderful and the ocean smells great. Jimmy and Liz hop onto the bed and they start jumping like two little kids and they're having such a good time.

Lets go get something to eat. They freshen up and change their clothes and head out the door and spot this little Sea Food Restaurant.

They go in and the waiter asks, table for two?

Yes.

You ready to order, folks?

Yeah, we'll have the grouper with fries and a couple of beers.

OK, I'll be back shortly.

Boy, what a great place Sanibel is. Wait till you see it in the morning. They have bicycles here and most of the people ride them or walk. When we get up in the morning we'll hop on the bikes and take a look around the island and see the sights. In the afternoon we'll take a ride over to Captiva, that's the next Island over. We can rent a motor boat and take a little cruise around the Gulf and have lunch on one of those small islands. This is like a little south sea island and we can go shelling on the beach.

The waiter returns with the groupers and drinks. Is there anything else?

No, this is fine.

This is good, how's yours, Liz?

Oh, it's really good.

They finish their dinner and Jimmy pays the check and leaves a tip.

When they get back to the hotel, Jimmy asks the hotel clerk to give them a wake up call at 7 in the morning. OK, have a good nights sleep. They go to their room and turn the light on and she goes to the restroom. When she comes out, he's sound asleep.

Poor Jimmy, he's had a tough week, I'm glad that I could help him out. He sure was worried about something. I wonder what could be that bad that made him so worried? Well, I hope everything turns out alright. Maybe getting away with me will be good for him and who knows. Some day we might even get married and he'll become a new man. Hopefully, we'll have a great time here.

Chapter 25

Chris calls Sal. How about meeting me at Gino's for a drink?

OK, I'll be there in about fifteen minutes. Sal walks in the door and sits next to Chris.

How's things coming along on your end, Sal?

Everything's going smoothly. Tony has all the permits and he's started clearing the property and he submitted all the plans and specs to the building department. Boy, he moves fast. The next thing is, they'll be starting on the foundation.

That's great news. How about all the doctors? Are they all on board, asks Chris?

Yeah, the word got out and now we have a waiting list to get space in the hospital. Yep, they're banging on the door to get in. This Medicare thing is going to be a gold mine. I think we better start looking for other places to build some more hospital's. We can put options to buy on a few properties that I know about. Once this hospital is up and running a lot of people are going to want to do the same thing. Chris, let me tell you, we got a head start on everyone and we can get the best spots in town at the right price. You and I can lock up these properties, but we have to keep this to ourselves. When Tony sees how good this is going, he'll be out there looking for himself. Remember, he's in business to make money too.

Yeah, I understand Sal, but we have a sweet little thing going with him. Lets keep it this way and we'll all make a ton of money.

Lets have a bite to eat and we'll talk some more about things.

Good idea, could we have a table?

Yeah, says the bartender. Hey, your table is ready.

OK, thanks.

The waiter comes by and asks, would you like some more beers?

Yeah, and I'll have spaghetti and meatballs and I'll have the same.

OK, I'll be back in a few minutes.

Now, Chris, we should start looking in the rundown neighborhoods, that's where this Medicare is going to really take off.

Sal, do you know anyone over in the Queens Borough President's Office.

Yeah, I know a couple of people there and I know Donald Mannheim, the Queens Borough President.

No kidding, that's great. Did you ever do any business with him?

As a matter of fact, Chris, I did.

OK, lets get moving on Queens too.

There's a few places out near Roosevelt Avenue and those neighborhoods are so run down that they're just about giving property away. Medicare will draw everybody in these neighborhoods.

The waiter arrives with their orders. Anything else, guys?

No thanks.

Chris, if we can get options on some of these properties and pick up a few from the city for back taxes, we'll have enough property to keep us busy for a long time. The Government is giving all sorts of tax breaks to hospital's to be built in low income neighborhoods. Now is the time to get in and make it while the making is good. This will be good for the next 15 to 20 years.

Sounds good to me. Lets get ready for the next hospital as soon as this one is finished.

Chris, It seems to be getting pretty hot between Tony and that little red head. The talk at the market on Arthur Avenue is that she's laid everything except the Atlantic Cable. I guess Tony don't know anything about that and I guess he'd drop her like a hot potato if he heard anything about it. I hope he don't, that could put a crimp in everything.

The other thing that could be trouble is Corporal. You know he don't like that kind of thing, one of his Associates going with some tramp that's doing everything that walks, crawls or talks. That causes gossip and especially on Arthur Avenue where he has his club. I don't know how we could break it to Tony.

Chapter 26

The train finally arrives in Fort Lauderdale and Charlie gets his bag.

Watch your step getting off.

Wow, the sun is so bright. Charlie has to squint to see. I better get a pair of sunglasses or I won't be able to see.

Hey, Charlie. Over here. I'm Bill. Carmine told me to meet you here.

Hi, Bill. Glad to meet you.

Come on, lets go to my place. How was your trip?

Not bad. I had a chance to catch up reading the newspapers.

We're about 20 minutes from here, you're right on time for lunch.

Good, I'm starting to get hungry. Wow, it's really hot down here.

Yeah, you gotta have a lot of suntan lotion or you'll get cooked. We're a block from the beach, you'll like it down here. You can relax and take it easy and we got a pool. When's the last time you've been to Florida?

About 10 years ago. Have you ever been to Fort Lauderdale?

Naw. we went to Miami for a week.

This is a nice place, not as crazy as Miami. Here we are, home sweet home.

They get out of the car and go into the house. We're home. Bill's wife comes out of the kitchen.

Charlie, this is my wife Kitty.

Let me take your bag. Sit down and make yourself comfortable. Would you like some iced tea or lemonade.

Yeah, iced tea would be nice.

Kitty brings him a glass of iced tea and goes back to the kitchen.

Carmine told me he would be calling today and if there's anything you want, just let me know. Another thing, if you answer the door, look out the peep hole before you open the door.

Kitty returns with a platter of sandwiches and a pitcher of iced tea. Help yourselves, hope you like them.

Bill says, if you wanna take a nap, that's your room right over there. There's a TV in there and we have cable.

Gee, thanks. Do you treat everyone like this? I feel at home already.

Great, just enjoy yourself and stay as long as you want. I have to leave for awhile but I won't be too long. Kitty will be here, so if you need anything just call her.

Bill drives down to the Beach Bar and Grill and parks his car.

Hey, Hank. Got a minute?

Sure, lets go into my office.

I just picked up that guy from New York and he's all settled in. Did Carmine call yet?

Naw, not yet.

OK, I told this guy Charlie not to open the door if anyone comes here, just look out the peep hole first to see who it is. I'll go home and jump into the pool for awhile.

Good, just give him anything he wants and keep him happy. I'll call you when I hear from Carmine.

As soon as Bill leaves, Hank gets on the phone and calls Carmine.

Hello, Carmine. It's Hank.

Did he get there yet?

Yeah. Bill picked him up and he's here now.

John, It's Carmine. He got there and everything's alright.

Good, I'll let you know when. In the meantime, everyone sit tight. Anything, call me, got it?

Yeah, I got it. Well, the clock is ticking.

John is sitting in his office talking to a few of his crew. Are you guys sure this is what's been going on?

Yeah, John, we were surprised to hear it too.

Well, I want you guys to double check this information, this could be bullshit just to get rid of Carmine and then the next thing we got the cops after us. Get hold of this guy that told you about Carmine and just act friendly to him. Take him down to the Spanish Steps and treat him real nice and when he's feeling real good, tell him that you're going to a party and then slip him a mickey and take him to the warehouse. When he comes to, give him a good going over and get everything out of him. When you're finished, get rid of him and dump him in the river. If Carmine was involved in that dope business, we'll take care of him too. Mum's the word, let me know what's happening. This has to be taken care of right away. Now, do you need any help?

No, we'll take care of it.

Chapter 27

Ernie and Vito meet over at the club on Arthur Avenue.

Vito, we better check out the store on Boston Post Road and show our faces, this way there's no question about who's who. While we're up there, we'll see about that guy Sammy. How about we put the word out that we're looking for somebody like Sammy to take over that store because Jimmy is moving up to another spot. You know he's going to get in touch with us, so when he does, we take care of him.

Hey, Tiny. We got a few things to take care of and we'll be back later on, but before we leave, sit down for a minute. Vito and me were talking about putting another guy on our crew. You've been here for quite awhile. How would you like to be one of our crew?

Sure, Ernie. I'd love that.

OK, as soon as we can find somebody to take your place, you're on. Do you know anybody that you could recommend?

Yeah, my cousin.

OK, Tiny, bring him over tomorrow morning, we'll have a talk with him. We gotta go now, see you later.

Boy O Boy. I've been waiting for this chance for a long time. I'll get in touch with my cousin right away.

Ernie and Vito drive up to the Boston Post Road Store.

Hey, Ernie. How you been, asks the old guy? I haven't seen you for a long time.

How's business, asks Ernie?

Not bad, it's moving along.

Jimmy's moving to another spot so we need somebody to take Jimmy's place. What do you think of that guy, Sammy?

I hear he's pretty good. He knows the business and he's always dropping in to see Jimmy. I heard he does a good business over there in Mount Vernon.

Put the word out that we're interested in talking to him.

Vito and me are taking over all the operations and Corporal is making a lot of changes, so if there's anything you want to talk about, you can get in touch with Vito or me. How long you been with us?

Over 8 years.

Do you like working with us?

Yeah, I do.

Well, you've been doing a good job here, so we're raising your pay by 300 bucks a week starting now.

Three hundred dollars, that's great. I don't know how to thank you.

Just keep up the good work and we'll be seeing you and don't forget, get in touch with that guy Sammy for us.

OK, and again, thanks.

Ernie and Vito leave and go downtown to the Spanish Steps.

Vito, watch. This guy Sammy will be calling by tomorrow. We'll see Angelo now and let him know how much the take is going to be every week and who to get rid of and who's coming to work here. The new Maitre d' is going to be Henri, he knows how to run a nightclub. Business should really pick up. With all the connections that Corporal has, he'll have all the top entertainers in New York and Hollywood begging to appear at the Spanish Steps. This will be the greatest nightspot in the whole country. Well, here we are. Let's go in.

They climb the stairs and Vito says, lets get rid of this carpet, the treads are starting to show.

Yeah, it's looks like hell.

They go to the office. There's Angelo, with some bimbo sitting on his lap.

Oh, hi. I didn't expect you.

Yeah, we can see that.

The girl gets off his lap and leaves the office in a hurry.

Please sit down, can I get you anything?

Naw, we just want to look around and have a little talk with you. Now, starting this week and every week, the take is 100,000 bucks and I want it delivered to Corporal every Monday morning. Understand?

Yeah, I understand.

Now, the new Maitre d' is going to be Henri, you know him, right?

Yes, I know him, he's the best in New York.

He'll be here later on today, and I want a list of everyone that works here. The people that are coming to work here will be showing up day by day, not all at once. I want you to show them the ropes so that everything changes slowly and smoothly and I want a list of the best people you have. We might keep them, but get rid of all the trouble makers as soon as the first group shows up.

Now, lets take a tour of the place, and by the way, no more broads in this office. When Henri gets here, he'll show you what has to be changed. This place has to be cleaned up. Vito wants that carpet on the stairs changed. He'll pick out the carpet and he wants it done fast. I guess that's it for now. Oh, and I forgot to tell you. Your new boss will be Moe Silverman. Any questions?

No, Ernie.

Ernie and Vito leave and drive back to the Zerega Club.

I don't think he was to happy. What do you think Vito?

He'll get over it. He still has a cushy job. He's not going to bite the hand that feeds him, but we'll keep an eye on him anyway.

Chapter 28

It's a pretty nice day. I'll go down to the Bronx and see Corporal and Ernie, but first I'll stop by the Yonkers Diner and get some breakfast. Moe gets in his car and drives to the diner. Corporal and Ernie are making some changes and big moves and I have a feeling that I'm moving up in the ranks. I wonder if Corporal took care of that thing I asked him about? That would be a big move up for me. He goes into the diner and spots a few guys from the Yonkers bunch and says hello to them and they wave back to him. The diner is a meeting place for most of the Yonkers crews and this morning is no different than any other morning. Everything looks OK with these guys. While he's having his breakfast, a few of the guys stop by to say hello on their way out.

After he finishes his breakfast he goes to the phone and calls Corporal. Ernie answers and Moe tells him that he's on the way down. Moe gets into his car and drives to the club.

When he gets there, he spots Amy walking along Arthur Avenue. I'd better keep quite about this. I didn't see anything.

He knocks on the door and Tiny opens it. Moe walks in and goes to Corporal and hugs end kisses him on both cheeks and then hugs everyone else.

Have a seat, Moe. Is everything OK up in Yonkers?

Yeah, seems alright.

I guess you heard. Ernie is the new Underboss and Vito is now my top Captain and Tiny is on Ernie and Vito's crew

That's great news, congratulations. He goes over and shakes their hands.

Moe, I took care of that thing for you. And something else. Moe, you are now running all operations at the Spanish Steps.

What? Holy smokes, thanks Corporal. I never dreamed of anything like that in my whole life.

He goes over to Corporal and hugs and kisses him.

Corporal tells Tiny, break out a bottle of Champagne. This is a great occasion and calls for a toast.

Tiny brings a bottle of Champagne and glasses and pours everyone a glass.

Corporal raises his glass. Here's to you guys, you deserve this. I never knew a bunch of guys like you. I'm proud to be your friend. You're the best friends that I ever had. I toast you.

Everyone toasts each other and they're all very happy. They all have been waiting for this moment. They are in solid with Corporal and they're all on the way up.

Meanwhile, Jimmy and his girlfriend are enjoying themselves, swimming and fishing and hiring a motorboat to go to those small islands and keys off the coast.

Hey, Liz. How would you like to live down here for the rest of your life?

Yeah, that would be nice, but not by myself.

Well, how about we get married and get away from that rat race and get a little place down here?

You really mean that?

Yeah.

I would love to marry you.

OK, lets get married tomorrow. We'll find a preacher and tie the knot.

Oh, Jimmy. I love you.

I love you too Liz. I decided that I'm not going back into that business, I got some money saved and we can get a little place and find a business. What do you think, Liz?

It sounds great.

Jimmy says, lets go and celebrate.

Back in New York. Tony is on the phone with Amy. I'm going to be gone for a few weeks, so when I get back, I'll see you and we'll make some plans to get away for a long weekend.

I'll stop by Conrad's tomorrow night when you get off, I want to give you some money for you and your kids.

OK, Tony. I'll see you then.

She calls her boyfriend. Pick me up when I get off, everybody is too busy to see little old me. I know you can take good care of me. I'll see you later.

Sal and Chris are having a bite to eat, and Sal is telling Chris, we can get options on two properties, both in Queens and I spoke to my friends in the Queens Borough Presidents Office. They said, everything can be taken care of. Just get the deeds to the properties and they'll take care of the rest. It's going to cost a little more this time because there's two properties, but we'll make a fortune on these two.

OK, sounds good to me. By the way, Sal. What's happening down at the Bronx Borough President's Office?

I really don't know, but I heard that the D.A. is really hot about getting some investigations started and that some private investigators have been watching Stanley Shaffer.

I also heard that Stanley was having some guys from the NYC Bureau of Public Works fixing up the street in front of his house and also fixing his driveway in broad daylight. He's got to be nuts. You got the Bronx D.A. looking to make a name for himself and he's pulling a stunt like this. I hope nothing comes out of this.

I got to get in touch with my friend down in the Bronx Borough Presidents Office and see if we can slip another zoning change in before the shit hit's the fan.

OK, how much do we have to put up for the options, Sal?

I'll let you know tomorrow, but I thought it might be cheaper for us to buy the properties now if we can get a good price on them. They've been sitting there for over two years. I think the time is now to get them.

OK, Sal. If you think this is the time, lets do it.

Alright, Chris. I'll be in touch tomorrow.

Chapter 29

John calls Carmine and tells him to come over to the night club about one o'clock.

OK, John. I'll see you then. I wonder what's going on with John? You never know with all this shit going on, I just gotta keep cool and do what I have to do. He drives over to Queens and parks his car in front of the club and he goes in and says hello to the two gumba's standing in front of John's office.

One of them opens the office door. Carmine is here.

OK, send him in.

Sit down. I want you to go down to Florida on Monday and take care of things. My two guys are going with you to make sure there's no trouble and that everything goes smoothly. Don't all sit in the same section. Your going to be picked up by Bill and Hank. They'll have everything ready for you guys to finish the job. Understand?

Yeah, I got it.

OK, here's money, don't use any credit cards. Bill and Hank have been taken care of. As soon as you're finished, you'll be taken back to the airport. The three of you, go back on the same plane. Call me when you're leaving Florida.

Now, this is what I want, he's going to be in a motel room, you knock on the door and he'll be looking through the peep hole. When he says, who is it? Pump two shots into the peep hole and when the door is opened, pump two more into his head and then leave. Make sure you have an extra gun with you just in case the one you're using jams. Wear rubber gloves and don't leave any shell casings laying behind. All of you take off your shoes and rubber gloves and put on other shoes that will be there for all of you. Give the guns to Bill and Hank and they'll get rid of them. Now, is there any questions?

No, I got it.

OK, give me a call tomorrow. I might have something else for you to take care of before you leave.

Ernie and Vito are at the club and they decide that Tiny is going to take care of this guy up in Mount Vernon.

Hey, Tiny. Come here. Did your cousin show up yet? We'd like to meet him.

Yeah, I was showing him around, I'll get him.

Hey, Arnie. Come in here. Ernie and Vito would like to meet you.

Arnie comes in and says hello to Ernie and Vito.

Arnie is huge, he has hands as big as hams, he must be six foot four inches tall and he must top the scale at over 300 pounds.

Arnie, can you drive a car?

Yeah, sure.

Can you cook?

Yeah, my mother taught me.

Tiny had a lot of good things to say about you.

Thanks, Tiny.

Well, would you like to work for us?

Yeah, sure.

OK, you're on. Tiny will show you everything. Welcome aboard Arnie. Be here at 8 tomorrow morning.

OK, I'll be here.

Seems to be a nice guy. Tiny, show him the ropes.

Now, the three of us are going to take care of a little business tomorrow. Tiny, do you have a piece?

Yeah. Bring it along, here's what's going down. We're going to whack someone and you're going to make your bones tomorrow. Nothing personal, it's only business.

Abe and Al are going over the days receipts. Since Jimmy left, there's a big improvement, the count is up by about 20 to

25 percent. The old guy is doing alright, he's giving us an honest count.

Yeah, says Al. What do you think?

Lets talk to Ernie, he might want to keep the old guy running it.

Chapter 30

Ernie and Vito are still at the club and the phone rings. Tiny answers it and tells Ernie, it's Sammy from Mount Vernon.

OK, I'll take it.

This is Sammy, I got your message.

OK, Sammy. You interested?

Yeah, when can I see you?

How about tomorrow, say around 11 in the morning?

OK, Ernie. 11 in the morning, see you then.

Ernie hangs up the phone and tells Vito. Sammy took the bait and he'll be here tomorrow. Now, we'll put everything on hold for a few days.

Tiny, everything is on hold for a few days, but bring your piece with you tomorrow. I want to take a look at it.

Arnie said he could cook, so have him cook something for all of us, and I told him to be here at 8 o'clock every day. Make sure that Arnie has a set of keys and gets to know everyone. Then I want you to impress on him that he never discuses anything about what goes on here. He always helps Corporal into the club and gets Corporal anything that he wants. Remember, speak to Corporal only when spoken to.

Now, Tiny. Vito and me will show you everything you have to know and do, When Vito has to take care of a few things, you pick up Corporal whenever he wants to go somewhere.

OK, I got it.

Meanwhile, Jimmy is getting a funny feeling. Nobody is trying to get in touch with him. He asks Liz to call her brother in Mount Vernon and see if everything is alright.

OK, Jimmy. What's the matter? You look like something is bothering you?

I don't know. I'm just a little jumpy and I'm wondering about things in New York. Let's use the phone booth outside to call your brother. Just ask about him and everybody and if anything is going on?

Hi, Eddie. It's me, Liz. How's Mom and everybody?

OK, I guess. I stopped by the numbers place and I was told that Jimmy is not there anymore and that he was at another place. The old guy that works there said he didn't know where Jimmy is.

Really, what else did you hear?

There's been some talk that there's going to be some big changes here in Mount Vernon as far as the numbers and sports go.

That's strange, Jimmy didn't mention anything to me about that.

Well, if I hear anything else, I'll let you know.

OK, Eddie, I'll call you tomorrow. She hangs up and tells Jimmy about what her brother told her.

Jimmy really looks worried now. Lets go back to the room. I gotta think. Something's not right. He turns on the TV and lays down on the bed and Liz lays down next to him.

What do you think is happening, Jimmy?

I don't know, but I don't think it's good. If something is happening, I got a lotta money stashed away. If I had to split, would you go with me?

Why would you have to split?

Well, I didn't tell you everything?

I figured there was something going on when you asked me to say that we met at the diner? What happened? Is that the reason we came to Florida?

Yeah, I got myself into some trouble with Corporal and the guys, and I was told to take some time off. That's when I asked Abe if it would be alright to go to Florida for a few weeks. He said that everything would blow over in a few weeks and it would be a good idea to take a few weeks off and go to Florida and that he would let me know when to come back. Things don't look so good, I think I'd better leave.

Well, what do you say, Liz? You want to go with me?

Where would we go?

There's a few places we could go to. California or maybe Texas. Lets think about this.

You know I love you and this would be a big move for both of us. I would have to leave my mother and my family forever. I just can't do that.

Yeah, I understand, Liz. We'll think of something, I'm sorry that I got you involved in this.

Jimmy tells Liz. Here's what we have to do. You're going back to Mount Vernon and back to your job. If anybody asks you, tell them that you and me broke up and if they ask you about me or where I am, tell them that I asked you to visit Boston with me. Tell them that I was acting strange and that I got drunk and we had a big argument and that's when we broke up and I left. You don't know anything about my private business. If anybody asks about you meeting me up at the Mount Vernon Diner. Tell them I asked you, but you couldn't because you were at the doctor that day. Now, pack up and get going, there's no time to waste. I have a feeling they'll be looking for me soon.

Jimmy, couldn't you talk to Corporal and those guys and tell them you're sorry?

No, that's not the ways it works.

There has to be another way, Jimmy.

I wish there was, Liz. Lets get going. Call the front desk and tell them you need a cab to go to the airport. Here's some money, buy your ticket to New York and use your credit card. If anybody asks, you tell them that you wouldn't take any money from me and you took care of your own ticket to New York. Tell them what a rotten time you had, and never again.

Jimmy, I can't say that.

You're gonna have to. These guys are bad. You gotta convince them that you and I are finished. Please do this. I'll always love you, but forget that I ever existed. Now get on that phone and tell the desk clerk to get a cab to take you to the airport. Get your bag and go over to the front desk and wait for the cab. When it gets here, leave in a huff and a puff. In a few weeks, you're going to get a check. Open an account down in Manhattan and don't try to find me. If anybody asks about me, just bad mouth me. Now leave.

Chapter 31

Arnie gets to the club at 8 in the morning and turns on the lights. I'm one of the guys. I'm going to do what ever it takes to get to be a Captain in Corporals family. When people see me they'll show me respect just like the rest of the guys in this family. Yeah, I'm here to stay.

Vito comes in and says hello to Arnie.

Hi, Vito. And Vito hugs him. I'll go and make some coffee, would you like some, Vito?

Yeah, sure.

Next in the door is Ernie and Tiny. They hug Arnie and he hugs them back.

Would you guys like some coffee? I just started making some.

Yeah, thanks.

As soon as it's made he brings a pot of coffee out and pours for the guys.

Where did you learn to make coffee like this?

My mother showed me.

Well, this coffee is great.

Thanks Ernie.

OK, Tiny. Show Arnie around and Tiny, did you bring your piece with you?

Yep, here it is.

OK, now go ahead and show Arnie everything.

Vito, this guy Sammy will be here soon, lets see what he's up to. I have an idea he's just looking around for his Boss, trying to find out what we have in mind. The son of a bitch is trying to play both sides against the middle. We'll pick his mind clean and then take care of him. We make the pitch to him that we need a new man for Mount Vernon and if he asks about Jimmy, tell him he's moving up and he took a little vacation before he starts. Let's see how fast he jumps at that. We make the offer real sweet, 1,500 bucks a week and a 5 percent bonus if he brings in more than 30,000 bucks a week. How's that sound, Vito?

Yeah, he'll grab a hold of that real fast.

Ernie remarks. Before we act, lets hear him out. Lets see what's happening with those idiots up in Yonkers and Mount Vernon. What a weak story they tried on us, having Jimmy come to us and say that the blacks in the projects are cutting in on our Boston Road business. Then having Jimmy tell this crap to Corporal. They all dug their own graves with that bullshit. Anyway, when we finish with this, we'll take care of Jimmy. I hope he enjoys the sun and surf. It'll be the last party he'll ever have.

Meanwhile, Chris and Tony are over at Ray's Boatyard waiting for Sal.

Chris, what do you think of Amy?

She's some dish. You got a beauty there, Tony.

Yeah, she makes me feel like a young stud again. I just can't get enough of her.

Yeah, I know what you mean.

How's everything with the wife and kids, Chris?

Great, the kids are doing well in school and the wife is busy with her organizations. She don't bust my balls about anything.

Hey, here comes Sal.

I got good news. I picked up two properties. I got the OK to start the rezoning process. As soon as they're rezoned, we submit the plans and the permits will be approved.

Tony asks, same deal?

Yep, says Sal.

Me too, says Chris.

Well, lets go over to the bar and have a drink on that good news. Here's to more great success. They drink and Tony orders another round. This is a great day. Lets keep up the good work, you get them and I'll build them.

Chris goes back to his office and calls his wife to see if everything is alright.

Andy comes in and says there's a woman on the line and that she has to speak with you.

Hello, This is Amy.

Hi, what's up?

I have something very important that I have to talk to you about. Could I see you over at Conrad's tonight when I get off at about 11 o'clock? It's very important.

OK, Amy. I'll see you then. I wonder what this is all about?

Chapter 32

Hey, Sammy. You ready to go down to the Bronx, asks Vinny? He's the Boss of Yonkers and Mount Vernon.

Yeah, I'm all set.

Now, don't get nervous, these guys are as stupid as shit. This jerk Ernie, that just got out of the can and that cripple Corporal think they got it all worked out to take over everything up here. Well, it's going to be the other way around. You just listen to them and go along with what they have to say. What ever they offer you, tell them you'll think it over and you'll get back to them the next day. OK, Sammy.

Yeah, I understand. Sammy leaves and drives to the Bronx.

This could be a sweet deal for me with those guys in the Bronx. I could tell Ernie that Jimmy is planning to hook up with the Mount Vernon bunch to take over Corporal's family and as soon as I heard about it, I was going to let you know. When I heard about you getting out, I began thinking about joining you and Corporal's family.

This could be the right time for me. Jimmy isn't around right now and they'll believe me, especially since that trouble Jimmy got himself into with them. Besides, it doesn't seem that I'm going anywhere with these jerks up here in Yonkers. Well, just about there. It's time to roll the dice.

Sammy parks his car and knocks on the door. Arnie opens it.

What do you want?

My name is Sammy and Ernie is expecting me.

Ernie, Sammy is here.

OK, bring him in.

Sammy follows Arnie in.

So, you're Sammy? Have a seat. Arnie, see what Sammy will have.

Would you like some coffee or something?

Coffee would be nice.

How about you, Boss?

Yeah, I'll have a cup of coffee.

OK, Boss. Coming right up.

Well, Sammy. What do you think?

I'm interested.

Good, did you mention this to anybody?

No, not yet.

Well, here's the deal. Jimmy is being moved up. We need a good man and we heard a lot of good things about you.

Excuse me, Boss. The coffee is ready.

OK, Arnie.

Sammy, this is Vito and Tiny. You'll be seeing a lot of them.

Hi, Sammy. They both say.

OK, tell us about you?

I've been with Vinny and his family for about 5 years and I run a place in Yonkers.

Why do you want to come over to us?

I know Jimmy for quite awhile and he tells me what a great family this is. The fact of the matter is, I need to make more money.

How much do you make now?

A thousand a week plus bonus.

We can give you more. How's 1,500 bucks a week plus 5 percent on anything over 30,000 a week?

Yeah, that sounds great.

What can you tell me about the Yonkers and Mount Vernon crew and their operation?

Vinny is the Boss and they got about 30 made guys and about 25 associates. They got all the numbers and a lot of the sports action and they also have a lot of the action at the Yonkers Race Track.

How about the bars and clubs?

They have just about all of them and most of the big money games are controlled by them. If you want to put money out on the street, you have to go through them. Just about everything in Yonkers and Mount Vernon is controlled by them. I heard that they're going to take over the Club Paddock.

And what else have you heard?

Well, I was going to tell you this today. Vinny is going to make a move on Corporal and you. Jimmy is in with them.

Really, where did you hear this from?

Jimmy tried to get me to join him and if I did, I would be moved up with him. Vinny has been trying to get me to find out more information on Jimmy and your crew.

Now, if you get anymore news about anything, let me know. When do you want to start?

How about Monday?

OK, you start at Boston Post Road.

Tiny, bring a bottle of brandy over here with some glasses and we'll all have a drink to our newest member.

OK, Boss. They all have a toast to Sammy and wish him luck.

Thanks a lot. I'll be leaving now.

Well, what do you guys think, Vito?

Before we do anything, we better talk this over.

You're right, Vito.

Let's go over everything before we tell Corporal. We don't have to worry about Jimmy for the time being and we round up all the family and make sure they stay put. We don't want to let this out yet, just tell them that we're making some changes and we'll let them know all about it soon.

Vito, get in touch with Moe and tell him to come here tomorrow.

Ernie calls Corporal and tells him he would like to see him.

OK, send Vito. I'll be ready in half an hour.

Vito, pick up Corporal. He'll be ready in half an hour.

Sammy is on his way back to Mount Vernon. I better go home for a while and get my story straight before I see Vinny.

Everything seemed alright. I think Ernie believed me. This could be a great move for me and if they're going to war I want to be on the winning side. I think that Vinny under estimated Corporal and Ernie. Well, I set the wheels in motion, no turning back now.

Corporal and Vito get to the Zerega club and Ernie goes to Corporal and kisses and hugs him and Tiny and Arnie do the same.

Arnie, I'm glad to have you on board, I've heard good things about you. Could I have a cup of coffee? Ernie tells me it's the best he's ever had.

Sure, Boss. Coming right up.

OK, Ernie, tell me what's happening?

Ernie tells Corporal about what's going on and the meeting with Sammy. Everything seems to be going better than I expected.

You handled everything very good. Now, we wait for a few days and let thing's develop. Did you start to get in touch with everybody?

Yeah, and we have Moe coming down here tomorrow.

Arnie comes to Corporal with the coffee and he takes a sip.

Ummm, this is very good coffee, Arnie. Where did you learn to make such great coffee?

My Mother showed me.

Well, you have a wonderful Mother.

Ernie, you were right, this is great coffee.

Tiny, Ernie tells me that Arnie is your cousin and you brought him in.

Yeah, Boss. He's a nice guy and he'll do everything he's asked to do.

Corporal asks Ernie, do you think this guy Sammy will keep his mouth shut about this meeting?

Yeah, he was sent down here to find out what he could. After we talked for awhile he let loose that he's looking to make more money. When I told him what we were offering, he jumped all over the chance to come over here. That's when he started spilling his guts about Vinny and Jimmy. I told him he could start on Monday. I'm sure he's going back to those guys to tell them he didn't find out anything new.

OK, let's start lining up all the operations that Vinny has up in Yonkers and Mount Vernon.

The next thing that we do is get up a list of our guys that can handle the action up there. Then we're going to open the books and take in the people that we need. I figure we should make about 20 and let in about 30 Associates. What do the both of you think, Ernie?

Yeah, we gotta have more people to handle all this extra business.

Right, I agree, says Corporal.

Now each of you give me a list of the people you think we should make and let in. Have it ready in a few days. Get me a list of all the made guys and Associates that we have. I'd like to have this family up to at least 300. Let's work out our plan of action within the next two weeks.

Find out where Vinny and the top guys live and hang out. We need to know this so that we can get them all at the same time. Find out if they're all going to any affairs or shindigs on the same day. They might even have a wedding or a big get together where we can take care of them all at once.

Sammy gets home, that was a pretty exciting day. I'll just take it easy for awhile and go over everything that happened today. I'm sure that Ernie bought my story.

Screw Vinny, all I am is the gofer. There's no future with these guys in Yonkers and Mount Vernon. They're a bunch of greedy shit heads. They think because the Yonkers Raceway is up here, they're better than everybody. The raceway is falling apart and all the business is going over to the Meadowlands. These jerks are so hard up for a buck they even tried to shake down Toys R Us and the manager called the FBI and five of those so called big shots got caught red handed with marked bills. All caught on video tape and then it gets splashed all over the newspapers. Well, those nitwits are going to be cooling their heels for the next five years. I must have been out of my mind to get hooked up with those retards. Anyway, I've made up my mind. They can kiss my ass.

Sammy calls Vinny. I didn't find out anything. They just wanted to know if I'd like to go to work for them since Jimmy is being moved up.

What? That's all, nothing else How come you didn't come back up here?

What for? There's nothing else to tell you.

Hey, don't get smart with me. Who do you think you're talking to?

I'm not getting smart with you, I told you that there was nothing else.

Yeah, forget it. I'll see you tomorrow.

Aw, I better slow down, the kid had a rough day. I flew off the handle. All this is making me a little nervous. Tomorrow is another day.

Chapter 33

Carmine just got a call from John and he has to run over to John's place real fast. When he gets there he sees John talking to a few guys that he don't recognize. When John is finished talking to these guys, he tells Carmine to come into his office.

Carmine. I want you to go over to Harlem and take care of two guys that were involved with Charlie. Here's a piece, check it out. They're at a cellar hangout near Pleasant Avenue and they're getting all boozed up with a couple of broads. Take those two guys with you that you saw on the way in. Hit Charlie's friends and the broads that are with them. They'll be there for the next couple of hours. Take these hoods with you and make sure you put them on before you go in. There's rubber gloves in the bag. Don't leave any shell casings laying around after you're finished. These guys know how to get in the back way. Leave the same way you got in. The door will be left open for you and nobody else but them will be there. No talking, hit them fast. Take care of the guys first and then the broads. Before you leave, put a round in each one's head, carry an extra piece in case you need it.

When you get to Harlem, you'll be dropped off at 117th street and when you're finished you'll all go to 118th street and there will be a gray Chevy waiting for you. The three of you will be taken up to the Bronx. Stay there until Casper and Doug come to pick you up and take you back here. Any questions?

No.

John opens the door. Bring those two fellas in here. OK, guys. Here's your guns and hoods and rubber gloves. Everyone take your pieces and look them over. The three of you are working together. You two know what's going down and this guy is in charge. He was just brought up to speed. Remember, hoods and rubber gloves on before you go in. Take the guys out first and then the broads next. Put a round into each one's head before you leave and don't leave any shell casings laying around. You guys don't have to know each other. Just do the job and leave. Anything else? OK, get going.

Boys, take these guys over to Harlem. You know what to do.

Carmine gets into the back seat with the other guys and Casper and Doug sit up front. They get over to Harlem and park on 117th Street.

You guys got everything?

Yeah.

Get out and walk up that alley and the door will be open. When you're finished, leave and walk to the waiting gray Chevy, don't run. See you guys on 118th street in a few minutes.

Carmine and the two guys get out of the car. Carmine follows them into the alley. He sees the open door and they put the hoods and gloves on. They check their guns and then walk into this smoke filled dimly lit rat hole. The music is blaring away and they're all laughing and drinking and carrying on.

No one seems to notice the three hooded guys that just walked in. One of the guys slams the door shut.

All of a sudden one of the women sees these masked guys with guns and she starts screaming and then they all start pleading for their lives. Please don't kill me, I have children. NO, NO, PLEASE DON'T.

Carmine and the other two start shooting the guys first and then they turn on the women. The men and the women fall to ground, blood all over the place. They walk over to the bodies and start shooting into their heads. The music is still blasting away and its is so loud that nobody heard the gunfire. They start picking up the shell casings and take off their hoods and gloves.

They step out and Carmine closes the door behind them and he follows the two guys to 118th Street. The gray Chevy is waiting there to pick them up and they walk to it and get in. They get up to the Bronx and are dropped off near the Yankee Stadium.

Carmine follows the guys into a building and they go upstairs and one of them knock on a door. A women opens the door and lets them in.

Two down and one to go.

He asks the woman if she has any beer in the house. She brings out three cans of beer and they all have one. These guys don't talk much, just as well, this isn't a social event. I'm glad that's over with.

What a mangy dump that was. You would think those guys would have had more sense than that. They should have left town. You can't hang around if John is pissed off at you.

Well, he should be happy with the results so far. I just have to take care of Charlie down in Florida and everything should quiet down. Boy, if anyone ever mentions dope to me again, I'll blow their head off.

Carmine is watching TV and there's a knock on the door.

The woman asks, Who?

Doug and Casper.

OK, guys. Lets go. Carmine, you go with me and you two go in the other car.

They get to John's place.

Doug says, you go in and I'll park the car.

Carmine opens the door and goes to John's office and knocks.

Come in and have a seat. How did everything go?

Fine, we did everything that you said. We were in and out in under three minutes.

Good, go home and take a shower and get rid of all your clothes and shoes. Give me a call tomorrow.

Chapter 34

Moe is thinking to himself, when I get the Spanish Steps moving, business should really pick up. Not only the sports but the high stakes card games. I'm going to have to get more people for both operations. That shouldn't be a big problem, I'll be making a fortune. Boy, things really are taking off since Ernie got back. Corporal is a great business man. He waited for Ernie to get out and now he's on fire. He held this outfit together like a field general. I guess I haven't seen the rest of what he has in mind.

For a guy that's disabled like him, nobody in his right mind would tangle with him. His wife Sally is such a wonderful person, she takes care of him like she was his mother. He really loves her. Nobody better ever say anything bad or insult her, they would find themselves floating down the river. Yeah, it was my lucky day when I joined Corporal's family. He's always been good to me.

Corporal is at the club with Ernie and Vito.

Ernie, hold up on things with Sammy. Lets take care of Vinny and his crew first.

Lou arrives and hugs and kisses Corporal and he hugs Ernie and Vito.

Lets go over to the table and talk a little. Lou wheels him over to the table and he sits down. He hands Corporal an envelope and he looks inside. Things seem to be looking up, it's nice and fat.

Yeah, Corporal, and the incinerators are just about ready to be installed in all the projects. And get this. They just passed a law that all apartment buildings in the five Boroughs have to have them within two years. And our guys have all the contracts with the city.

Well, that's very good news. Lou, you earned your stripes. I'm making you a captain.

Ernie and Vito, come in here and bring Tiny with you. Tell Arnie to open a couple of bottles of champagne and bring six glasses here. Sit down, all of you. Arnie brings the champagne and Corporal tells him to pour out six glasses.

Well, boys. Lou has just been promoted to captain and I want you all to have a drink and toast him on his promotion to Captain in our family. They all hold up their glasses and drink a toast to Lou. Corporal shakes his hand and hugs and kisses him. All the others do the same.

Tiny and Arnie, this should be a great honor for you to be part of this celebration. One day, the both of you will be standing where Lou is standing now. I expect you to be a big part of this family and to rise up like Lou, Ernie and Vito. I'm proud of all you guys. Here's to you, my friends.

Well, it's been a long day. I think I'll go home now. Vito wheels him out and they leave.

Lou has another drink with Ernie, Tiny and Arnie. Time to go. He says goodnight and leaves.

Lou gets into his car and drives home. Wow, I never expected to be promoted to Captain. What a great day this has been. Corporal is on the move and I'm part of it. The sky's the limit now with these guys at City Hall and they have all this other stuff coming up and I'm going to handle it all for them.

Hey, Manny. What do you think John will say when we tell him about Carmine and his cousin, Paulie?

The shit's gonna hit the fan. I didn't think it was gonna get this big.

The Bosses are really gonna go nuts when they hear about this, says Sergio. Well, we're nearly there. I wonder what else he'll want us to do?

Sergio parks the car in front of John's club and they both go in. John's two gumba's are there and one of them knocks on the office door.

Yeah, what is it?

Sergio and Manny are here.

OK. Have a seat. How did everything go?

Good, we did everything like you said, he's with the fishes now.

Did you find out anything about Carmine?

Yeah, he was one of the top dogs.

I was hoping that he wasn't. Anything else?

Yeah, we found out that his cousin Paulie is hooked up with Carmine too.

OK, anything else?

Naw, that's it.

OK, guys. You did a good job. Keep this to yourselves and get over here tomorrow about 1 o'clock.

John gets on the phone and calls Sonny in Harlem.

This is John, is Sonny there?

Hold on a minute.

Yeah, John. What's up?

Are you busy right now?

No.

Can you come over now? I'd like to see you.

Sure, I'll be there in about a half an hour.

OK, Sonny. See you.

I wonder what's going on? John would never call if it wasn't really important.

John calls his two gumba's. Come in and have a seat. I want you two to go down to Florida with Carmine tomorrow and take care of that little matter. When you finish, have Carmine sit up front in the car. The driver will stop on the way back to the airport and he'll say they have a flat tire. Everybody gets out to give the driver a hand and as soon as Carmine gets out. Put a couple of rounds into the back of his head. Turn him over and put two more into the front of his head. Then get his wallet and airline ticket. After that, toss him into the water and make sure you pick up the empty shell casings and then leave. Do the two of you understand everything?

Yeah, Boss.

OK, hang around for a little while. I'm expecting Sonny from Harlem. Show him in when he gets here.

Sonny parks his car and goes in.

Come in. Have a seat, Sonny.

Casper closes the door and Sonny asks, what's up?

My guys took care of that guy Willie last night, but before they did, Willie told them that Carmine was one of the guys running the operation and that Paulie, Carmine's cousin, was involved with them too.

Gee, he had us all fooled and he's he's gonna take care of my son in law.

Look, Sonny. This is why I asked you to come over here. We got all this under control. He's going to Florida with my guys tomorrow and they're going to take care of Charlie. When they finish him my guys are taking care of Carmine. We'll clean up this mess real quick and the cops will be satisfied. As far as Paulie goes, I'll have someone on this right away.

OK, John, thanks for letting me know about everything.

Don't worry, Sonny, everything will be fine.

OK, John. I'll be leaving now. Keep in touch.

Sonny leaves and John calls Moe up at the Paddock in Yonkers.

Hey, Moe. this is John, got a minute?

Sure, for you I got more than a minute. What can I do for you?

Are you going to be there for awhile? I'd like to see you.

Sure.

I'll be up there in about an hour.

John calls his two gumba's into his office and he tells them to get the car. We have to go up to Yonkers. One of them gets the car and parks it in front of the club.

OK, Boss. The car is here.

Lets go boys. Head up the Deegan Highway and get off at the Yonkers Racetrack.

When we get rid of Paulie, that should be the end of all this crap and we can get back to business. Well, just another few miles and we'll be there. Make a left here and park in front of the Paddock. I'll be out in about 20 minutes.

Hey, John. Lets go into my office and we can talk.

They both have a seat and Moe asks, what's up?

I have a little problem that has to be fixed. Can you take care of a guy downtown for me?

When?

As soon as possible.

Who is he?

His name is Paulie and he has an after hours place in Manhattan.

Where does he live?

In the Bronx. Can you do this right away? I'll double the payment.

OK, Let me make a call.

Timmy, can you and Gingy come over to the club right away?

Yeah, we'll be there as soon as I pick up Gingy.

OK, bring your tools.

They're coming over now.

John. Tell them what ever they ask you. They're the best. While we're waiting, lets have a drink at the bar. Here's to happy times and they toast each other.

The door opens and Timmy and Gingy walk in.

Hey, guys. Lets go into my office. They all go in and sit down.

This is John and these guys are Timmy and Gingy. Now, here's what's going on. John has a little problem and he would like to have it taken care of right away.

Timmy asks, where does this guy live?

In the Bronx on Pelham Parkway.

Where does he hang out?

He has an after hours place in upper Manhattan.

Can you get him to meet someone at say, down in Manhattan?

Maybe.

When can you get in touch with him?

I'll make a call right now. John calls Sonny, this is John. Can you get in touch with Paulie to meet with you this evening?

OK. Where?

Hold on a minute. John asks Timmy, where?

Timmy says, tell him, the diner on 125th Street under the West Side Highway.

John tells Sonny.

Yeah, I know where that is. Hold on for a minute. OK, I just spoke to Paulie, he'll be there at 8 o'clock.

Timmy says, have Sonny wait outside until Paulie gets there. Then tell Paulie he's got to get something out of the car. Tell Paulie to go inside and he'll be there in a minute. We'll wait outside until Sonny leaves and we'll take care of the rest.

John tells Sonny and he hangs up.

OK, guys, you got everything you need?

Yep, we'll call you when we're finished.

They leave and Moe tells John. That's it, they're the best. You don't have to worry. You can stop by tomorrow and drop off the money.

OK, how much?

Double, 50,000.

OK. Thanks Moe. I'm sorry it had to be on such short notice. See you tomorrow.

John leaves and gets into the car. OK, guys, back to Queens.

Chapter 35

Carmine is having a beer and watching TV and just taking it easy. I'll finish this up in Florida and then I'm taking a vacation.

The phone rings and it's John. Get dressed and take a cab over here right now.

OK, John. I'm leaving right now. He puts his clothes on and turns off the TV and lights. He gets on the elevator and when he gets to the lobby he goes out and hails a cab.

Take me to Queens Boulevard. Keep going until you see the Queens Boulevard Night Club. The cabbie parks in front of the night club and he gives him the fare and a 5 dollar tip. He goes into the club and John is waiting there with his two gumbas.

OK, guys. You're going to the airport and taking the same plane. Sit in different seats, pay in cash and don't stand in line behind each other. Put about 7 or 8 spaces between each of you. Got it?

Yep.

Take a cab to the airport. Call me before you leave and let me know what flight you're on so I can have you picked up. When you're finished, return to the airport and get back to New York. Remember, don't leave anything behind and pick up the empty shells casings. OK. Get going.

John looks at his watch. They'll be on their way to Florida by the time Paulie gets hit. As soon as Carmine calls me with the flight number and arrival time I'll call Florida and let those guys know the flight number and time that Carmine and the boys will get there.

The phone rings, it's Carmine. OK, John we'll be on flight 418 and we should land about 9:26.

Call me when you get there.

Right, talk to you later.

In the meantime, Timmy and Gingy are heading downtown. It's about 7:30 pm

Timmy tells Gingy, we should park up around Broadway and then get over there about 5 minutes to 8. This way nobody sees us sitting around to long. Remember, put this stocking over your head and put your hat on. Wear these rubber gloves and don't speak. Once the shooting starts, everyone will make a dive for the floor. Just walk in. Shoot him twice in the head and twice in the chest. I'll do the same. Turn and walk out. Any questions, Gingy?

No.

It's post time. Lets go. They park and turn off the lights.

Sonny arrives and parks on the opposite side of the diner, gets out and goes over and stands in front of the diner and waits. A car pulls up and parks in front of Sonny's car.

Paulie gets out and goes over to Sonny. He talks to Paulie for a moment and then walks to his car. Paulie goes inside the diner and sits at a booth and waits for Sonny.

Outside, Timmy tells Gingy to put on the gloves and the stocking and his hat. Timmy does the same and they walk over to the diner.

Sonny is still in his car as they walk in.

There's some people sitting in the booths. Timmy and Gingy walk up next to Paulie just as he's lighting up a cigarette. Paulie never sees it coming. Timmy and Gingy start shooting. People start diving for the floor. Paulie is spread out all over the booth and there's blood all over the place. They turn around and walk out. Nobody is moving or making a sound. They all keep hugging the floor.

Sonny is gone and Timmy and Gingy get into the car and take off the stocking and rubber gloves and head up to the Bronx.

They stop by the German Stadium for a drink and put the stockings and gloves into the garbage dumpster.

What'll you have?

A couple of beers.

Here you are, guys.

Well, here's to us. Man, that was a sweet one. Nice and clean. I'll go to the phone booth and call Moe.

It's Timmy, all done.

Good, stop by tomorrow.

Moe calls John.

Hey, John. It's done.

Good, see you tomorrow.

John calls Florida. They'll be in at 9:26 on flight 418. Did you move Charlie?

Yeah.

Good, my guys got all the details, they'll let you know when they get there. Do you have all the tools?

Yeah, everything is ready.

Chris is leaving to meet Amy over at Conrad's. He gets there a little early and has a drink at the bar. He's sitting there and Amy walks up behind him and covers his eyes with her hands.

Guess who?

He pretends not to know and he spins around on the bar stool.

It's me, Amy. Are you surprised?

Yeah, I am.

Amy throws her arms around him and gives him a big kiss on the lips.

Umm, that was nice, what a surprise.

Yeah, I've been waiting a long time to do that to you, Chris.

You have?

Yeah, for a long time.

Lets have a bite to eat.

Sounds good to me, she says.

They go into the restaurant and the waiter leads them to a corner table. He gives them both a menu and asks if they would like to have something to drink?

Yeah, a nice bottle of red wine.

Gee, you look beautiful, Amy.

Oh, thank you, Chris.

The waiter is back with the wine and he pours two glasses.

Here's to us, Amy.

And she says, here's to romance.

Well, lets have a good time then. What time do you have to get home, Amy?

I don't have to go home tonight. I have a room here at the hotel.

You do.

Yeah, would you like to go up and see it later?

Yeah, I sure would.

OK, and if you get tired you can lay down and rest. Would you like that?

Oh yeah, I sure would.

The waiter comes by. Would you like to order now.

Yes, I think I would like a T-bone steak with mushrooms.

And you, sir?

That sounds good. I'll have the same.

The waiter pours another glass of wine for both of them.

She moves over close to him and starts to rub his thigh. He's starting to get worked up and she knows it. She's an old pro at this, only he doesn't know it.

The waiter brings the steaks and asks if there's anything else?

Yeah, bring another bottle of wine.

Yes sir, coming right up.

This is delicious. Have you heard anything from Tony, asks Chris?

No, nothing at all. I hope that naughty boy behaves himself. He's such a bad boy at times. Well, we're here and he's not, lucky me. I've got what I wanted for a long time. Now this will be our little secret, won't it, Chris?

Oh, yeah. It sure will be.

The waiter asks. How about some dessert?

Yes, I would, some strawberries with whipped cream.

And you, sir?

An espresso.

How do you like working here, Amy?

I hate it, every drunk in the place grabs my ass and I have to pretend to like it. The money is good but it's not a career move. Sometimes a nice guy like yourself comes in and asks me if I would like to go out with him. But it's the same old thing, the only thing they want is to hop into the sack with me and I never see them again. But you and Tony are not like that. You are real gentlemen.

The waiter comes by with the dessert and espresso. Will there be anything else?

No, let me have the check, please. They finish and Chris leaves the money on the table.

Come on, Chris. Let me show you my nice room. She takes his hand and leads him to the elevator. They get off and she takes the room key out of her purse and gives it to Chris. Could you open the door, Chris?

Yeah, he takes the key and opens the door. He turns on the lights and closes the door and she puts her arms around him and starts kissing him.

Oh, baby. Come over here and sit on the bed with me. She tells him to get comfortable. Then she goes to the rest room and takes a shower and puts on a see thru gown.

When she's finished he goes in and takes a shower and then wraps a towel around himself and comes out. Amy pushes him onto the bed and she starts to dance in front of him.

Tony got himself a hot little tomato here. What a great little body. I guess Tony won't mind if I hop onto to that little beauty for awhile especially since he's not here. What he don't know won't hurt him. After all, what are friends for?

Chapter 36

Carmine is looking out the window and the plane is gaining speed going down the runway. All my problems will be over pretty soon. The plane is up in the air and I'll be in Florida before I know it. The gumba's are busy looking out the windows and the stewardess is coming around with refreshments. I think I'll have a scotch and soda to steady my nerves.

Meanwhile, Bill and Hank are waiting at the airport to meet Carmine and the gumba's.

The plane should be landing soon, Hank. As soon as they get here, we'll go and take care of Charlie. This way no one has second thoughts about this and they won't get cold feet.

Yeah, says Hank, as he lights a cigarette. Don't waste time, just go there and do it. Carmine won't be thinking about anything else. OK, the plane should be landing in a few minutes. Bill, check to see that we have everything, gloves and three guns.

Yep, everything's here.

Carmine gets off the plane followed by the two gumba's and walks into the terminal. He goes to a news stand and buys a pack of cigarettes and lights one up and then walks outside followed by the two gumba's.

Carmine, yells Bill. Over here.

The three of them go over to Bill and get into the car.

Bill asks, how was the trip, Carmine?

Pretty good, nice and smooth.

Here's what we're going to do. We're going to take care of Charlie, says Bill. Carmine, you're going to knock on the door and put the gun right up to the peep hole. Charlie will look out the peep hole and when you hear him say, who's there? Fire twice. Hank will open the door and Carmine, you will put two more rounds into the back of his head. Make sure you pick up the empty shell casings and put them into the bag. Hank will close the door and lock it. Here we are.

Carmine and Hank get out and walk to the door. Carmine puts the gun up to the peep hole and then knocks. Nothing happens, he waits for a few seconds and then knocks again, still nothing.

The two of them look at each other.

Hank starts to panic. Something's wrong. Stay here, Carmine.

You two, Hank yells to the two gumba's, run to the back and take a look and if he tries to get away, waste him.

Carmine points the gun at the peep hole and knocks again. Suddenly the door opens. Carmine and Hank are caught by surprise. There's Carmine holding the gun straight at Charlie's head and Charlie looking wide eyed at him. For a moment, they're frozen and terrified.

Two shots ring out and Charlie falls to the floor.

Quick, roll him over and Carmine pumps two more into the back of his head.

Hank, pick up the shell casings and lets get out of here. Close the door and lock it.

The two gumba's come running and Carmine tells them to get into the car. Hank and the two gumba's get into the back seat and Carmine sits up front with Bill.

The car speeds away and Bill asks. What happened back there?

When I knocked on the door, Charlie was supposed to come to door and look out the peep hole and say, who's there? Nothing happened and I knocked again. Still nothing happened. Hank and me were still standing there and I gave it another try and knocked again and all of a sudden the door opened and there's Charlie standing there without saying a word. That scared the hell out of me. I didn't expect that, says Carmine. If he had a gun he would have killed Hank and me.

Hank is so shaken he can hardly talk. I thought we were gonna die right there. I was frozen in my tracks. It's a good thing he didn't have a piece in his hand or it could have been the other way around. What an experience that was. I'm glad it's over.

Me too, says Bill. Now put all the guns and gloves into the bag along with the empty shell casings.

Carmine still can't calm down. I never had such a fright in my whole life like that. I'd better get a drink to settle down. I'm getting too old for all this crap. I gotta take a long vacation.

Bill points, that lake is loaded with alligators. Oh, Oh, I think we got a flat tire. He gets out and goes to the front driver's side.

OK, guys. Get out and give me a hand with this flat.

Everyone gets out and the gumba's walk up behind Carmine as he's looking at the tire.

What's going on here? There's no flat.

He looks up and the two gumba's are pointing guns at him. His eyes are bugged out and he starts pleading for his life. Hey, guys, don't do this to me. Please give me a break.

The gumba's open fire and Carmine falls to the ground. They walk over to him and put a few more bullets into his head.

Get his wallet and airline tickets. OK, drag him over to the lake and toss him in. The alligators will take care of the rest of him.

The gumba's take his body by the feet and head and swing him back and forth a few times and let go. He sails about 10 feet out into the lake. Everyone gets back into the car and they drive to the airport and drop off the gumba's.

Bill and Hank head to the closest gin mill to have a drink. This was the wildest hit that I ever was on. Hank is still shaking.

Yeah, me too. Those guys from New York are nuts. That was the end of the line for those two guys.

Chapter 37

Hank calls John, everything is all taken of down here and your two guys are on their way back. They should be there about 6 o'clock.

Thanks, Hank. Any problems?

Nope, no problems.

OK. I'll keep in touch.

This should keep the cops and everyone happy, especially Sonny. Well, the boys will be in shortly and I'll get the rundown from them. I have to go and see Corporal and Ernie up in the Bronx soon. They got something they want to talk to me about. I'll check with everybody and make sure that things are running nice and smooth.

Corporal and Ernie are at the Zerega club talking about how things are running.

Ernie, is everyone satisfied about the moves and promotions that we made in the family?

Yeah, I'm pretty sure they are.

Well, I asked John and Sonny to come up here so we can talk over a little business and I want them to know that you are taking over most of the day to day operations of the family.

I heard that some of those guys in Brooklyn and New Jersey are thinking about expanding their operations over here in New York. If we can work out some mutual agreements with John and Sonny, we'll let those family's in Brooklyn and New Jersey know that if they make a move on any of our family's, they'll get hit by all of us and we'll wipe them out. Sonny, John and us will meet some time this week. What do you think Ernie?

Sounds pretty good to me.

Now, how are you coming along with this problem up in Yonkers and Mount Vernon?

I got a few guys finding out about Vinny and his top guys and I found out that they get together once a week and have a little poker game. When I find out when and where, we'll take out all the top guys and Vinny in one shot. When that's done, we walk in and take over all their operations. If anyone doesn't come over, we get rid of them.

How about that guy Sammy?

When everything is over, we take care of him too. I want to have him hang around for awhile, see what else he has to say.

OK, Ernie. It looks like you have everything mapped out.

How about the collections, everybody giving the right count?

Nobody is short changing us and they're all on time. The Spanish Steps should be up and running soon along with the gaming and sports action. We're putting Al in charge of all that action and Hanri is right on top of everything. His envelope is always on time and never light. It looks like he put life back into that place. Angelo had a long run there at the Spanish Steps and he better be satisfied with his new position. I don't hear any bitching and moaning from him.

How about the bank and Abe?

He's the best. He runs it like it was a real bank and he makes a lot of money for us.

Well, I'm happy to hear that from you, Ernie. After we settle all the family business. Let's promote Abe to Captain. What do you think, Ernie?

I think that's a great idea. He's always been loyal.

Well, Ernie. You're doing a great job and I appreciate all that you've done.

How about your new helpers, Vito and Tiny?

They're good, we can depend on them and they have no ambitions, only the family and you.

That really makes me very happy, Ernie.

It was kinda rough around here while you were away. But you're back now. I haven't been feeling too good for awhile so when this family business is finished, I'm gonna check into the hospital and get a tune up. My Doctor has been after me for awhile, so I'll make him happy and go into the Hospital.

Ernie, I know you're up to the job and you can take over. It's about time to hand the family over to you. Start building the family the way you want to operate it and I'll start to stay more and more in the background. Just keep it to yourself for now. When you think you're strong enough, step up to the plate and let them all know that you're in charge. Remember, don't trust anyone, they'll all test you. When they do, act fast and take care of them and don't show any mercy. Be ruthless and you won't have any trouble from any of them. I'll always be there for you, Ernie, you can count on that.

Thanks, Corporal, and I'll always be there for you.

Chapter 38

Jimmy is on his way to Miami to get the money that he stashed in a bank. Nobody knows about it and he put it in under a different name. Good thing that I got that name and Social Security card, it makes life much easier for me. I know that they're looking high and low for me, but they'll never catch up to me as long as I'm careful. From now on, I'm John Martin. I can't make any slip ups. I have to stay away from casino's and clubs or anywhere that those guys hang out at. They got eyes all over the place. I think I'll head out to Cleveland, Ohio and open a little business.

I got to remember, I'm John Martin. Just go into the bank and get my money. Can't forget the briefcase and put on the glasses. He parks the car and goes into the bank.

Good morning. May I help you?

Yes, I want to open my safe deposit box.

Would you please sign the register? Follow me. May I have your key? She opens the metal door and pulls out a big box and hands it to him. Here's your key. Would you like one of the private rooms, Mr. Martin?

Yes, thank you.

She opens the door to the private room and leaves.

He starts to fill up his briefcase. It's a good thing I got a big box. Good, all done. He goes to the attendant and gives her the key.

She puts the box back into the vault and locks it up with his and her key. Is that all, Mr. Martin?

Yes, thank you.

124

The new John Martin walks out of the bank with his briefcase and drives away. There's a nice looking motel. He parks
and get's his bags.

Are you checking in?

Yes.

The desk clerk finishes checking him in.

OK, Mr. Martin. That's room 2153.

Jimmy goes to his room. There should be close to 800,000
bucks here. I'll put some of this cash into a few of these banks
and I'll fly to Cleveland and put the rest into a few banks up
there. He finishes counting the money and packs up the bun-
dles of cash and goes out and gets into his car. When he's finished putting some of the money into three banks, he goes
back to his motel and takes a shower and gets dressed and
checks out. I'll return the car and I'll get on a late flight to
Cleveland. Then I'll check into a hotel near the airport and get
a bite to eat. In the morning I'll put the rest of this money into
a bank and then take a look around.

He checks out of the motel and drives to the airport and
returns the car and then goes to the ticket counter.

Can I help you?

Yeah, a ticket to Cleveland, Ohio.

Coach or first class?

Coach.

Next flight is at 9:15, flight 453, leaving from gate 21.

OK, and he pays her. Lets see, I got about 45 minutes. I'll
go to a pay phone and make a hotel reservation.

Good, that's all set. When I get there I'll have something
to eat and hit the sack. I'll be as fresh as a daisy in the
morning.

Now boarding for flight 453, have your tickets ready.

He goes to his seat by the window. Everyone is seated and
the plane begins to taxi out to the runway. It stops and waits for
a few minutes. All of a sudden it starts moving down the runway, faster and faster and it's lifting off the ground and heading straight up for the sky and it makes a turn. He's looking out
the window at the cars with their headlights on driving up and

down the highway. The plane straightens out and then starts to climb again like it was a rocket and he's off to Cleveland. Wow, that was better than a roller coaster, the last time I was on a plane it was smoother than this. The guy flying this plane must have been a fighter pilot.

Chapter 39

Chris gets to his office early. Hi, Andy. Any messages?

Yeah, Tony called.

Go down to the candy store and get the News and Mirror.

Here's the papers, Chris.

He turns to page five. There's an article about the Bronx Borough President's Office being investigated for corruption and that indictments are expected to be handed down soon. The Bronx DA has had an ongoing investigation into corruption in the Bronx Borough President's Office for some month's now. There's a rumor that the target is the Bronx Borough President Stanley Shaffer and that he has ties to organized crime. When contacted, the Bronx DA's Office had no comment.

It seems to be getting a little hot down in the Bronx Borough President's Office. I don't think I'll call Tony right now, the DA is just trying to make a name for himself. Well, I'll just keep an eye on things.

Chris calls Amy, she answers the phone.

Hi, Chris. I was just thinking of you.

You were? I was thinking of you, too.

Oh, how nice.

Guess who I was just talking to, Amy?

Who?

I was talking to Tony and he asked me to take good care of you until he gets back.

That was nice of him, then get over here and take care of me right now.

OK, I'll be there in about two hours.

What? Two hours. What am I going to do for two hours?

Chris answers, I'm certain you'll think of something.

You naughty boy, get over here as fast as you can to our little love nest. Room 304. I'll be waiting.

Boy, she's something, no wonder Tony's nearly out of his mind with her. I might as well have some fun with her while the getting is good. Tony will be back in about a week and the party is over. If this ever got out, my business and friendship with Tony would be over with. I'd better be careful and not let her get inside my head.

Ernie and the guys are at the club, the phone rings and it's Sammy.

I got some information on the Yonkers bunch.

Come over, Sammy.

Hey, guys. Sammy's coming over. Arnie, when he gets here pat him down and don't say anything. I'll do the talking.

Hey, Ernie. He's here.

Let him in.

Sammy comes in and Arnie puts him up against the wall and pats him down.

Hey, what's going on?

Arnie is just learning the ropes. I told him to pat everyone down that comes in here.

Uh, OK. I found out where Vinny and his Captains are having their card game. It's tomorrow night at the Pizza place on Broadway and Ludlow. They usually have it at another place but they're fixing it up and it's going to be closed for awhile.

Thanks, Sammy. We'll check it out.

Ernie calls Corporal, Sammy was just here and I'd like to talk to you.

Send Vito over now. I'm ready.

OK, he'll be there in a few minutes.

Vito gets there and calls on the intercom. It's me, Vito.

Come up and give me a hand.

They get to the Zerega Club and Vito wheels him in.

Ernie, lets go in the back and talk.

He sits next to Corporal and tells him that Sammy was just here. He told me where Vinny and his guys are going to have their card game.

What do you think, Ernie?

I think it's a set up. This jerk is trying to convince us that these guys are going to have a card game tomorrow and it's going to be a piece of cake. Let him think that he sold us on that. He's just trying to play one against the other. He'll go back and tell them that he just set us up and they can wipe us out as soon as we walk in. I've got a few people on it and we should have it all worked out pretty soon.

Corporal, I'd like your permission to bring Moe and his guys in on this. They're the experts when it comes to these sort of things. Moe and me and his crew can take Vinny and his guys out fast. Ernie continues, after that, I'd like to take Arnie and Tiny with us. They're still wet behind the ears and they can gain some experience and we'll get rid of Sammy.

Corporal replies, I like the idea, go ahead and do it. That's one of the reasons I picked you to take over this family.

Corporal tells Ernie, I have John and Sonny coming up here tomorrow and I want you in on this meeting. If they haven't already heard, they'll know that you are the Underboss of this family and that I handpicked you to take over this family. When they come here, just listen and we'll talk after they leave.

Now, take me out to the front so I can talk to the guys for awhile.

The guys really love Corporal. He never looks down his nose at them and he's just like one of the boys. He's not like some of the bosses that got made because they married into one of the bosses families. Those jerk's don't last too long. They bring it on themselves when they get whacked.

Chapter 40

The Bronx DA Robert Gallo is as happy as a pig in shit. It seems that a lot of people are buzzing about the newspaper articles that were leaked by the DA's Office. The DA knows a lot about what's been going on in the Bronx Borough President's Office and quite a bit about Stanley Shaffer and his ties to organized crime, but they don't have any hard evidence yet. Never the less, they're all in a great mood. They've put the first crack into that wall of silence.

Stanley Shaffer is shitting in his pants since they splashed those pictures in the newspapers showing the Public Works employees paving his driveway and a big dump truck with N.Y.C. Public Works on its sides, pouring concrete on his sidewalk and NYC Public Works employees with shovels and rakes working on his driveway. He must think that it pays to advertise.

Anyway, all those young attorneys that want to be known as crusaders and crime busters are slap happy. They think that they are on their way to busting the biggest government conspiracy between government officials and organized crime since Al Capone. Yeah, this guy Gallo has them all fired up. Everybody better watch their ass.

Al is spending a lot of time down at the Spanish Steps, he sees a lot of potential for high stakes games and a great opportunity for sports betting. Midtown is the place for growth. We got our foot in the door and nobody is going to come up against us. This is like Las Vegas in the heart of Manhattan. I gotta sit down with Corporal and Abe and go over all the figures with them. This could be bigger than we ever thought.

Lou drops in at the Zerega and greets Ernie and the others. How's Corporal? He's fine.

Ernie, could I have a word with you in private?

Sure. Lets go in to the back room.

He hands Ernie a big envelope. I have those five no shows that Corporal wanted. Just let me know the names and I'll take care of things for you.

OK. I'll let you know tomorrow. How's everything coming along, Lou?

Pretty good, Ernie. We're working on a big one right now, I'll let you know how everything is going after this next meeting with the Mayor and his guys.

Do you need anything, Lou?

No, not right now.

Well, I'll be going now, Ernie.

Abe stops in and hugs Ernie and the others and he and Ernie go into the back room. He hands Ernie a big white canvas bag.

Everything OK, Abe?

Yeah, everything's good. How's Corporal?

He's fine.

OK, that's good. I got to get back for the rest of the collections.

Next, Angelo comes in and hugs Ernie and the others.

Lets go into the back, Angelo. How's everything at the Spanish Steps?

Much better since you and Henri took over. Angelo hands Ernie a big fat envelope.

Ernie opens the envelope and looks at the $100 bills. Looks good.

How's Corporal? Good.

OK, Ernie, I have to be going.

Al comes in and hugs Ernie and the others. Lets go into the back room. When they get back there Al hands Ernie a big fat envelope filled with cash.

Looks good.

I gotta talk to Corporal and you along with Abe.

OK, how about tomorrow?
That will be fine.
Be here about 10 in the morning.

Chapter 41

The phone rings. Sonny, I just called to remind you about our meeting with Corporal.

Yeah, thanks John.

If you want I could stop by and pick you up.

Aw, that's alright. I have to do a few things after we're finished.

OK, Sonny. I'll see you up there.

Sonny gets into his car and starts driving up to the Bronx. On his way, he's thinking about his daughter. She's gonna flip when she hears about Charlie. She really loved the guy, but he was such a son of a bitch. This would never have happened if he had listened to me. He could have risen to the top and taken over my spot when I retired. Aw, no great loss, I never liked that jerk anyway. Always chasing after those sluts and whores in Harlem. He never had any respect for anyone. Just because he was married to my daughter, he thought he could get away with anything. He made me look bad. Well, everybody in Harlem will take notice of this when they deliver his dead ass back here and if anyone tries to do anything like this again, the same thing will happen to them.

I wonder what Corporal has on his mind. He's a real smart guy and a man of his word. I have all the respect in the world for him. He'd do anything for a friend, but cross him one time, you're dead. He loves his wife Sally and he adores her and she loves him and would die for him. Anyone that would disrespect her would get killed. No one in his right mind would ever think of doing anything like that.

Well, here we are. John parks right behind him and they both go in.

Hey, Corporal.

Hi, John and Sonny. They all hug and kiss each other.

Lets go into the back room. Arnie brings in coffee and espresso and bagels.

This is Arnie, fellas. He's the new addition to the Family. Arnie, say hello to John and Sonny.

Hi, nice to meet you fellas and he hugs them both.

That's a pretty big guy, Corporal.

Yeah, he's Tiny's cousin.

The reason that I asked you up here is, two of the families from Brooklyn and New Jersey are planning to make a move on us. They've been bragging about taking over all our operations. What I'd like to propose is that we form an alliance and warn all of them that if a move is made on any one of us, they'll be taken out right away. So if they're wise they'll stay in their own back yards.

Yeah, it sounds pretty good but does this mean we all become one Family?

Naw, not at all. We all keep our own identity and our own operations. We just let everyone know that if anyone gives us any trouble, the full force of our Families will come down on them. What do you think, John?

Well, we've always helped each other in the past. I think it's a good idea.

Sonny agrees. I'm in, it's a great idea.

They all put their hands on each others hands and it's done.

Arnie, bring a bottle and some glass's and pour some drinks. Corporal toasts to the success of this alliance and to this wonderful friendship of ours. Here's to all of us.

Ernie, come over here and have a drink with us.

John and Sonny, you know that Ernie is the Underboss of this Family and I want the two of you to be the first to know that Ernie will eventually be made the head of this Family.

Hey, that's great. Congratulations, Ernie. They all toast Ernie.

Thanks, I'll carry on the same way that Corporal has for all these years. You'll always have my support, you can count on it.

They come over and hug and kiss Ernie and he does the same.

Sonny says, I have to get back to Harlem to take care of some business.

Me too, says John.

Ernie, now we have the biggest army in all of New York City. I'm happy that they accepted you to become head of our Family. Now, we can talk from a position of power. The only thing that we have to be careful about is from our own ranks. If you find a Judas, get rid of him and do it fast. Now, we take care of that bunch up in Yonkers and Mount Vernon and Sammy too. One other thing, leave a message for everybody in Yonkers.

OK, Corporal. I got something very special in mind for Sammy.

Has anybody heard from Jimmy?

No, not yet.

Put the word out that we want him. We might as well clean up everything while we're at it.

Kenny calls Chris. Sonny's son in law will be getting in about 6 tonight.

OK, have Bob set up everything when he gets here. Call Sonny and tell him everything will be ready for tomorrow afternoon.

Your wife, Eileen called and said that she has to go to a meeting at the school tonight and Amy called and asked if you could stop by this evening. A few people stopped by and left insurance checks for the funerals that we had last week. Carmine's family called and said that they haven't heard from him in a week and could you find out if anybody has seen him down in Harlem?

Jimmy is checking things out in Cleveland and most of it looks like the South Bronx. Brother, it doesn't look so promising. I'll go back to the hotel and look through the newspaper to see if there's any business for sale, but it looks like the whole city is headed for a rummage sale.

I must have been crazy to get mixed up with Sammy, now I have Corporal after me. What a sweet life I had. I'd give anything to go back to New York again, but that's out of the question. As soon as I got spotted, I'd be dead within a hour. I'll stick around here for a few more days and see if I can find anything.

Jimmy heads back to the Hilton hotel and goes into the bar and grill. He sits down at a booth in the back of the restaurant and the waiter comes over.

I'll have a ham and swiss on rye and a beer. He looks around the restaurant. Only a few people here. I guess it's too early for anybody. They all must be working right now. I wonder what the night life is like around here? Maybe I'll come down later tonight and check it out. The waiter comes back with Jimmy's order. He's sitting there eating his sandwich and just looking out into space. All of a sudden, he sees a women that he thinks he knows walking through the lobby carrying a briefcase. Where do I know her from?

She's from New York. Yeah, now I remember. I knew her down at the Jersey shore in Wildwood. She looks a little different now, very business like. Yeah, she was always in a bathing suit or wearing jeans and a tee shirt. Man, she's still looks good. She doesn't know what I was involved with. I'll go over and say hello. What was her name? Now I remember. Christina Malloy.

He walks over to her and says hello, remember me?

She looks at him. Jimmy? Yes, Wildwood, New Jersey. Oh, yes. I remember now. That was a long time ago.

And you're Christina Malloy.

Yes, and you remembered. How nice to see you again. What brings you to Cleveland?

Business. And how about you?

I'm just finishing a business trip and I've got to be back on Monday.

Are you staying here, Christina?

Yes, I am.

How about you?

Yeah, I'm staying here too. How about having dinner and talking over old times?

OK, I'll just go and freshen up and I'll meet you back here at about seven.

Great, I'll see you then.

Wow, what a small world. She's still a knock out. Hmm, maybe Cleveland isn't such a bad place after all. Jimmy goes back and finishes his beer and pays the check and leaves a tip. He goes over to the front desk and asks, is there any entertainment here tonight?

Yes, there's an orchestra and dancing starting at 8 o'clock. You can make a reservation over there at the dining room. He goes over a makes a reservation for two for 8 o'clock.

What luck, meeting her. I wonder if she's seeing someone or if she's married? Well, I'll go upstairs and shower and get ready. This could be my lucky day.

Chapter 42

Moe is driving down to the Spanish Steps and thinking to himself. This is a great move for me. I can bring a lot of people into New York and show case them at the Spanish Steps. A lot of their careers are starting to slide. What better way to get a shot in the arm than appearing at the Spanish Steps. We get them to appear there at bargain basement salaries and we get top notch entertainment. We'll have them waiting in line to get into the place. Those show people from Hollywood and Vegas will be banging on the doors trying to appear at the Spanish Steps.

Well, here we are, he goes in and there's Henri.

What's happening?

Just waiting for the help to show up for work. We have a great show lined up for tonight.

Lets go into the office and talk. Now Henri, get in touch with all the show people that you know. Let them know that we're going to show case anyone that has great talent and that this is going to be the show case of the world. If they want to be seen and promoted, this is the place. I'm getting in touch with all my contacts to get the word out. Do the same. I want this place to double its profits in the next six months. We have the talent to do it and it means more money in your pocket.

Moe, that's a great idea. This place has been making money since Corporal and Ernie got rid of all those stiffs and it's becoming the most popular place in town.

Yeah, we got the name and the location, so lets do it. Give it another couple of weeks and start charging more to get in and boost the price of everything in the place. Cigarettes and pictures go up 25 percent. We're going to put in a souvenir shop for the customers, coming and going, so there won't be any traffic jams.

Moe adds, forget the cover charge. Put a big sign outside. NO COVER CHARGE. That always chased tourists away. Make them want to come in. They don't care about the prices inside. They expect to pay more for a great show and good food and drinks. Make sure there's real booze in those drinks and don't try any bull shit in this place. We want everybody to be happy and they'll tell everyone that they know that this is the greatest place in the world.

If I find out that anyone is messing with anything they'll be out the door. The bartenders and the waiters and waitresses better not get caught clipping anyone. And the cashiers, the count better be right, or they'll be out the door. But they'll get something extra on the way out. Understand?

Yeah, I'll get the word out.

Also tell them not to be the first one to be caught. That one will be made an example of. If they don't believe me, test me. I want you to tell that to everyone that works here.

I'm leaving now, take care of everything. Tell Angelo what I said.

I think that Henri had some ideas of his own, but he changed his mind, he don't want to be the first one caught.

Chris is going over to Conrad's to meet Amy. She's one hot little chick. She could take on an Army and still want more. Anyway, Tony can take over when he gets back. I kept my promise and took care of her for him while he was away.

She's waiting for him in the lobby.

Oh, Chris. I've been waiting here so long for you.

She kisses him and he asks if she would like to have a bite to eat?

No, not right now, lets go up to our little love nest first. Like Tony said, take good care of me. If you don't, I'll tell Tony. And he'll be very annoyed with you.

When they finish, he takes a shower As he's drying himself off, he looks in the mirror and there's hickey's all over him.

Holy shit, how am I going to explain this? What the heck is wrong with this woman? If Eileen sees these things, she'll cut my balls off. He goes out and asks Amy, why did you do this?

Don't you like them? I think they look cute. Every time you see them, you'll think of me. From now on, promise me we'll get together at least once a week.

But I thought this was for only while Tony was away.

Oh, no, I can't let you go like that, that wouldn't be fair to you. I know you want me and you can have me every week for the rest of your life.

But, what if somebody finds out?

They won't, you know how to keep a secret. You'll find a way to keep your promise to me, won't you? Now, you made me work up an appetite. Maybe we can have a little dessert when we finish eating, won't that be nice?

I feel sick, how do I get out of this?

Chapter 43

Sonny's son in law is laid out in Chris's Funeral Home and the family arrives. Chris says hello to Sonny and his daughter and asks them to follow him upstairs. They walk over to the casket. Sonny is holding on to his daughter and they're looking at Charlie. He looks pretty good for a guy that just got murdered. She starts crying softly and Sonny takes her over to the sofa.

The rest of the family go over and pay their respects to Charlie. People are saying, who could do such a thing? He was such a good boy. He came from one of the finest families in Harlem. Friends of the family start to come in and it's getting pretty crowded. They all go over to Sonny and his daughter and each one give her an envelope, then they make sure they all sign the register, because they know that Sonny will check it and it wouldn't be good if their name's weren't in the book.

One of the women paying her respects is looking at Charlie in the casket and is heard to say, everything looks so nice. Florida was so good for him, he's got such a nice tan and he's so healthy looking.

John and some of the other bosses come in and offer their condolences to Sonny and his daughter.

Chris excuses himself and asks Bob if he has anything to cover the hickey's that he got last night.

Come on down to the embalming room and let me see. Open your shirt and show me. Holy shit, what happened to you?

It's a long story. Do you have anything to cover these things up with?

Let me see. Bob opens up his instrument bag and takes out a bottle of makeup. I'll try some of this. Hey, not bad. Once it dries, nobody will notice that you were nearly eaten alive.

What is that stuff, Chris asks?

It's the cosmetics that I use on the bodies.

WHAT? You use this on the dead bodies?

Sure, it does the job.

Chris thinks, how the hell did I get myself into this fix, being covered by makeup that they use on dead bodies.

Here Chris, I'll give you some of this, you'll need it until those things go away.

Thanks, Bob, lets go get a bite to eat. They go down to the diner and order a couple of sandwiches. Bob, do me a favor. Don't ever mention this to anyone, promise.

OK, my lips are sealed.

Meantime, Corporal and Ernie are at the club and Moe shows up. Moe goes to them and hugs and kisses both of them.

I went down to the Spanish Steps last night and had a talk with Henri and laid out the plans for the Spanish Steps and all the help, including him and Angelo.

When do you want to put that souvenir shop in?

Right away.

OK, what kind of souvenirs?

Tee shirts, sweat shirts, jewelry, beer mugs, and you name it, with Spanish Steps printed on everything. If Disney can do it and make a fortune, so can we.

I like that idea, NO COVER CHARGE. Why didn't anyone think of that before, remarks Corporal?

Ernie says, none of them knew how to run a Night Club. Now that Moe is running it, watch how it's going to take off.

OK, Moe, do you need anything else?

No, we just have to hire a few more people to work in the souvenir shop.

Corporal asks, how about we have some Chinese food and then we get ready to take care of our other business.

Hey, Arnie. Tell the guys that we're having Chinese and ask them what they would like to have and then go to the Chinese restaurant and bring it back.

OK, Corporal. Arnie finds out what everybody wants.

After they finish eating, Moe tells Ernie, we better get going and pick up Timmy and Gingy.

Ernie tells Corporal, when we're finished, I'll be back here to pick up Arnie and Tiny. Sammy and Al will be here before I get back, I won't be too long.

Moe and Ernie leave and drive to the Paddock. Moe parks the car and they go in. Timmy and Gingy are already there.

Hi, guys. Lets go into the office.

They sit down and Moe asks, everyone got their gear?

Yeah, they say.

Now, when Timmy and Gingy give us the OK, we put the masks and gloves on and go over to them. Timmy and Gingy go in first and we follow. It's 7:15 now, time to go. Ready?

Yep, lets go.

Timmy and Gingy get into their car and Moe and Ernie follow.

They get to the Hotel and park their cars. Timmy and Gingy get out and go into the lounge. Moe and Ernie park overlooking the door next to the lounge.

Vinny and his crew should be getting here pretty soon. The sun is going down and everything is in place. Now, we just wait.

Moe looks at his watch and it's about 5 minutes to 8.

Two cars pull in and park.

It's Vinny and his crew. There's six of them and they go into the Hotel.

Now we wait for about 10 minutes until Timmy and Gingy give us the OK.

The minutes go by very slowly, it's like forever.

Finally, Timmy opens the door and waves them in. Moe and Ernie get out of the car and put on their gloves and masks and head for the door.

OK, we're in. Lets do it.

Timmy and Gingy push the meeting room door open and go in with their shotguns blazing away and Moe and Ernie are right behind them blasting away.

Vinny and his crew are all falling to the floor. All six of them never knew what hit them. Some of them are squirming and moaning as they lay on the floor bleeding to death. Timmy and Gingy pull out their automatics and start shooting while Moe and Ernie are putting the finishing touches to them and then they put a bullet into each ones head. They make sure that they pick up the empty shell casings and they all look at Moe. Everyone gives a thumbs up and leave.

Nobody is around and they walk to their cars and take off the masks and head to the Paddock. They go in and Moe asks them if everyone is alright.

Yep.

OK, guys. I'll see you tomorrow.

They leave and Moe asks Ernie, how about a drink?

Yeah, that's a good idea.

Moe pours a couple of stiff ones and they down them in one gulp.

Do you want another one, Ernie?

Naw, that was good. I still have to take care of a couple of things, thanks.

They leave and head down to the Zerega Club. Moe parks the car and they go in.

Corporal is still there having a drink with Sammy and Al. Ernie and Moe go over to Corporal and hug and kiss him.

All finished boys?

Yeah, all finished.

Ernie tells Tiny and Arnie. I want to see you for a minute.

Do you have your pieces ready?

Yeah, we got them.

Ernie opens a drawer and takes out a hacksaw and a gun and puts them into a bag.

Here, Arnie, take this bag and hold onto it.

OK, lets get going.

Tiny and Arnie get into the back of the car with Sammy between them and Al gets into the front with Ernie. They get onto the Bronx River Parkway and head downtown.

Ernie tells them he has to make a stop and he gets off at Fordham Road. He drives to Pelham Parkway and pulls into a construction site. It's where Chris and Sal's Hospital is being built.

OK, guys. Get out. Arnie, bring that bag. They all get out and go into the construction trailer.

Sammy, sit over there for a minute. I don't want you to get dirty.

Al, come outside with us.

They close the trailer door and Ernie tells Arnie to give Al the gun.

What's this for?

Your going to kill Sammy.

WHAT?

Now take the gun and go in with Arnie and Tiny and all of you are going to shoot and kill Sammy.

Al doesn't know what to think, everything is happening so fast. If I don't do it, they'll kill me. I have no choice. He takes the gun and follows them in.

OK, you rat son of a bitch, you played your last bullshit game with us. We are going to kill you, aim for his chest.

Sammy is screaming and pleading for his life. No, please don't, I'll do anything you tell me, only please don't kill me.

OK, you'll do anything I tell you, then die.

Ernie fires and the rest of them all shoot Sammy in the chest.

Alright, Arnie. Give Al the hacksaw.

Al, cut his head off and put it in this bag.

WHAT?

I said cut his head off and make it snappy.

OK, guys, when Al is finished cutting the head off, get that big piece of plastic over there and wrap the body in it, then take it outside and dump it in the hole where they're going to pour cement in the morning.

Al is still hacksawing Sammy's head off and the blood is getting all over him. He finishes cutting the head off and puts it in the bag.

Lets go, Al. Take that bag with you and put it into the trunk but put this piece of plastic in first. I dont want blood getting all over the trunk.

Al grabs the bag with Sammy's head and when he gets outside he starts throwing up. He's barfing like crazy.

OK, are you finished throwing up? Lets get going.

Ernie looks to see if Arnie and Tiny did a good job of stuffing Sammy's body in the hole.

Lets go. They all get into the car and leave.

They pull up right outside the Bronx Zoo entrance. Now you two are going to stick the head up on that iron picket fence right in front of the Bronx Zoo entrance.

Arnie and Tiny get out of the car and take the head out of the bag and stick it up there real tight and they make sure he's looking across the street at the Howard Johnson Restaurant.

Chapter 44

Back in Cleveland, Jimmy is waiting in the lobby for Christina.

Wow, here she comes, she's beautiful.

Hi, Jimmy.

Hi, Christina. You look beautiful. We have a reservation.

He gives the host his name and tells him that he has a reservation.

Follow me, please. He leads them to a front table right up by the dance floor. Is this table alright?

Yes, it's fine. Thank you.

The waiter comes over with the menus and hands one to each of them. Would you care for a drink?

Yes, a glass of red wine.

And you, sir?

The same.

I'll be right back. He returns with the drinks.

They give the waiter their order.

Well. Here's to us, Christina. They touch each others glass and drink.

Gee, what a small world this is.

Are you married?

No, I'm divorced.

How about you, Jimmy?

No, I never got married.

Any children?

No children, answers Christina.

So where do you live now?

Alexandria, Virginia.

And where do you live, Jimmy?

I just left New York, but I'm thinking of moving here. I'm not sure though. I don't know much about Cleveland. I was looking around today and I didn't see much at all. I just sold my business and I'm looking to get back into some sort of business.

What do you do for a living, Christina?

I work for a marketing company in Washington, D.C.

That must be an exciting job.

Yes, I guess you could say that.

The waiter returns with their orders. Will there be anything else?

Yeah, bring a chilled bottle of white wine.

The orchestra starts to play and Jimmy asks, would you like to dance?

Yes, I would.

They start dancing and Jimmy is having memories of the wonderful times that they spent on the Jersey shore a long time ago. They stay on the dance floor for another dance and the two of them are holding each other tightly. The music ends and they sit down and finish their supper.

The waiter stops by and asks if they would like dessert?

Hey, Jimmy. How would you like to share a Mud Pie with me? I haven't had one of those for a long time.

Yeah, that sounds good. Bring a Mud Pie with two spoons.

Coming right up.

Jimmy pours her and himself another glass of wine and they toast each other.

I'm happy that we met again. What happened?

We lost touch with each other. I went to college and things sort of changed. I met this guy and we got married and we were very happy, but things started to change after about three years. He had a good job and so did I, but my job required a lot of travel and it started to play on him. He wanted me to get a different job where I wouldn't have to travel, but I wouldn't listen, so he quit his job and left. I haven't heard from him since and I guess I never will. So much for success. So Jimmy, why didn't you get married?

I just got wrapped up in business and I guess it never entered my head to get married.

The waiter shows up with the Mud Pie and two spoons.

Would you like to stop in the lounge for a drink, asks Jimmy?

Yes, the night's young and I'd like to spend more time with you.

Jimmy pays the check and gives the waiter a nice tip.

They go to the lounge and have a few drinks and a few dances.

Oh, Jimmy. I missed you, seeing you again just gave me goose bumps. Do you have anything to do for the rest of the week?

No, answers Jimmy.

Christina asks, would you like to stay together for the rest of the week?

Why sure, that would be wonderful.

Oh, that'll be great, just like old times. Lets drink up and go to my room.

OK, he says. Lets go.

Chapter 45

Down at City Hall, Lou is there to complete the signing of the contracts for the incinerators in all the City Housing projects. This is a big prize for Lou and it means big money for the Corporal Family. The Mayor and all the City big shots are here and there's going to be a big party over at Kelly's afterward. There's been talk that Lou might get the contract to build Freedom Land up in the Bronx. That would really be big time. Lou is making the rounds and shaking lots of hands. Finally they all go into the conference room and sign all the contracts. Lou and the Mayor shake hands for all the cameramen. Flash bulbs pop and then they all head for Kelly's across the street from City Hall.

It's a very nice day and Corporal is feeling pretty good.

Vito, go by the main entrance to the Bronx Zoo before we go to the Zerega. As they approach the entrance to the Bronx Zoo, there's a crowd forming and there on a iron picket is Sammy's head looking at the Howard Johnson Restaurant across the street from the Zoo.

Wow, look Boss, there's a head stuck on top of that iron picket. Holy shit, that's Sammy's head.

Yeah, I see. Well, Sammy finally got people to look up to him. Lets go over to the Zerega now.

After all the hugs and kisses, Corporal asks, How's everything this morning? Great, they all say. Lets all sit down and have some coffee and bagels.

Well, Ernie. I saw your handy work, it's very creative. Did anyone pick up the newspapers this morning?

Yeah, here they are.

On the front page of the Daily News, the headline reads. Murder in Yonkers, and a picture under the headline showing six dead men laying on the floor. The article reads that it appears that this is a mob rubout. All six men were shot to death and they all had bullet holes in their heads. The Yonkers police are investigating. The other newspaper, The Mirror, had Mob Hit on their headline.

OK, Ernie. You can be expecting calls from Yonkers pretty soon. They'll be running around like chickens without their heads on. Moe should be here soon and we'll get his take on how this should be handled.

OK, Corporal. They'll all be kissing ass when they hear about Sammy.

Where's Al?

He'll be here soon. He got a little sick last night, but Tiny and Arnie are real troopers, they handled things like old pros.

I'm proud of you guys, you're going to make it to the top here in this family.

Ernie, give them both an increase of 300 bucks a week.

Did you guys hear what Corporal said?

They're speechless. They both go to Corporal and Ernie and hug and kiss them and thank them.

Moe arrives and he hugs and kisses everyone.

Did you see the morning papers?

Yeah. I heard about Sammy. News travels fast. All those guys up in Yonkers are shitting in their pants. We'll be hearing from a lot of them pretty soon.

Well, Moe. What do you think we should do with the business up in Yonkers?

There's a few ways that we could approach this. We could walk in there and take it all over and get rid of everyone or we could let everyone keep operating under separate Franchise's with us. This way there's no family up there and we're the only ones that anyone can do business with. Everyone pays us ten percent of their take every week and if anyone steps out of line, they get hit with a ten thousand dollar fine and if it happens again, they're out. Vinny's family is officially disbanded. They can apply to become Associates with this family, but someone in this family will have to vouch for them.

Corporal asks, Ernie, what do you think?

It sounds pretty good to me. I like the Franchise and we don't have to put a lot of people in there to run the business. Lets try it out for awhile and see if it works for us.

Yeah, that's a good idea. What do you think about Moe running this operation, asks Corporal?

I'm for that, I think that Moe is the right guy to take over this operation.

You're going to have to have some help, you pick out the people that you need and let me know who you want, Moe.

I want Al.

Are you sure? He was a little shaky last night when we took care of Sammy.

It was his first time. Let me talk to him, and if I notice that he's not ready we'll get someone else. I need Abe, he's the best bank operations man in the business.

OK, Moe. I know that you'll want to give some raises out. That's fine, you handle this anyway you want. There's plenty on your plate.

Now, Moe, I'm having Ernie take over the family when I step down. I want you to replace Ernie as the Underboss.

What? I can't believe it. Oh, thank you, Corporal, What an honor. I never dreamed of anything like this ever happening to me. I'll never let you down.

Ernie and me talked it over and we both want you to have this.

Thank you, Ernie. And you'll always be able to depend on me.

I know you mean it, Moe.

Arnie, bring out a few bottles, and have Vito and Tiny join us.

Chapter 46

Arnie and Tiny just opened the club and they're cleaning up. Ernie comes in and says hello to the guys.

How about some coffee, Ernie?

Yeah, that's a good idea.

In comes Moe, he hugs Ernie and the guys.

Did Al get here yet?

No, not yet.

He goes to the phone and calls Al, this is Moe. I'm here at the Zerega.

Hi, Moe. I'll be there in a little while, I'm just leaving now.

Moe sits next to Ernie and has a cup of coffee.

I don't think Al is feeling so good. What makes you think that?

Aw, it was his tone of voice, like he still was half asleep.

Well, we'll see what's bothering him when he gets here, says Ernie. We should be hearing from some of those guys in Yonkers pretty soon and has anyone heard anything about Jimmy?

No, not yet, Ernie.

Vito comes in and says hello and hugs everyone.

Vito, we gotta go downtown later on.

OK, Moe.

Al arrives, he says hello and hugs everyone and goes over and pours himself a cup of coffee.

Moe asks, are you feeling alright, Al? You look like you're dragging it?

Aw, I think I might be getting a cold. Thanks for asking.

OK, you're welcome. Ready to go to work?

Yep. Lets sit over here. We have to go over everything. You know we took over all of Yonkers and their operations. Now we have to reorganize everything and absorb all this new business.

First thing, the Spanish Steps, it's off to a good start. Then, we get everyone and everything in line.

Lets get those guys from Yonkers in here and find out everything that they have. We want a list of everyone and every business that they're involved with. They have to bring all their records in. Anyone that drags their feet will get a visit from us. Now, Al, lets get one of them in here and have him give us a run down on everything they're doing.

The phone rings and Arnie answers it, it's a guy from Yonkers, says he's one of Vinny's crew and would like to talk to Ernie.

He hands the phone to Ernie.

Yeah, who's this?

This is Pete, I'd like to sit down and talk with you guys.

When?

As soon as possible.

OK, come down to the Zerega club now, and come by yourself.

I'll be there in twenty minutes.

Moe, guess what? One of the Yonkers guys is coming down here now.

Which one?

He said his name is Pete.

OK, I know him. He's low level, but he and a few others have all the action at the track.

Good, lets see what's on his mind.

Al, we're going to hang around for awhile. We have to attend to a little business before we leave.

The phone rings again, Arnie answers it.

Ernie, there's another guy calling from Yonkers, says he would like to talk to you.

Yeah, who's this?

This is Victor, I'm with the Yonkers group.

What's on your mind?

I'd like to talk with you.

When?

As soon as possible.

OK, come down to the Zerega club about 12:15 sharp and come by yourself.

Gee, Moe. They'll be standing in line to see us.

OK, everyone stay until we're all finished with our business here. Arnie, you answer the phone, and give it to Vito. Don't yell anything out, just tell Vito quietly.

Ernie, someone is here.

Let him in.

Arnie opens the door and asks, who are you?

I'm Pete.

OK, turn around and put your arms up. Arnie pats him down. OK, go in.

Vito comes over and tells Pete to sit down over here.

Ernie sits down next to Pete.

Hi, I'm Ernie.

Pete extends his hand and they shake.

What can we do for you, Pete?

Vinny got hit the other night along with all the top guys in our family. Right now, the Yonkers family has no leadership and I would like to come over to join up with your family. The rest of the family would also like to come over and join up too.

Well, Pete. Tell us a little about yourself and your business?

I run all the action at the track and around lower Yonkers.

Tell us what kind of action and where in Yonkers?

From the Bronx line up to the track on Yonkers Avenue on the west side and over to the east side from the Bronx line up to Yonkers Avenue along the Bronx River Parkway.

Ernie continues to asks him a series of questions.

When will you have those lists for us?

Tomorrow.

OK, be here at 10 tomorrow morning. They shake hands and he leaves.

Ernie turns to Moe, what do you think, Moe?

Hmm, very interesting, lets wait until we hear from this other guy Victor.

Hey, Arnie. You did a good job handling that guy. Keep up the good work. Anyone comes through that door, give him that same treatment, except our guys.

Ernie, there's another guy here.

OK, Arnie. Show him in.

Arnie opens the door. Who are you?

I'm Victor. Come in. Arnie closes the door and tells him to turn around and put his arms up. He pats him down, OK, put your arms down.

Vito comes over and tells him to sit down over there.

He sits down and Ernie comes over and sits next to him.

Hi, I'm Ernie.

Victor extends his hand.

I'm Victor, and they shake hands.

Well, Victor. What can we do for you?

You probably know that Vinny and his top guys got hit. We have no leadership and I would like to be associated with this family.

You mean to say no one's in charge or running your family?

Yeah, all the bosses are dead.

OK, tell us a little about yourself?

I'm running things over in Mount Vernon.

What kind of things?

Numbers, sports, shy locking, carting and just about everything else.

Can you bring us a list of everything you control?

Yeah, sure.

And can you give us a list of everyone and the business's that you deal with?

Yeah.

Ernie tells him the same thing that he told Pete.

OK, Victor. When will you have those lists for us?

Tomorrow.

Good, be here at one o'clock sharp. They shake hands and he leaves.

Well. There it is, what do you think, Moe?

Lets wait until tomorrow and see what else happens. These guys are worried. They must think that we're going to step in and chase them out. From what both are saying they'll be willing to accept any deal we'll toss out to them. Let's take a look at those lists tomorrow and see what they show us.

OK, lets break and have a bite to eat.

Chapter 47

Moe is making sure that everything at the Paddock is running smoothly. He's going over everything with his accountant to make sure all the figures are right and that all the bills are being paid. The accountant tells him that everything is up to date. All the help seems happy with the way the business is going and they're all making money.

Al is coming to see Moe, they have a lot to talk about. Al is trustworthy and knows his business, but there's something bothering Al and Moe's gotta know what it is before they go any further. Al walks through the door and they say hello to each other.

Come into the office so we can have a little talk. Have a seat. We got a lot happening right now and I want you in on all of it. Here's the question, can you handle it or not? And what's bothering you?

Yeah, I can handle it but the other night is still on my mind.

You mean being in on a hit is bothering you?

Yeah, it is.

Well, just to bring you up to date, when you got involved with this family that meant you became a part of this family. You got a share of the rewards and you have to help the family out when called on to do so. Did you think that you could just pick and choose to do what you want? We have a leader to head and run this family and we do what we are asked to do. You'd better understand this or get out. It's as simple as that. Nobody twisted your arm to come into this life or this family.

But the other night nobody told me ahead of time what was going to happen. I never thought that I would have to do a thing like that.

So, if you knew ahead of time, you wouldn't do it?

No, no, I didn't mean it that way.

Well, Al. I like you, and I trust you, but the fact of the matter is this, make up your mind right now that you'll do what's asked of you without question or get out. Now, what is it?

Al is thinking fast, if I say no, I'm dead. I'd better say yes, and if I do I know they'll send me out to take care of someone right away.

I'm in.

OK, Al. Lets get down to business and don't ever let anyone see you act that way again. That's the reason you and me had this little talk. People were starting to wonder about you. I went to bat for you, so don't you ever let me down.

OK, Moe. I won't and thanks.

Meantime, Jimmy is having a great time in Cleveland with his old girlfriend. He checked out of his room and moved in with Christina.

Hey, Honey. How about we take a tour of the city and take in the sights?

That sounds wonderful, the two of us together again. Oh, Jimmy. I'm having such a great time. Lets go and see what's out there. They get ready and have some breakfast and then they leave.

There's a tour bus right outside the hotel and they get on it. That's 30 dollars for the two of you. He pays the tour guide and he hands them a tour map.

Lets just enjoy the ride and then we'll find something else to do. The bus starts off and the tour guide is on the speaker pointing out all the points of interest.

They're talking about all the good times that they had at the Jersey Shore. Boy, those were good times, no worries, sun and fun, rock and roll the whole summer. Gee, it would be great to go back to those times and get out of this rat race.

What are you going to do if you don't find anything in Cleveland, Jimmy?

I don't know. I haven't made up my mind yet. How about you, Christina?

Well, it's back to the grind. I don't have any plans for anything. All my family is up in New York, and I really don't want to go back there. Well, at least I have a good job so I'm happy about that.

Wow, this place is pretty well beaten up. Just a bunch of factories that look like they're ready to fall apart. It's very depressing. Lets rent a car and go out to this amusement park that's on this tour map.

OK, that sounds like fun.

They get back to the hotel and go inside to the car rental booth.

Jimmy rents a convertible and they hop into it and off they go in the direction of the amusement park. They leave the city and get out into the country side.

It's pretty nice outside the city, remarks Jimmy, I wonder if there's anything going on out here? So far, nothing but farms. There's a sign up ahead. Fun City Amusement Park, 30 miles. Well, we're on the right road. They pass through a few small villages and then there's another sign up ahead. Fun City 10 miles. A few more houses and buildings start showing up. Some small general stores and gas stations and a few motels come into view as they get closer to Fun City. Now there's some restaurants and some more stores. Looks like there could be some business opportunities around here, I gotta keep this place in mind. They finally arrive at Fun City. Nice looking place, a lotta people here. Jimmy parks the car and they go in.

That's 10 dollars, the tickets are for the rides, and if you want more, we have ticket agents walking all over the place selling them.

They get on the Roller Coaster and then on the Bumper Cars and then on the Merry Go Round.

How about a Cotton Candy? They're like two kids having such a good time. She hasn't had a nice time like this since they were at the Jersey Shore. It sure turned out to be a great day.

Jimmy says, if you like, we could stay here for another day, there's some motels just down the road that we could stay at.

OK, I'd love that.

Well, everything seems to be working out for Jimmy. This could be the place for him to settle down in.

Chapter 48

It's pretty nice today, remarks Corporal, as he is being driven to the club. Looks like things are shaping up. Ernie and Moe really took care of business pretty fast. Just a few more loose ends to take care of. Some of the bosses are going to be bitching about Moe being made Underboss because he's Jewish. I don't want to cause a problem for Ernie or Moe. I don't think we'll have a big to do about Moe, everyone knows that I made him Underboss, so we'll keep this in the family and have a private affair for him and Ernie and family members only.

Well, as soon as all of our business is straightened out, Sally and me will take a nice vacation and then I'll go into the hospital and get taken care of. Yeah, Sally always wanted to take the train out to California and see the Rocky Mountains and the Grand Canyon. When we get to California, we'll take a trip to Hawaii. Why not, she deserves the best. When I get home today, we'll talk about it.

Vito turns into Arthur Avenue and all the shop keepers wave to Corporal as he goes by. They all know and respect him. He's a living legend. Vito parks the car in front of the club and Arnie comes out to help Corporal into the club.

Everyone comes over to Corporal to hug and kiss him. Ernie and Moe go into the back room with him and sit next to him.

How's things, asks Corporal?

Pretty good, replies Ernie, a lot of excitement. It seems like everyone in Yonkers and Mount Vernon would like to join up with us. A couple of them were down here yesterday. We told them to come back today with all the information about their operations.

OK, guys, lets see what they have and then we can decide what to do with them.

There's more Associates and guys hanging around here than usual. I guess they're hoping to get in on some of the new action.

Yeah, there's going to be more than enough to go around.

Arnie tells Ernie that Pete from Yonkers is here.

OK, Arnie, you know what to do and then bring him in.

Arnie opens the door and lets Pete in. Turn around and face the wall and put your arms up and he pats him down. OK, put your arms down and follow me.

Pete follows Arnie into the back room and walks over to Corporal and takes his hand and kisses it.

Corporal tells him to have a seat.

Ernie and Moe sit on each side of Corporal and Ernie asks, did you bring all the information and reports?

Yeah, here they are and he hands them to Ernie.

He takes a quick look, where's the figures?

Did you want them too?

Lets get something straight, when I ask for something, bring it. Now, get out of here and don't come back without them. Be back here at 3 sharp.

Pete gets up and leaves fast.

Holy shit, I thought I was going to get killed, I'd better never pull that crap again with any of those guys. They mean business. When I looked into Ernie's eyes, I was looking at death. I'll get those figures and be back at 3 o'clock.

Corporal says, well, it looks like you scared the hell out of him. He'll get the news out fast. When's the next one going to be here?

Ernie answers, one o'clock.

Moe, is everything going alright, asks Ernie?

Yeah, everything is good.

How about Al?

We had a little talk yesterday? He's alright now.

How about Jimmy? I'd like to get that over with, asks Corporal?

Ernie answers, we're following that up too, we got a few leads on him. Sooner or later he's gonna slip up and we'll nail his ass.

Lou is doing good, he has all those contracts signed and our take on those windows and incinerators will double. And he mentioned this thing about Freedom Land. He's got an in with the Mayor and his staff. They like Lou, he's a good earner and they trust him.

How's things with Abe?

Very good. He got everything under control.

Everything else OK, Ernie?

Yeah, everyone is on time with their envelopes and they're all giving us a good count.

Very good, says Corporal. Lets see what this guy Victor brings us?

Arnie comes over and tells Ernie, Victor from Yonkers just got here.

OK. bring him in, you know the drill.

Arnie lets him in. Turn around and face the wall, put your arms up. Arnie pats him down. OK, turn around and follow me.

Victor follows Arnie and he goes to Corporal and takes his hand and kisses it. He bows and Ernie tells him to sit down.

Ernie asks, did you bring the information?

Yeah, and he hands it to Ernie. He looks through it quickly and pulls out a few pages. It's the report on the earnings and all the operations in Yonkers and Mount Vernon. All the names of the made guys and the Associates are here and what they do and how much they bring in.

OK, we'll go over everything and we'll get together again. Now, let me ask you a question? What would you like out of this?

Well, I'd like to keep my operations.

OK, we'll talk about it. If we need anything else, we'll let you know.

Victor gets up and goes to Corporal, thank you for seeing me and kisses his hand.

Well, Ernie and Moe, what do you think?

Lets look at the report and we'll compare it with the one that Pete brings us.

They have a bite to eat and when they finish Pete shows up with the report.

Arnie puts him through the drill and takes him to Ernie.

Ernie goes through the papers real fast and pulls out a couple of pages and looks at them.

Seems like it's all here. Moe and me will look them over and get together with Abe.

Vito, take me out to the other room, says Corporal. I want to talk with the guys for awhile.

Chapter 49

Ernie and Moe are at the Zerega club waiting for Abe to show up.

Moe says, I went over those papers and I think there's a lot missing. Those figures don't add up. We're going to have to put some of our people in there to see what's going on. Al is the guy to put in there, he's sharp and he'll be able to spot anything that they left out. This guy Victor is a snake, I think after things get going we should get rid of him.

You're right, says Ernie, I didn't like that jerk the minute I laid eyes on him.

Arnie calls out. Ernie, Abe is here.

OK, let him in.

Hey, Abe. How you doing?

Good, and they all hug each other.

Arnie brings over some coffee for them and asks if they would like anything else.

No thanks, Arnie.

So, Abe. Did you get a chance to go over those papers, asks Ernie?

I think most of that information is bullshit. For a big bunch operating in a city the size of Yonkers with no competition, these guys aren't showing us anything.

Moe and me agree, we were thinking that we should send Al in there to look everything over and then put our own people in there to operate everything once we get a handle on their operations. Keeping any of those guys would only bring trouble. Let them think that they're still running the show and when we know the operation and everybody is comfortable with us, we take over and get rid of them. Let's get Al on the job right away. Don't give them the idea that we are a little slow to act. Right now we have the element of surprise. Get enough of our people to start working at all the places and have the guys that run these operations introduce us as their new partners and that we'll be picking up the collections from now on.

OK, Vito, you handle that.

OK, Boss.

Keep your eyes on all those idiots and don't let them handle any money. Pay them at the end of every week and keep them in the dark about everything. Tell our guys not to get chummy with any of those guys and never to discuss family business with any of them.

Abe. Does everything else look alright?

Yeah, the take from the Spanish Steps is picking up. All the other operations are good and on time.

Down at the DA's Office, things are starting to pick up. They have some information on Stanley Shaffer from one of the people that work in the Bronx Borough President's Office.

It seems this guy got arrested for selling cocaine and he's looking at 15 years if he gets convicted. He wants to cut a deal and said he's got enough on Shaffer to put him away for a long time. He's over at Rikers Island and he's really shitting. He's never been arrested before and Rikers is a zoo, he can't handle it. Lets get over there right away and have a talk with him.

On the way over to Rikers, DA Gallo and his Assistants are discussing the arrest of this guy that works for Shaffer. What have they got on him? Possession of over 20 kilos of cocaine with intent to distribute. Wow, that's heavy. If he's got something good on Shaffer, we can put Shaffer away for a long time. Well, here we are. The guard at the gate checks their ID's and waves them on to the ferry. They get escorted into the prison and taken to a interview room. The prisoner is waiting there for them.

My name is Mario Gallo. I'm the Bronx District Attorney.

My name is Edward Grimes.

I heard that you wanted to talk to me.

Yeah, that's right.

OK, lets hear what you have to say.

You know that I got arrested for possession of cocaine, so I want to cut a deal. I know about Stanley Shaffer and some of the deals he's involved with. A lot of them involve Organized Crime figures and I have the proof.

Tell me about some of these things, says DA Gallo.

Not until we cut a deal, says Edward.

OK, what kind of deal do you want?

Complete immunity from prosecution and get me out of here now.

Hmm, that's a tall order, you've got to give me something real big for that, replies DA Gallo.

I'll give you Stanley Shaffer and a lot of people in his office.

Well, let me see. I can have you moved into protective custody.

No good, if that's all you can do, forget it. I'll do business with someone else.

Who?

You'll find out.

I'll be right back, says DA Gallo. He tells his assistants to come with him. They go outside and he tells them, if we can't cut a deal and get him out of here today, he'll slip out of our hands and the FBI will be here before you know it and they'll take over and we'll look like chumps. He's got us over a barrel, we have to make a few calls and cut a deal with him. Go in and tell him that we're working on it, get him coffee and donuts and cigarettes and tell him we'll get him out of here today.

The Assistant DA's call around and get in touch with the Chief Judge of the State of New York and they convince him to give this guy complete immunity from prosecution and to house him in the Concourse Plaza Hotel under protective custody, provided he will testify against the Bronx Borough President and anyone indicted along with Stanley Shaffer.

The Judge agrees. He'll sign the order and have it delivered to you today.

OK, guys. Lets draw up the papers and get him released into our custody.

They go back into the interview room and tell Edward that he's going to be released into their custody. Now, if you don't keep your side of the bargain and you give us a bullshit story, you'll be back here in general population and we'll get the word out that you're a rat.

Don't worry, you'll love what I'm giving you as soon as I see those papers.

They show the Warden the release papers and off they go with Edward to the Concourse Plaza.

Chapter 50

Chris is on his way to his office and he's thinking, I'd better get rid of this lunatic, she's liable to pull anything. How stupid of me to get involved with this nut job. Well, Tony will be back in a couple of days. I'd better come up with something good to get out of this mess. If any of this gets out, I'll be up the creek with Tony. He gets to his office and goes in.

Hi, Chris. There's a couple of messages for you on your desk.

He sits down at his desk and looks at the messages. There's one from a friend of his, Dennis, he's a detective with the DA's office.

This is Dennis, who's calling?

It's Chris, I got your message.

Chris, are you at your office?

Yeah.

I'll call you right back.

I wonder what this is all about?

The phone rings, Chris, this is Dennis. Do you know a guy by the name of Edward that works in the Bronx Borough President's Office?

I don't think so.

How about a guy named Sal, he's a builder and investor.

Yeah, I know him.

And how about a guy named Tony, a state contractor and builder?

Yeah, I know him too.

Chris, I got to talk to you right away. Meet me at the Stadium Deli on 161th Street by the Yankee Stadium.

OK, I'll be there in about 20 minutes.

Chris tells Andy, I'll be back in awhile and he gets into his car and drives to the Stadium Deli. He goes in and he sees Dennis waiting for him.

Hi, Chris. Lets go in the back. A guy by the name of Edward that works in the Bronx Borough's President Office got busted with a load of coke. The DA got him and is keeping him under an order of protective custody. This guy is going to testify against Stanley Shaffer and a lot of other people. The grand jury is going to hand down indictments against Shaffer and some others. They'll most likely issue arrest warrants for him and the others in a couple of days. As soon as I heard about this I called you and I'll let you know more as soon as I can.

Thanks, Dennis. Can you stop by my place in the morning?

Sure, I'll see you then.

Wow, he thinks to himself, it looks like the shit is going to hit the fan. I better call Tony and Sal and I'll call Amy and tell her something came up and I have to lay low for awhile, maybe she'll just go away when she thinks there's trouble happening. Well, here we are. He goes into his office and closes the door and calls Tony.

Hello, Tony.

Hi, Chris. What's happening?

Not good, a friend of mine called me a little while ago and told me that the Bronx Borough President Shaffer is going to be indicted and arrested in a few days and other people are going to be indicted along with him. I won't know until tomorrow who they are.

What happened?

A guy working down at the Bronx Borough President's Office got busted with a load of coke and he cut a deal with the DA to testify against Shaffer in a corruption case against Shaffer.

Did they give you the name of the guy that got caught with the coke?

Yeah, some guy named Edward.

That's the guy we were working with.

Chris, that guy never met you or me. Get a hold of my lawyer and let him know what's going on. If that guys in custody and made a deal with the DA, he'll spill his guts. No sense getting nervous, lets find out about everything. Call my office and tell my secretary to give you my lawyer's name and number.

I'll call her right now and let her know that you'll be calling.

Call me back when you find out more.

Chris calls Tony's secretary and she gives him the lawyers name and number.

He calls Tony's lawyer and tells him about Tony and what's happening.

Alright, let me know when he gets here and when you hear anything else.

Chris gives it some thought. In the meantime, I'll make a few calls and see if I can find out anything else. We better be very careful about our other projects. As soon as I hear from Dennis I'll know what to do. My name isn't going to come up and I doubt that they have anything on Sal or Tony. I'll bet this is a crock of shit. The DA wants Stanley Shaffer and he gets his name in the papers. Then he gets to be a big hero as a gang buster and runs for a higher office. But we don't want him tripping over us. Once this is over, everything goes back to normal. That jerk Shaffer is a greedy son of a bitch, getting his house and his picture in the papers and having his driveway paved by the NYC Public Works Department.

Chapter 51

Jimmy and Christina are having the time of their lives. They're starting to take up where they left off a long time ago.

I'm going to have to go back to Virginia tomorrow, I've got to get back to work. What about you, Jimmy?

Well, I'm not sure.

OK, when you make up your mind, why don't you come visit me in Virginia?

Yeah, that's a good idea. I have to take care of a few things before I do that. You know something, I never got your phone number or your address.

Well, I thought you'd never ask, let me give you that right now and don't lose it.

How do I get in touch with you, Jimmy?

Well, as soon as I get settled, I'll let you know, but I'll keep in touch with you.

You promise?

Yeah, I promise. I'm not going to lose touch with you again.

I've had such a good time being with Christina, I would love to stay with her, but I can't get her involved with any of my business. Those guys will be looking for me for the rest of my life. I gotta be real careful and not make any mistakes. Anyway, I'll try not to think of those things for the rest of our time together. I don't want to spoil this great time that we're having.

Meantime, Ernie, Moe and Al are having a meeting at the Zerega. We have to pick out our own guys and put them to work up in Yonkers and Mount Vernon.

You're right, Moe. We got about 20 of them coming here today. We'll let each one know where he's going and who he's going to work with.

Arnie calls out, there's some guys coming now.

Tiny, go over there and give Arnie a hand, if any of them are packing, take their guns and weapons and put them away. Let them in, one at a time and Tiny, have them sit out in the front room.

Arnie lets the first one in, turn around and put you arms up. He pats him down and takes his gun. Go over there and sit down.

How about my gun?

You'll get it back when you leave. Arnie does the same with every one and when he finishes he tells them that Ernie and Moe will be there in a minute.

They come in and say hello to all the guys sitting there.

This is Moe and I'm Ernie, if you don't already know who we are. That fella over there is Al and you already met Arnie and Tiny on the way in. We'll get right down to business.

Our family has taken over all operations in Yonkers and Mount Vernon. You've been told to come here to let you know where you're going to be working in Yonkers and Mount Vernon and with who. Moe is going to explain everything to you and Moe is the head of everything in Yonkers and Mount Vernon. Al is Moe's assistant, if there's any questions, you can bring them up after Moe and Al are finished. I'll hand this over to Moe now.

Moe greets them and starts telling them that they've been picked to work in Yonkers and Mount Vernon. Your going to work with those guys up there and learn everything there is to know about what they're doing. We'll let you know where you're going and who you're working with. Your cut will be 15 percent of the gross and you're not to talk about family business with anyone, ever. At the close of every day you deliver the money and receipts to Abe and we are open every day except Sunday. Make sure the count is correct and never light. Basically, that's it. Do what you're told to do. If you don't, you're out. Understand? I didn't hear that to good. Now, I'll ask again, Understand?

YEAH, WE UNDERSTAND, they shout out.

Don't ever have anyone of us have to repeat ourselves again.

Now Al is going to talk to you.

I'm Al and I'm Moe's assistant. After we finish, we're going to hand each one of you your assignment and who you're going to work with. Everyday before you close, put the take and the receipts in the bag and seal it. If there's anything that looks fishy with those receipts put them in a separate envelope along with the take and receipts. Just do your job and don't have any conversations with those guys up there. And here's a warning to everyone. If you get any ideas about clipping, DON'T. Any questions? None. OK.

Tiny will call out your name, step up and get your assignment. When you report to your location, be on time. If you had a weapon when you came in, you can pick it up on your way out.

Ernie, Moe and Al sit down and have a cup of coffee.

Good job. You made them know that you meant business. They'll think twice before they pull any shit. Sammy will be a reminder of that.

Corporal has been asking if anyone's heard about Jimmy. He wants to get that out of the way before he goes on vacation. Lets put the pressure on his old girlfriend and his family and see if they give us some information.

Moe, how's things coming along at the Spanish Steps?

We already started the renovations and it should be all finished in two weeks, replies Moe, and I got a lot of new acts and people from Vegas lined up to appear at the Spanish Steps.

Sounds good, says Ernie. I'll get in touch with Corporal and let him know.

Chapter 52

Chris is at his Funeral Home in Harlem. It's packed with mourners and Sonny is there to make sure that there's no trouble. After all, this is his daughter's husband that's being buried. She's up stairs receiving all her friends and relatives and people who came to pay their respects. The Priest shows up to say prayers before going to the church. He goes over to her to say a few comforting words, then he walks over to the casket with her and everyone joins in to say prayers for the deceased. When the Priest finishes, everyone walks past the open casket to say goodbye to Charlie.

All the mourners then go downstairs and wait on the sidewalk. The chauffeurs and the pallbearers take the flowers down to the flower cars and then go back up to the chapel. Chris and the widow along with Sonny go downstairs and he asks them to wait with the rest of the mourners. He goes back upstairs and closes the casket and the pallbearers lift the casket onto their shoulders and follow Chris. He goes over to the widow and Sonny and stands with them. Then the pallbearers walk past them and put the casket into the hearse.

Chris gets into the hearse and leads the way to the Church. There must be well over 100 cars in the procession. Cops and squad cars line the way to the church. When the Mass is over, the casket is put into the hearse and everyone gets into their limousine's and cars and follow the hearse to the cemetery. When they arrive at the cemetery the gravedigger's take the casket from the hearse and lower the casket into the grave.

The mourners walk to the open grave and the Priest says a few prayers and they all toss flowers on top of the casket, then everyone returns to the limousines and cars, but Sonny lingers for a moment.

He mutters to himself. You son of a bitch, I wouldn't be standing over your dead ass here at this cemetery if you did what you were told. Well, good riddance to you.

Thanks for all your help, Chris. I'll never forget. I'll be in touch. They all leave and Chris returns to Harlem.

Kenny tells him, there's a couple of messages on you desk. He goes into his office and looks at the messages, Dennis called and Amy called.

He calls Amy.

Hi, Chris. I hope you didn't forget me.

No, how could that happen?

Well, when will you be here?

In a couple of hours.

OK, I'll be waiting for you. I have something very important to tell you.

Yeah, what is it?

I'll tell you when you get here, so you better hurry up.

OK, I'll see you.

He picks up the phone and calls Dennis.

Meet me at the same place.

OK, I'll be there in about 15 minutes. Chris gets there and goes in.

Dennis is waiting for him. They sit down and Chris hands him an envelope.

Thanks Chris. The DA has been talking to this guy Edward since yesterday and I found out that they got pictures of him and Shaffer and Sal on a payoff at the Concourse Plaza Hotel. Edward had pictures taken just in case anything like this were to happen. Not only that, he tape recorded all the meetings he had with your guy Sal and himself and Shaffer. I understand that he won't turn any of those things over to the DA until he gets to court and is given immunity and is acquitted. He don't trust the DA. He's going to be kept at the Concourse Plaza Hotel on the top floor. That's all I got for now, I'll keep you up to speed.

Thanks, Dennis. I'll be seeing you.

Chris goes up to his Bronx office and calls Sal and gives him the news.

Chris, don't worry. We'll straighten this mess out as soon as Tony gets back. Look, we'll hook up tomorrow and talk about this. In the meantime, take it easy.

Chris calls Tony.

Hi, Chris. What's up?

I just heard from my friend. This guy Edward got more than we thought he had. He tape recorded every meeting he had with Sal and he did the same with Shaffer. He also had pictures taken of Sal paying him and Shaffer off.

Wow, that son of a gun, who would have thought he would have done a thing like that.

OK, I talked to your lawyer.

I did too. I'm going to lay low for awhile. I'll stay out in Queens for awhile.

Chris leaves and heads over to Conrad's Cloud Room. Amy is waiting for him at the bar.

Chris, you finally got here.

Let me have a drink, how about you, Amy?

Alright, I think I'll have another one. Well, here's to us, lover, and they touch glasses. Lets drink up and head to our little love nest.

Wait a minute, Amy, hold on. What's this important thing that you're going to tell me?

HA HA HA, this is funny, someone said that they saw me with a guy at Conrad's having dinner. That's so funny, because it was you. Wait till Tony finds out that it was you. HA HA HA. The jokes on him. Tony asked you to take me to dinner and to take care of me. You took good care of me, didn't you? Well, lets go upstairs and you can take good care of me again.

Chapter 53

John sent a couple a guys over to Conrad's Cloud Room to have a talk with Conrad about purchasing his food and liquor and restaurant supplies from his company but Conrad told them to get out.

OK, Quint. I want you to go back over there and see him again, but this time I want you to tell him that we can offer him protection insurance along with his restaurant supplies and food and liquor. Take Casper and Doug with you and show him what we mean. John calls his two gumba's in and tells them to go with Quint. They leave and go over to the Cloud Room.

Quint goes in with Casper and Doug and calls out to Conrad.

Conrad comes out of his office. Wow, look at the size of those two monsters. I told you the other day that I don't want to do business with you.

Well, I'm here to offer you protection insurance along with your restaurant supplies. You never know when someone could come in here and start breaking things and maybe hurt you. Show him what I mean.

The two gumba's walk into his liquor store room and start busting up all his liquor bottles and then they start breaking tables and chairs.

Stop, stop, don't do this or I'll call the cops and have you arrested.

When they're finished, they grab Conrad and give him a beating.

Conrad gets up, please, don't, no more, I'll do what you want.

Quint tells him, see, I told you that you really need protection insurance. If you had it, this wouldn't have happened. Now you have to replace all this. But don't worry, we want to help you. Sit down and tell us what you need to open up tonight. Just to show you how nice we are, we're going to give you a line of credit and you won't have to lay out a nickle right now. And we're going to give you protection insurance and you'll never have to worry about anybody doing anything like this again. Just sign these contracts and we'll get this stuff over to you right away. We'll bill you at the end of each month for your supplies and protection. Conrad signs the contracts. That's good, see how easy it is to do business with us? Oh, by the way, to show you how really nice we are, I'm sending you a few guys, they'll be your new bartenders and bouncers. I'll give you their names tomorrow so you'll know who to make the pay checks out to. Well, let me get going and I'll get this over to you so that you can open up on time. We want to be as helpful as possible. Remember, you can count on us. And thanks for the big order.

They leave and go back to John's place.

How did you make out?

Wonderful, he didn't know that we had so much to offer. He even signed a contract that we're his exclusive supplier for all his supplies. And he signed up for our protection insurance policy. He was so pleased with our service that he asked if we could get him some help. I told him we'd be delighted to secure two bartenders and two bouncers for his supper club.

Quint asks John if he could call John's supply company to have the order delivered right away.

Sure, Quint. Service with a smile. We do what nobody else can do. Good job, send four of our guys over there tomorrow.

Conrad doesn't know what to do. He's hurting all over. Some of his workers help to clean up the mess. The truck from John's supply company arrives with the liquor and tables and chairs and the place is looking like new again and he's ready to open the doors for business.

I'll let the manager take over for the night. I've got to go home and rest after that experience. I never thought those guys had an eye on this place. They would have killed me if I didn't do business with them. I'll get together with my accountant tomorrow and see what he has to say.

I could ask those fellas, Tony and Chris for some advise. They're hooked up with those Bronx guys, maybe they could help me out. That fella, Tony, goes with Amy. If I treat her real nice, he might put a good word in for me. OK, I'll go along with those guys for the meantime. I could go to the cops and have them all locked up. Oh, man, every bone in my body hurts.

Chapter 54

Jimmy and Christina are back in their hotel and are just talking about what a nice time they had these past two days. You know, I was thinking, I really don't have much to do for the next week. He calls down to the front desk and tells the front desk clerk that they are finished with the car and just put it on my bill. What would you think if I tagged along with you and went up to Arlington or Washington?

Jimmy, that would be great.

Are you sure? Do you have a boyfriend that might get a bit jealous?

No, nothing serious going on.

OK, lets see if I can get on the same flight as you. He goes to the front desk and asks if he could use the house phone to make a call to the airport. Sure, and here's the number for the Airport.

Christina, whats the airline and flight number that you're going on?

Western Air and the flight number is 918 leaving at 10:15am.

Western Airlines, please. Hi, I would like too make a reservation on Western Airlines for tomorrow on flight number 918 leaving at 10:15am going to Washington, DC.

OK sir, name.

He gives her his name.

Coach or first class?

Coach.

OK, how will you be paying?

Can I pay at the Airport?

Yes, I can hold this until 9am tomorrow.

I'll go to the Airport and pay for this today.

OK, sir. You can pay for this at the Western Airlines counter and they will issue you the ticket.

Well, it looks like I'm going to Washington with you. Lets go to the Airport and get that ticket. They go outside and hail a cab. Take us to the Airport. It takes about 25 minutes to get there. He pays the cab driver and they go into the terminal and to the Western Airlines ticket counter.

Can I help you?

I want to pay for my ticket and he gives her the information.

That will be $85.00.

He gives her a 100 dollar bill and she gives him the ticket and his change. Jimmy and Christina leave and go to one of the fast food restaurants to get a bite to eat.

Well, I didn't think that I would be heading for Washington tomorrow. Strange how life is, you just can't figure out what life has in store for you. Well, lets go and find out.

They go back to the hotel and freshen up. What do you say that we go to a movie? Lets see what's playing. He looks in the paper and says, nothing much. Hey, look at this, an ad for the Racetrack. Did you ever go to the horse races?

Yes, once, it was a lot of fun.

Well, would you like to go now?

Sure, lets go. They grab their things and out the door they go. Jimmy hails a cab and he tells the cab driver to take them to the racetrack.

The cab parks in front of the race track and he pays the driver along with a tip. They go to the ticket booth and pay for two tickets. The place is packed and he gets a racing form and hands it to Christina.

She glances at it. Look, My Lucky Day.

He's a long shot, lets go and put a few bucks on him. They go to the 20 dollar ticket window.

Here's a 20 dollar bill. Just tell the ticket agent, My Lucky Day to win.

She goes to the ticket window and puts the 20 dollars on the counter. My Lucky Day to win and he punches the button and her ticket pops out.

Now, lets go and watch the horses run. They go down to the rail and wait.

The horses are being put into the starting gate and now they're ready. The bell rings and they're off. The crowd is roaring, everybody is yelling and screaming for their horse to win. Now the horses are rounding the half way mark and the crowd is really roaring. People are waving their arms and getting excited. Here they come, down the home stretch, racing toward the finish line and My Lucky Day is moving up real fast. The jockey is beating My Lucky Day harder and harder and My Lucky Day is really pouring it on. In one final burst of speed he crosses the finish line and wins by a head.

The crowd roars its approval and Christina is jumping and screaming and hugging and kissing Jimmy. That horse was like greased lighting.

Jimmy looks at the tote board and My Lucky Day pays $52.50 to win. Honey, you just cleaned up. Lets go and get your winnings.

Wow, I never won anything in my life.

They go to the ticket window and she hands over the ticket and the ticket agent counts out her money and hands it to her.

Well, lets go to the club house and celebrate. Now, don't get hooked on gambling. It's alright to go once in a while, but don't make a habit out of this. So, here's the racing form, pick out the next horse.

The waiter comes by and they order two mint juleps.

That was so much fun, but don't worry, I won't get hooked on gambling

The waiter comes back with their drinks and Jimmy pays him along with a nice tip.

OK, I picked this one.

Go to the same window and put down 20 dollars and tell him the horses name and say, 20 dollars to win and don't forget to take your ticket.

Jimmy is enjoying his drink but a guy is passing by and recognizes Jimmy.

Holy smokes, the whole world is looking for Jimmy and he's sitting right here at the track like nothing is going on. I'd better get to a phone and call Ernie and tell him. There's no phones allowed inside the track so he has to run down three fights of stairs, then run outside to find an empty phone booth. He finally finds one. Boy, I'm ready to drop dead from all this running around, I'm all out of breath. He takes out a hand full of change and calls Ernie.

Hello, this is Nappy, let me talk to Ernie.

He's busy now.

Tell him it's important and I gotta talk to him.

Ernie, it's Nappy, and he's gotta talk to you, it's very important.

OK. it better be important.

Yeah, this is Ernie, what is it?

Ernie, this is Nappy. I'm in Cleveland at the racetrack and Jimmy is here too. He didn't see me.

What? Cleveland. Try not to let him out of your sight. Keep up with him and let me know where he is. Now get back there and don't let him spot you.

Nappy hangs up the phone and pays to get back inside the track again and runs up the three flights of stairs and into the clubhouse. He looks around and Jimmy is still sitting there with a woman.

Wow, I feel like I'm going to pass out. I better get a drink of water.

He asks the waiter for a glass of water.

Are you alright? You look like you're going to have a heart attack.

I'm alright, I'm just out of breath.

OK, I'll be right back.

I'm getting too old for all this bullshit.

The waiter returns with a glass of water.

Nappy offers the waiter a few dollars.

No thanks. Do you want some help?

Naw, I'm starting to feel much better. Thanks for bringing me the water.

OK, I'm glad that you're feeling better. The waiter leaves and Nappy is starting to feel much better now.

The race goes off and the crowd starts to roar again.

Your horse is starting to catch up. He's moving up pretty fast.

As the horses make the turn, the rest of the field start to pass the horse that Christina bet on. The winner passes the finish line and her horse finishes last.

Aw, that's alright, you can't hit a home run everyday.

Yes, you're right, but I had so much fun.

So did I. Lets get going before the crowd starts to leave.

They get up and pass by Nappy and head for the exit.

Nappy follows them out.

Jimmy hails a cab and he tells the driver to head to their hotel.

Nappy hops into a waiting cab and tells the driver to follow that cab.

Jimmy and Christina get to the hotel and Jimmy pays the driver.

They walk into the hotel and Nappy's cab pulls up in front of the Hotel and he pays the driver and follows Jimmy and his girl into the hotel. Before he can get to the front desk to find out what room they're in, they're gone.

Excuse me. Those two people that were just here getting their room key. What room are they staying in?

Sir, we never give out that information and if you're not a guest here, don't let me see you loitering around here or I'll notify the house detectives and have you thrown out of this hotel.

Oh, boy. Wrong move. I'll just have to wait outside then. He goes outside and gets a newspaper to appear that he is waiting for someone.

Just my rotten luck, it's starting to rain. Gee wiz, now it's really started to come down. I'll be drowned out here. Why didn't I mind my own business. After he's been out there in the rain for awhile, he starts to sneeze. Darn, I'll wind up with pneumonia. It's going to be a long wait, this turned into a bad day for me. Why did I have to come to Cleveland for a vacation to get away from everything?

He looks through the window of the restaurant and sees the two of them having dinner and a bottle of wine while he's starving to death and getting drowned at the same time out here.

Chapter 55

Chris is on the phone with Sal. We gotta move on this thing, it's getting serious.

OK, Chris. Nothing can happen until they start arresting people. See you tomorrow.

The phone rings. This is Dennis. Can you meet me at the same place in 20 minutes.

Sure, I'm leaving now. Chris is driving down to 161st Street and thinking, this thing is really getting out of hand. If this guy Edward is going to spill the beans, we'll all be in deep shit. I'd better get a hold of myself and not start falling apart. Well, we have to take it day by day. Look at Sonny, talk about tough luck, he had to handle all that trouble or he could have wound up in a box himself. Well, here I am.

Hey, Chris. Lets go into the back. How's everything?

Good, how about yourself?

Fine. Here's what's going down. Shaffer is going to be arrested tomorrow in his office. The DA is going to make a huge deal out of this. He's basing his whole career on Shaffer and so is everyone in his office. The press and TV will all be there as the DA personally arrests and handcuffs Shaffer in his office. Then they'll march him outside like a prized catch and hand him over to the cops. They'll bring him down to the local precinct and book and fingerprint him as the press and TV are snapping pictures and all of this is going to be on live TV and radio. All of the Press, TV and Radio stations are being alerted that a major event is going to happen tomorrow.

Shaffer doesn't have a clue. This is going to be a spring board to success for Gallo and his office. The DA doesn't really have too much at this point. All he really has is this guy Edward. He's counting on him to get Shaffer convicted, but in the meantime he's putting on this show so that he can get all the publicity he can. If all this goes down and Shaffer beats this, so what, all that anybody will remember is that DA Gallo and his office are working hard for the public to fight crime. Then he can run for Governor and who knows, maybe get elected. Nobody really gives a shit, this makes headlines and this is all about DA Gallo and his march to success.

Yeah, you're right. Thanks, Dennis, and Chris slips him an envelope.

Thanks, Chris. I'll be in touch with you.

Back in Cleveland, Jimmy and Christina are having dinner in the Hotel dining room while the music is playing. This is wonderful and we won all that money at the track. Wow, I can't wait to tell my Mom and Dad all about it.

Yeah, it sure was a great day and we got here before it started raining. We better hit the sack soon, we got an early day tomorrow. They finish and go to their room and turn on the TV and fall asleep.

Meanwhile, Nappy is outside waiting and it's still raining cats and dogs. He's soaked and he's hungry, I can't take this anymore, I'll wind up in the hospital. I'm getting out of here. I'll never do anything like this again. If they're ever looking for anybody, don't count on me. He gets a cab and tells the driver to take him to his hotel.

Well, Chris. How's everything going along with our business, Tony asks?

It seems like everything is right on schedule. Queens is just waiting for Sal to get over there and start the ball rolling. There's a little problem up in the Bronx, but it's going to be taken care of.

What kind of a problem?

Chris tells Tony all about Stanley Shaffer and how he's getting arrested today.

Holy shit, that little weasel, he brought all this down on himself. He would shake down his own mother if he thought he could get something out of her. So, they plastered his picture and his house in all the newspapers getting his driveway paved by city workers and having a NYC Department of Public Works truck deliver the material to do it. You got to get me a copy of those newspapers, as a matter of fact, get a dozen copies. I gotta have one framed so that I can hang it in my office. That jerk, I knew he was a greedy little bastard, but this takes the cake. Tony starts laughing out loud. This really is hot shit, he can't stop laughing. They all start laughing, it's catching.

Chris is thinking, it's really funny when you think of it. Here I thought Tony was going to be in a panic, and he's laughing his ass off. Tony still can't get over this. They finish breakfast and Chris takes care of the check and they go back to the boat.

Don't worry, I'll check with my lawyer, we'll get this whole thing straightened out. We have a lot of friends up in the Bronx. They go on board the boat and Tony says, lets have a drink.

Chris, did you do me that favor and take care of Amy and take her out to dinner?

Yeah, Tony. I took care of her.

Thanks, Chris. She's a great gal, isn't she?

Oh, yeah. She sure is.

Tony gets in his car and takes off and Sal and Chris get into Chris's car and leave.

Wow, I thought Tony would act differently, he thought the whole thing was hilarious. Come to think of it, it is. You know Sal, we forgot that Corporal has so many judges in his pocket up in the Bronx. Why were we so panic stricken? Tony is well connected also, and we forgot, this is the Bronx.

Chapter 56

Hey, Amy. It's Tony. I'm back.

Oh, Tony. I missed you. It's great to hear your voice, when am I going to see you?

Later on today.

OK, let me know when you can get away and I'll leave work early.

That sounds good, don't let to many guys pinch your behind or you'll have bruises all over that pretty little ass of yours.

Oh, Tony. You say the craziest things, you know you're the only one that can do things like that to me. My little ass belongs to you.

I know, I can't wait to see you and get my hands on you.

Oh, you wild thing you. I can see that I'll be riding a wild bronco tonight.

You can bet on that, I'll see you later.

Jimmy and Christina are all packed and ready to go. He checks all the drawers and bathroom to make sure they didn't leave anything behind. They get the bellboy to take their bags down to the front desk.

We're checking out, he tells the desk clerk.

OK, here's your bill. Oh, by the way. When you came in yesterday, a man came up to me and asked what room you were staying in. I told him that we do not give information out on hotel guests and I had him removed from the hotel. He waited outside in the pouring rain well past midnight.

Really, what did he look like?

Average height, in his forty's and he wore a suit and he had a hat with a turned up brim and he spoke with a lisp.

Oh, man, Jimmy thinks to himself, that's sounds like it was Nappy. How did he find me here? Thanks, he hands the desk clerk a ten dollar bill.

Thank you. I hope that you the two of you had a pleasant stay. Please come again.

The bellboy comes over to him and says the taxi is waiting for them, they go outside and the bellboy and the taxi driver put the bags in the trunk of the cab. Jimmy tips the bellboy and looks up and down the street to see if anyone is hanging around.

Take us to the Airport. On the way, Jimmy is wondering. How did that guy Nappy find me and how come I never spotted him? It must have been at the racetrack yesterday. There was so many people there. I gotta be more careful and stay away from crowds. Son of a gun, I knew that I should stay away from tracks and casinos. How stupid of me, little slip ups like that could get me killed. That rain saved my ass, and good thing that hotel clerk chased Nappy out of the hotel. That must have been something. Nappy standing outside in that pouring rain, he must have landed up in the hospital. Well, here we are at the airport.

They check their bags and go into the terminal. He spots a lounge and they sit in a back booth to keep out of sight.

I had such a wonderful time these past days, I hope it never ends.

Yeah, me too. As soon as we get to Washington, I'm gonna start to look for a little business to buy and if I'm lucky, I should be able to find something in the Washington area.

Your right, there's plenty of opportunities there, you could start with a business broker. Usually, the seller pays the commission, so you don't have to waste your time running all over the place looking for something. They do all the work for you.

Yeah, you're right, I'll start tomorrow. It's time to check in, so we better get going.

Sal calls his lawyer and he tells him to come to his office. He gets there and they start going over everything.

Now, what do they have on you, Sal?

I was doing business with this guy Edward to help me get a piece of property rezoned.

Is that it?

No, he claims that he has a tape recording of a meeting between him, the Bronx Borough President and me and that he has pictures of us at the Concourse Plaza.

What happened there?

I slipped two envelopes under the napkins and they took them.

Did you have any conversations with them about the rezoning?

No, we just had a bite to eat and left.

Well, I'll find out if there's anything else and if they're going to subpoena you. It's possible, this DA Gallo is going to fluff everything up and make it seem like this is going to be the biggest criminal case that ever happened in the Bronx. He's one hungry son of a bitch and he's desperate to make a big name for himself. Election time is coming up and if he can keep this in the newspapers up to that time he probably will get elected again and he wants to run for Governor and hold himself out as a crime buster.

Now, if they do subpoena you, take it and bring it to me. From what you tell me, there's nothing to worry about, just stay away from the Bronx Borough President's Office and go on with your business. I'll be in touch as soon as I hear about anything.

Chapter 57

It's such a beautiful day in New York City. Lou tells the cabbie to stop here, I'm going to walk the rest of the way. Lou is enjoying his walk to the New York Athletic Club. It's great to be walking toward the NYAC on this wonderful day and the promise of becoming a millionaire after this meeting at the NYAC with the Mayor of New York City. The doorman opens the door for him and he goes to the elevator. Second floor, please. He gets off and goes into the Tap room.

Over here, Lou. The Mayor calls out to Lou.

Lou goes over to the bar where Mayor Williams is.

Hi, Mayor Williams.

Hello, Lou. Have a drink before we go into the private dining room. The bartender comes over and Lou orders a bourbon. Lou, here's to you. And they both toast each other. How's things coming along, Lou?

Oh, everything's right on track, your honor.

Yes, things look very good on this side too. The head waiter comes over to the Mayor and tells him that everything is set and that he and his guests can come into the dining room and be seated.

The Mayor calls out to all the invited guests and asks them to follow him into the dining room.

Come along and sit next to me, Lou. Mayor Williams sits at the head of the table and Lou sits next to him.

Some of the biggest bankers and investors in New York City are here with their lawyers. They all sit down and the waiters pour wine into the glasses.

Mayor Williams starts introducing everybody and he introduces Lou as the head of a group that is going to build Freedom Land up in the Bronx. After we've all eaten Lou is going to tell you all about Freedom Land.

The waiters start serving them. There's a lot of talk going on while everybody is enjoying their food and wine. The waiters come out and start serving coffee and dessert and the Mayor stands up to announce that Lou will give you some of the highlights about Freedom Land.

They all applaud and Lou starts telling them about Freedom Land and the plans and projections and what kind of returns this will mean to them. He takes questions and invites them all to take a tour of the location. The questions are many and there's lots of interest shown. At the end of the presentation, there's enthusiastic applause. They all promise to get back in a day or so.

Mayor Williams walks out with them and says goodbye to everyone.

He asks Lou and his Deputy Mayors to stay and join him at a table in the Tap Room.

Patty, the manager comes over and says hello to Mayor Williams and his Deputy Mayors.

Hello, Patty. I'd like you to meet Lou.

Hello, Lou. I'm Patty and it's my pleasure to meet you. Would all you fella's have a drink on me?

Why sure, replies the Mayor.

Patty gets the drinks and serves them himself. Well, here's to all of you and he toasts them and all toast him. I'll be getting back now and I'll be seeing you before you leave.

That was nice of Patty. Well, what did you fella's think of the meeting?

All the Deputy Mayor's agree that it was great.

Mayor Williams tells Lou, I got the high sign from Harold Stevens, he's the biggest Investment Banker in the City of New York and he's the head of that Consortium.

Now, Lou. We have the green light from him so tell your people to get everything together with the contractors and unions. Tell them we would like to have all the contracts signed, sealed and delivered in two weeks. I want to make a special announcement to the people of New York City that I have paved the way to build Freedom Land.

OK, Your Honor. I'll have all the contracts signed before then. That's a promise.

Great, Lou. Well, I've got to get going, keep me posted, Lou.

They all leave and Lou hails a cab. Take me to Arthur Avenue in the Bronx.

Al drives over to the Zerega and meets Ernie there. They hug each other and have a seat.

How's things going, Al?

So far, so good, It seems that it's quiet up there in Yonkers, but I got a bad feeling about that guy Victor, we gotta keep an eye on him.

Yeah, I don't like that guy either. Anyway, how's the collections coming along?

Good, Al reaches into his briefcase and hands Ernie a big brown envelope.

Nice, things are picking up. Angelo should be stopping by in awhile with his envelope. Moe really turned that place around.

Al, Corporal's been asking about Jimmy. We got a call from Nappy. He's visiting out in Cleveland and he spotted Jimmy at a racetrack. He followed him to a hotel in Cleveland and then he lost sight of him. He thinks he got on a plane the following day. He don't know where he went. Here's what we want you to do. Go up to Mount Vernon and pay a visit to his girlfriend and her brother. Ask them if they know where Jimmy is? Her brother plays the numbers up on Boston Post Road. Just be friendly and if they hear anything about him, just let you know. Keep up the pressure until they tell you something. Pay a visit to his mother and if she asks why you want to know, tell her you're worried about him, he hasn't called us and if she hears from him, ask him to call us.

Chapter 58

The sun is just coming up as Stanley Shaffer and his wife are taking their daily stroll around Riverdale. It's a beautiful morning in the neighborhood. A few people are out taking their morning walk and the birds are chirping away. It's a nice place to live and there's not much crime up here. Stanley and his wife like to walk down by the Hudson River, it's like the country in upstate New York. One would never guess that this part of Riverdale is in the Bronx. The view of the Hudson River is spectacular and Marian Shaffer is thinking, how wonderful life is for us.

We are blessed. Stanley is the Bronx Borough President, we have a beautiful home in the best neighborhood in New York City, we are well respected by all our neighbors and our future is secure. Oh, I feel so good this morning. Stanley is such a good man, he's always helping everyone and the people of the Bronx are so lucky to have such a great man as my husband as their Borough President. He is loved by them all. They continue their walk in the neighborhood and some people are starting to head for work and they wave and say hello to Stanley and his wife. It looks like Riverdale is starting to wake up and come to life and it's getting ready for another day in New York City.

Stanley is feeling good, it's nice to be recognized by all these people and to know that they all love and respect you. I feel like I'm walking on top of the world. Look at Marian, she is glowing, as proud as a peacock. It really makes me happy to see her like this.

Well, we both started off like everybody else in the Bronx, poor. We struggled and we had children. She always encouraged me, we'll all get through these hard times, she would tell me. I finally finished College, working and going to College at nights. I got a job with the City and worked my way up. I took all the exams that came up for higher positions in the City and I joined the Democratic Party. I finally landed a good job through the Bronx County Democratic Leader, Jim Buckley. We got to know each other very well. He made me his assistant and he taught me all about politics. Knowing him was one of the best things that ever happened to me. He had me appointed Deputy Commissioner of the New York City Water Department. Wow, what a job that turned out to be. I got to meet and know all the bigwigs in the City and State. Jim Buckley was my mentor, he brought me along like I was his son. Things really picked up for Marian and me and the kids. We got a three bedroom apartment up on the Grand Concourse, that was a big step up in our lives. As the years went on we were able to send our kids to good schools and put money away. I had great benefits working for the City and Jim Buckley introduced me to Investment Bankers who showed me how to invest and make money through the stock market and good investments. We were starting to become wealthy and our style of living was starting to change. Me being Deputy Commissioner of the New York City Water Department opened a lot of doors socially for us. We were invited to so many wealthy peoples homes and powerful politicians affairs that we were always on the go. It was becoming like a whirlwind kind of life. We hardly spent any time at home anymore.

There came a time when Jim Buckley told me, it's about time for you to take the next step up. You're ready to become The Bronx Borough President. You're running for that office on the Democratic ticket. And don't worry, you'll win, hands down. Congratulations Stanley, your going to be the next Borough President of the Bronx.

Wow, I couldn't believe it. I couldn't wait to get home to tell Mariam and the kids. A little Jewish kid from the Bronx becoming The Bronx Borough President. I had to call my

Father and Mother as soon as I got home. Life was really getting good. Now here I am, taking a nice little walk with my wife in Riverdale and everybody that we meet saying, Good Morning, President Shaffer.

Chapter 59

Everyone is showing up early at the District Attorney's Office this morning. There's a sense of excitement in the air and they're all waiting for DA Gallo to arrive. He finally gets there and now all the talking dies down and DA Gallo walks to the front of the office and greets them.

Good morning, everyone. I see that everybody is here bright and early. Well, this is the day that everyone of us has been waiting for. We are going to clean up the Bronx and get rid of all these crooked politicians and gangsters that have corrupted the Bronx for so long. The District Attorney's Office is not going to be known as the do nothing District Attorney's Office anymore. We will be respected and praised for doing our job and keeping crime out of the Bronx. We have started a campaign to rid the Bronx of all crime. This is a war against the forces of evil and we will win this fight. All of us will come to be known as the champions of the citizens of New York City and we will protect the rights of everyone that lives in the Bronx.

There's a loud cheer in the DA's Office. DA Gallo is on a roll now and has them all fired up, they're ready to go out and kill the Dragon that prays on the people of the Bronx.

He goes on as the cheering subsides. You are the future of the Bronx and New York State. We will carry this fight on to the Capitol of New York State. This has become a crusade and thousands of attorneys will join us in this battle against crime and corruption. We are the vanguard of this movement that cannot be stopped. I am proud that each and everyone of you have joined me on our march to victory and you are the leaders of a new tomorrow. This will not end here, we will continue until we have conquered and taken over the corrupt political system that controls all of New York State. This is only a small step in our fight for full victory in the State of New York. Now, I ask you to roll up your sleeves and join me. This is not going to be easy, they will try and fight back with everything that they have, but we have justice and the people of the Bronx on our side. Everyone of us will go on to achieve higher office and govern with fairness and impartiality. Now, my dear and loyal partners, lets get ready to meet the Press and the TV and Radio and the people of the Bronx and New York State and the rest of the nation. They will all take notice of the New District Attorney's Office and the fight against crime. Are we ready to go out there and destroy the enemy?

They scream, YEAH, LETS GO GET THEM.

The screaming and the cheering continue and everyone in the courthouse building and outside on the street hears this commotion and is wondering what's happening.

The cheering and screaming dies down and DA Gallo has them and himself all whipped up and ready to go on to claim his eventual quest to be the Governor of the State of New York. Now, we'll be going up to the Bronx Borough President's Office soon. Everyone, calm down and I'll let you know when we're ready to go.

The whole office is ready, they would follow him into a raging battlefield if this were the Army. All the Assistant DA's are having visions of becoming Mayors, Congressmen, U.S. Senators, Governor's and perhaps, The President of the United States. Their careers are all set, nothing can stop me from getting to the top, they're all thinking.

DA Gallo is waiting for Stanley Shaffer to arrive and get to his office. He wants this to be very exciting and melodramatic and to catch everybody by surprise. The Press and TV and Radio will make this the biggest news event that ever happened in New York City.

Oh, Boy. This really will get me elected Governor of New York State, thanks to Stanley Shaffer. Nothing personal, it's only business.

Chapter 60

Stanley and his wife Marian finish their walk around the neighborhood. The housekeeper is making breakfast for them and they both go into the kitchen and have a cup of coffee.

Marian, I was thinking. I was approached by a big cable corporation and they offered me a position as Vice President of their corporation. It's a pretty good offer. The salary is good with a lot of benefits, stock options, health benefits, chauffeured car, memberships to the best clubs in New York City, bonus, big expense account, profit sharing and a 10 year contract. I know what they want in return, a license to put cable in Riverdale. They've been trying for years to get the license, but they've always been turned down. I could make it possible for them to get that license. I've been thinking of not running for reelection again. What do you think, Marian?

Well, Stanley. You do what you think is right. Whatever you decide, I'm with you.

Thanks, Marian.

The housekeeper serves them their breakfast and when they're finished, Stanley gets up to take a shower and get ready to go to his office. While he's taking his shower, he's thinking, it's getting pretty hot at the office. I made a big mistake by having the City workers fix my driveway. That caused a big stir, and then Edward getting arrested for possession of cocaine. I hope he's not shooting his mouth off, he could start a lot of trouble. After he finishes his shower he goes to the phone and calls Cabletime, the cable company that offered him a job.

Hello, Arnold Matthews office. This is Stanley Shaffer, I'd like to speak to Mr. Matthews.

I'll see if he's here, one moment please.

Stanley, this is Arnold Matthews, how are you?

Fine, and you?

Great, Arnold, I was thinking about that offer. Are you busy right now?

No, I'm free right now.

Good, could you meet me at Ehring's Tavern on West 231th Street at say 11 o'clock this morning?

Why yes, Stanley.

Oh, by the way, Arnold, bring your attorney and the contracts and be ready to sign them.

OK, Stanley, I'm on my way.

Stanley calls his lawyer, Bill Campbell. This is Stanley Shaffer, is Bill there?

Yes, he is, hold a minute.

Hello, Stanley, What can I do for you?

Bill, I'd like you to meet me at Ehring's Tavern on West 231st Street at 10:30 this morning, you know where that is, right?

Oh, Yeah.

I'll fill you in when you get there, don't be late.

OK, I'm leaving now.

Marian, I'm leaving now, I've got to meet some people and I'll call you later on.

OK, dear. You have a good day, love you. I love you too, see you later.

Stanley gets into his car and drives to Ehring's Tavern and parks in front of the Tavern.

Eddie the owner is there behind the bar. Hi, Stanley. How are you?

Great, and how are you, Eddie?

Real good, thanks.

Eddie, I'm meeting a few people, could I have one of those tables in the back?

Sure, come with me.

Stanley follows Eddie and he seats him at one of the back tables. Would you like a drink or something while you're waiting for your friends.?

How about some coffee?

I'll be right back.

Bill, Stanley's lawyer comes in and sees Stanley sitting at the table in the back.

Hi, Bill. Have a seat.

Eddie brings the coffee.

Stanley asks Bill, how about some coffee?

Yeah, that sounds good.

Eddie, could you bring some more cups and a pot of coffee?

Eddie brings the coffee and Bill pours himself a cup.

Now, Bill, some people from Cabletime are meeting us here and they've offered me a position as Vice President of the Corporation. They're bringing the offer and the contracts with them. Now, let me fill you in on the rest of this.

Cabletime has been trying for a long time to get a license to install cable in Riverdale but they've always been turned down. Now you know why they are offering me this job.

Yes, I understand.

I would like to accept this job because I'm thinking of not running for reelection. Nobody knows that, just you and me. Can you handle this?

Sure, lets see what these people have to offer and we'll go from there.

Now I told them to be prepared to sign the contracts today. I didn't mention that you would be present. But that shouldn't matter. If they want something, they'll have to sign on the dotted line.

You're absolutely right, says Bill. If everything is to you're satisfaction, lets get it done today.

OK, Blll, here they come.

Hi, Stanley.

Hi, Arnold. This is Bill Campbell, Bill is my Lawyer.

Nice to meet you, Bill.

Arnold introduces his Lawyer, this is Charles Bentley.

Hello, Mr. Shaffer and hello, Mr. Campbell.

Everybody sits down and has a cup of coffee.

Arnold, I brought Bill up to speed and now I guess he has some questions he'd like to ask you.

Mr. Arnold, I understand that you have offered Mr. Shaffer a position with your company as Vice President.

Yes, that's right.

And could you tell me, Vice President of what?

Yes, Public relations and marketing.

And what kind of a package are you offering?

I have it here, would you care to look it over?

Yes, I would, thank you.

Arnold hands the proposal over to Bill and he starts to read it and make some notes. He reads it slowly and starts asking Arnold some questions.

Is this contract for 10 years based on performance?

Well, yes.

Before we get to the rest of it, lets talk about this. Arnold, you know that this is a loophole so that your company can slip out of this contract whenever they want to.

It is? I guess I didn't read it carefully.

OK, before we go any further, maybe we should get everything corrected and not have to haggle about every word and paragraph. Mr. Shaffer came here with the understanding that you were ready to do business and get these contracts signed today.

I would like to have a word with Mr. Shaffer. Excuse us for a minute.

Lets sit over here. Stanley, these snakes are trying to get over on you, this shits not worth the paper it's written on. Here's what I think.

These guys are desperate and maybe they thought you were to. Lets play hardball with them. We tell them what we want and to get it in writing and have their CEO and CFO both sign these contracts and we want it done within the next two hours.

Stanley, they need that License for Riverdale and they can't leave here without it. Believe me Stanley, they'll do it, and they'll have it done within the next two hours or I'll eat my hat right in front of you.

Stanley starts laughing quietly, OK, I'm with you Bill. Let's do it.

They go back to the table and sit down.

Mr. Matthews and Mr. Bentley. Mr. Shaffer and I have discussed this offer that you made to Mr. Shaffer. I've made a few notes and this is what Mr. Shaffer will accept.

Bill hands it to Arnold, he reads it and thinks, this guy Bill is to slick for me. If I start to squawk, they'll pack up and leave and there goes my job. I'll give them what they want and get that License and then I'm finished with this whole thing. Those guys at Cabletime said, get that License, we don't care what it takes, just get it done. Well, I'll get it done.

OK, Mr. Shaffer and Mr. Campbell. I've read these notes and I'll have this contract written up with these corrections right away.

Don't make any mistakes, this is a binding contract and make sure that they don't try to put any loopholes in it. You have two hours. We'll meet you back here.

Arnold and his lawyer, Charles Bentley, run to the phone and call their office.

Quick, let me talk to my secretary. This is Arnold, take this down, he starts dictating the contract to her. Make sure there's no mistakes or errors in this contract. I'm going to stay on the phone until this is done. He can hear her typing.

OK, I'm done, she says.

Read it back to me.

She reads it back to him.

It seems OK.

Proof read it, and she does, it's perfect.

OK, have the CEO and the CFO sign it. As a matter of fact have them sign every page. I'll hang on, hurry it up.

He's waiting, it seems like forever. Finally, she comes back.

It's all signed.

Did they sign every page?

Yes, they signed every page. Anything else?

Yes, I want you to take a cab and get up here right away. Here's the address, write it down.

She writes it down, got it.

OK, hurry up and tell the cab driver to make it snappy. I'm waiting here for you .

She runs to the elevator and gets on. It stops on the ground floor and she runs out of the building and hails a cab. She tells the cabbie to take her to West 231st street in the Bronx and make it as fast as you can.

The driver goes as fast as can, good thing its not the rush hour. They get there in 20 minutes and she pays him and gives him a five dollar tip.

She gets out of the cab and goes in and sees Arnold standing at the bar.

Hey, you made good time, lets sit over here with Charles.

She gives Arnold a big brown envelope. He opens it up and takes out the contracts. He looks them over.

I wish I had a contract like this, he's got everything but the kitchen sink in here.

Charles, do you want to look these over?

Sure, he starts reading the contracts. It looks good.

Well, Charles, they should be back here in a few minutes.

Hi, fellas. Everything alright, asks Bill?

Yes, everything is here.

Shall we sit in the back and go over these papers.

This is Miss Crowley, she just arrived with the contracts.

Thank you very much, Miss Crowley.

They sit down and Arnold hands the papers to Bill and he starts to read them. He takes out his notebook and starts checking everything in the contract to make sure that it's all correct.

It seems to be all there, Mr. Shaffer, would you like to take a look at it?

No, that's OK. I'm certain that it's fine.

OK, now if you gentlemen will sign all the pages.

They sign and then Bill says, OK, Mr. Shaffer, you sign all the pages now.

Stanley signs and then Bill signs as witness.

Well gentlemen, all signed. How about a drink on a successful day for Mr. Shaffer and Cabletime?

Eddie comes over and takes the order and he returns with the drinks.

Here's to all of us, gentlemen, and they all toast each other.

Well, we have to be going, It's been a pleasure.

Arnold and Charles stay. I need a drink, so do I, says Charles.

Outside Stanley and Bill are saying goodbye. I'll be seeing you and thanks, Bill.

Your welcome and I'll be seeing you too, Stanley.

Oh, by the way Bill, you don't have to eat your hat.

Chapter 61

It's turning out to be a great day for Stanley Shaffer. He and
his lawyer nailed down the position as Vice President for me at
Cabletime and I'll be set for the next ten years. I'll go down to
the office and see if everything is running smoothly and I'll
call Mariam and then we'll go out tonight and celebrate. Maybe
take in a Broadway play and then dinner at the Four Seasons.
Yeah, it's a great feeling not having to worry about getting
reelected. Politics is getting to be a hairy business. Everybody
and his brother is looking to take my job away. I'll get the
license approved for Cabletime to get into Riverdale and then
I'll either resign or announce that I'm not running for another
term as The Bronx Borough President.

He turns the corner and heads for the Courthouse under-
ground garage. I wonder what's going on over there? All those
TV Cameras and TV station trucks lined up on the street.
Somebody must have gotten killed. Stanley parks in his spot
and takes the elevator up to his office. He opens the door to his
office and goes in and says hello to everybody. Seems to be
awfully quiet in here.

He walks into his office and calls his secretary. Any messages for me?

No, sir.

Is everything OK?

She goes to the door and locks it.

Why did you lock the door?

Mr. Shaffer, I have to tell you. The District Attorney is
coming up here to arrest you.

What?

Yes, they've been waiting all day for you to get to the office. Please, don't tell them that I told you.

Thank you for telling me. They'll probably be here any minute now. Call my lawyer and then call my wife and tell my lawyer to come down here right now.

OK, sir.

Right then, someone is trying to get in. Then there's a pounding on the door. Open this door or it will be broken down.

Go ahead and open the door, Miss Simmons.

She goes to the door and opens it.

What's the meaning of this, shouts Stanley?

DA Gallo rushes in. Mr. Borough President, as District Attorney of the Borough of The Bronx, I am personally arresting you. You are now under arrest.

Cops and reporters are pushing into the office.

DA Gallo tells the cops to read Stanley his rights.

A cop starts reading him his rights as reporters are trying to ask him questions? Are you guilty? Others are shoving TV cameras into Stanley's face and bulbs are flashing all over the office.

DA Gallo is trying to speak and get the attention of the reporters and TV cameras.

I am The District Attorney of The Bronx and I...................

The reporters push him aside. Nobody is interested in DA Gallo. They're only interested in getting a statement from Stanley Shaffer.

There's shouting and cursing and complete pandemonium going on. DA Gallo tells the cops to clear the office out. The cops tell all the reporters and TV cameramen to clear the office and wait down on the street. They'll be coming down shortly.

DA Gallo goes over to Stanley. Mr. Shaffer, turn around, I'm putting the handcuffs on you.

Mr. Gallo, could you put the handcuffs on with my hands in front of me?

The Police Captain steps in and says, it'll be alright. He picks up Stanley's coat and hands it to him. Here, Mr. Shaffer. Nobody will notice the handcuffs.

Thank you, Captain. What a nice thing to do. That was an act of kindness that I'll never forget.

DA Gallo tells Stanley he is being taken to the Police Precinct and he'll be booked and fingerprinted.

They get down to the street and there's a big crowd of people looking on as the TV and Newspaper reporters are asking questions and taking pictures. DA Gallo is trying to get the attention of the TV cameras and the Newspaper reporters, but nobody is paying attention to him. All eyes are on Stanley Shaffer, The Borough President of the Bronx. The cops put Stanley into the back of a Police Car and take him to the local Police Precinct. When they get there, they help Stanley get out of the Police Car and lead him into the Police Station.

The handcuffs are taken off and he's put him into a holding cell. After a while, one of the cops unlocks the cell door and tells Stanley to follow him and they go into a small room that has a camera and a stool.

Mr. Shaffer, sit here and hold this in front of you up around your chest. The cop hands the name board to Stanley and he takes Stanley's picture holding it with his name and prisoner number on it. Stanley Shaffer 15487506.

OK, Mr. Shaffer. Follow me please. He leads him to another small room and a cop tells him, give me your right hand. The cop takes his hand and takes each finger and presses it into a black ink pad and then presses each finger onto a fingerprint card and does the same to his other hand. When the cop is finished taking Stanley's fingerprints, he hands him a bottle of liquid soap and tells him to wash the ink off his hands and then he gives him some paper towels to dry his hands. When they're finished, another cop tells him to follow him back to the holding cell.

Stanley goes into the cell and the cop slams the cell door shut behind him.

BAAAAAAM, it's shut.

Stanley sits down on a wooden bench and looks around the cell walls. JJ was here 1961. Joe Blow from Kokomo 1956. All sorts of names and things are written all over the walls. This is an awful place. I'll bet this place hasn't been cleaned since it was built.

A cop and his lawyer, Bill Campbell appear outside his cell. The cop opens the cell door and Bill goes in.

Bill, thanks for coming so quick.

Stanley, I going to get bail set for you as soon as I can get hold of a judge. It could take a couple of hours. Are you feeling OK?

Yes, but this is like a nightmare, things happened so fast.

Here, have this. Bill opens his briefcase and takes out a pastrami sandwich and a bottle of Cream Soda. This should hold you over until you get out of here.

Now, some of these schmuck's might come in here and try to talk to you. Just tell them to speak to your lawyer. You have nothing to say. We'll get together tomorrow. Remember, this is all bullshit. You are still the Bronx Borough President. I'll be outside on the phone and as soon as I get the papers from the Judge, I'll drive you home. Enjoy your sandwich in the meantime.

Thanks, Bill.

Bill goes to a phone and calls Stanley's wife, Mariam.

Hi, Mrs. Shaffer. This is Bill Campbell.

Hi, Bill. How's Stanley?

He's fine. He'll be home in a few hours and he'll tell you all about everything then.

OK, thanks Bill.

Bill gets in touch with the Judge and the Judge calls the Precinct Captain and tells him that he's releasing The Bronx Borough President, Stanley Shaffer on ROR, (released on his own recognizance).

The Captain tells the Desk Sergeant, release Stanley Shaffer. Bill and the Desk Sergeant go to the holding cell and the Sergeant opens the cell door and tells Stanley he's free to go. They leave and Bill drives Stanley home.

Thanks Bill, see you tomorrow.

Chapter 62

Chris and Sal meet each other at the diner on Boston Road.

What do you think, asks Chris?

My lawyer said to sit tight and not to do anything until this whole thing starts to unfold. Tony should be here any minute now. Have you heard anymore from your friend down at the DA's office?

No, he told me that he would get in touch with me as soon as he hears anything. Here comes Tony, lets see what he's got to say.

Hey, guys. I spoke to my lawyer, he told me not to worry about anything. From what he was able to gather, the only thing they have on Shaffer is getting his driveway paved by city workers from the Department of Public Works.

This guy they have in protective custody is the only witness they have and that could be a crock of bullshit. And Gallo, the DA, is desperate to get anything on somebody so that he can claim he's doing something about cleaning up the Bronx. He don't have any evidence on anyone and this guy is not going to give up anything until he gets to court and they give him immunity from prosecution. So, the only one that could do anyone any harm is that guy from the Bronx Borough President's Office that's in protective custody.

Outside that, there's nothing, but DA Gallo is trying to get headlines in the newspapers about himself. As far as Sal and myself getting involved or indicted, it's not going to happen. We have plenty of time to see how this thing is going to play out. If they decide to go to trial with this, it won't be for at least six to twelve months.

Stanley Shaffer is out on ROR and we'll see how far they'll go with that.

Chris, why don't you get in touch with your friend down at the DA's office and see what he's heard?

DA Gallo is going to try to keep this thing in the newspapers for as long as he can. He's up for reelection and he needs all the publicity he can get.

Aside from that, Sal, how's everything going with our projects in Queens?

Very good, says Sal. We have everything in order, lets go over everything and make sure we're ready to go to The Queens Borough President. The last time I spoke to them, they said to just make sure that we own the properties and have title to them and have all the necessary papers in order and they'll have them rezoned.

They have this Federal Revitalization Program to give financial help to depressed neighborhoods. That means, they'll cut through all the red tape and in this case, these areas are so rundown they'll rezone them right away without holding any hearing. So, we'll have those properties rezoned right away and they'll issue the building permits after that.

OK. Sal, do you need anything from us?

Not yet, I'll let you know. I'm going back to my office and I'll go over everything for Queens.

Chris says, I'm get touch with my friend down at the DA's office.

Tony says, I'll stop by Pelham Parkway and see how we're coming along with our Hospital. OK, guys. Lets all touch base tomorrow, same time, same place.

Chris goes to his office.

Anything doing?

There's a few messages on your desk.

He goes into his office and sits down at his desk and takes a look at the messages. Eileen, his wife and Dennis called. Nothing important, let her know if he'll be home for dinner.

Dennis. It's Chris.

Meet me at the same place.

Chris hops into his car and gets there in about 20 minutes. Dennis is waiting for him.

Lets go into the back. DA Gallo is going to offer this guy Edward a deal that if he gives him all the evidence right away he'll drop all the charges and he can walk. He said he'll talk to his lawyer and think it over. The DA said he'll give him until Monday or he'll take the offer off the table, so he has the weekend to think it over. So far, nobody has seen any of this evidence. This could be a bluff, this guy Edward might have nothing.

Thanks, Dennis. Chris hands him an envelope and they both say goodbye.

Chapter 63

Chris and Sal meet each other at the Boston Road Diner for breakfast.

Sal, this guy Edward is being offered a new deal if he turns all the evidence that he has over to DA Gallo.

Yeah, what's the deal?

All charges against him will be dropped by the District Attorney's Office and he will be set free if he'll give up everything that he has and that he will testify against everyone that's connected with or doing business with him and Shaffer and the Bronx Borough President's Office.

Wow, this could be pretty serious. Tony should be here pretty soon. Did you mention this to him yet?

No, not yet. Here he comes now.

What's happening this beautiful, wonderful morning? How about something to eat first, and then we can get down to business.

They give their orders to the waitress and she returns shortly.

As they're finishing breakfast, Chris and Sal start telling Tony about what's going on at the DA's office.

Yeah, I already heard about that from my lawyer.

You did, how did he find out about that so fast?

He's got his connections down at the Bronx County Court House.

Well, since you already know about this, what do you think?

Well, first of all, thanks for being so kind to let me have breakfast before breaking the news to me. That was very considerate of you guys. Lets go over to my yacht.

Tony's boat looks like it's getting ready to sail around the world. They go on board and Tony says hello to the Captain and tells him that they are going to be busy for awhile in the lounge. We don't want to be disturbed.

OK, Sir.

Tony opens the lounge door and they go in. How about a drink?

Naw, it's a little to early for me, they both say.

OK, here's the deal. We have to do something about this guy Edward. He's a loose cannon and we don't know if he's got something or not. The DA really wants to get Shaffer, but if this guy Edward does have something, we could all be up the creek. So, lets talk about this problem. Chris, how well do you know this friend of yours in the DA's Office?

Well, I've known him for quite a while and he's always looking to make some extra money.

You think he might be interested in helping us out?

He might be, let's see how I could approach him.

This probably would be a job for Moe to handle. Find out from your friend Dennis if he knows who's guarding this guy at the Concourse Plaza. If he goes along with the plan, we can give this to Moe and he can take care of it.

Tony says, here's what I was thinking. Dennis can have his friends go into the adjoining room to watch TV and Moe's guys can toss this guy Edward out the window. It sounds pretty simple but everything has to be done right. If Dennis and his guys go for it, it's done. The papers get hold of it and they'll play it up that the guy jumped out the window. These guys guarding Edward say they were in the other room watching TV and Edward was in the bedroom. When they went to check on Edward the window was open and they looked out and there he was, down on the sidewalk.

The DA will think that Shaffer had something to do with it and after a while it'll just blow over. The DA Gallo will get all the publicity that he wants and he'll get reelected and move on. What do you think?

Yeah, it sounds pretty good to me, says Sal. And I think it sounds great, says Chris.

Chris, get a hold of your friend Dennis. Have dinner with him and then have a talk with him.

OK, I know just the right place.

Can you handle this by yourself? Do you need one of us to go with you?

No, I'll handle this by myself, we don't want him to get nervous, he trusts me.

Now, the question of money is going to come up. Offer him fifty thousand dollars and he takes care of his two partners.

That's a lot of money, says Chris, but I'm sure when he hears that, he'll go for it.

Are we all agreed?

Yeah, Chris and Sal both say.

Now, lets have that drink. Tony pours the drinks, bottoms up.

Chapter 64

Amy is heading to Conrad's Cloud Room to go to work. When she gets there Conrad goes over to her and asks.

Amy, could you ask your friend Tony if I could speak to him for a minute?

Sure, he'll be here later on tonight.

Oh, thanks Amy, I really appreciate that.

Amy is wondering, Conrad looks a little worried about something. He's been treating me real good lately and he gave me a one hundred dollar a week raise. It seems like he's trying to get on my good side. Well, I'll find out what that's all about after Tony speaks to Conrad and Tony is going to tell me all about the vacation that the two of us are going on. I can't wait to hear where we're going. With all the money he has, he can take me anywhere in the world. He's all mine and I'm going to make sure that he stays mine. Nobody is going to steal him away from me.

Moe tells Al, you seem to be a lot calmer lately. How's things up in Yonkers and Mount Vernon?

Things seem to be alright so far.

Have you heard of any trouble happening up there?

Nope.

Well, keep your eyes and ears open, remember, we just took over and there could be some hard feeling about what happened.

Yeah, you're right, but everyone seems to be happy and they're all making more money than before.

How's our guys doing?

They doing good, they seem to have been accepted by everyone that comes to play the numbers.

OK, that's good. When those guys come in with the daily receipts talk to them and see if you notice anything different about any of them. Remember, they're around money and some of them could get bad ideas.

Here we are at the Spanish Steps. They get out of the car and Moe hands the keys to the doorman and they go in. They climb the steps and head to the office. Moe opens the door and there's Hanri sitting at the desk with one of the showgirls on his lap.

What's all this?

The showgirl gets up off his lap and runs out of the office.

What was that girl doing on you lap?

Hanri struggles to get to his feet and his face turns red like a beet. I'm sorry, Moe. It won't happen again. I promise.

Hanri, I'm surprised at you, taking a girl into our private office. That's what the word means, Private. There's a lot of very important papers in here and that's the reason no one but us are allowed in here. I'm telling you, I'm giving you a pass this time and don't ever let this happen again. Do you understand me?

Yes, I understand you.

OK, now go and find Angelo and the both of you come back here.

Hanri goes out fast to find Angelo.

Al, when they come back, take over and read them the riot act. I want them to know who you are and for you to gain their respect right now. Don't let them ever bullshit you. Remember, you're my right hand man and don't ever get too friendly with any of them. If they think they can get over on you, you'll lose that respect and they'll never fear you. Keep this in mind "familiarity breeds contempt". Don't forget it.

There's a knock on the door.

Come in, yells Moe.

Angelo and Henri both come in and Al is sitting at the desk.

Come over here. He doesn't offer them a seat, he lets them stand there in front of the desk. I'm Al. If you don't know it already, I'm in charge of the Spanish Steps under Moe. Things around here are going to change and if you can't change with them, you're out of here. We don't ever want to see anything like what we saw today. This is not a game like when the cat's away the mice will play. We want loyalty from you and everyone that works here. We're loyal to you and we expect the same from everyone that works here.

Hanri, I'm disappointed in you. I've heard so many good things about you. Everyone in the business respects you as a great manager, you being the top dog in the City of New York and running the Spanish Steps, the greatest night club in the world, and when I saw you with that slut sitting on you lap, it crushed me. I thought to myself, is this the great Hanri with a common whore sitting on his lap? How degrading. Have you lost all your self respect. This will never get out, we still have respect for you. Pull yourself together and get out of the gutter.

And you, Angelo, when Ernie and Vito came down here to pay you a visit, you showed the same lack of respect. I'm going to tell you this one time. We don't care what you do outside of the Spanish Steps, that's your own business, but while you're inside here, maintain your dignity and remember that whatever you do reflects on the Spanish Steps. This is a world class nightclub with a great reputation to uphold, not some two bit clip joint. Now get your acts together and remember, we're in business to make money. If you don't like your jobs, leave.

Hanri, I want you to get the word out, if anyone doesn't like it, show them the door. You can go now.

Angelo, you stay here.

Hanri leaves and he's sweating like he just took a shower. Wow, I thought Al was going to kill me. Holy shit, he's worse than Moe and the rest of them. He would kill you on the spot. I'll never pull anything like that again. My whole life flashed in front of me, I thought for sure that was the end.

OK, Angelo. I want to know if there are any trouble makers working here?

Not really, there's the usual bitching and moaning going on, but no trouble.

Any problems at all?

There was a little trouble the other night.

What kind of trouble?

A few guys from New Jersey started loud mouthing and saying that the show stinks and that they weren't going to pay the check and that their crew was going to take over the club and that they were going to run us all out of town.

Do you know who they were?

One of the waiters knew who they were.

When that waiter comes to work, find out from him who they were. And what happened to those guys?

My bouncers brought them out to the cashier and made them pay the bill and then they threw them out.

Now Angelo, I want you to inspect the club every night before you go home and make sure there's no faded table clothes or napkins and that there are no damaged tables or chairs. Silverware and cups and dinnerware are in good shape. If there's any pealing or cracks or fading on the paint, have it touched up or repainted. We want to have this place looking like it's the first day that it opened and we want to have it looking that way from now on. That goes for uniforms and the people wearing them. Now, tell them that's the way it has to be. Everybody and everything has to be squeaky clean. We want everybody to look full of energy and ready to go. No more people dragging themselves around.

Al asks, how's the business going?

Great, ever since we got rid of the cover charge, the lines to get in here are getting longer and longer. The receipts have increased by about 40 percent and the way things are going they'll go up by another 40 or 50 percent. We cut the shows down to about one hour and we put on some short order cooks and they really know how to get the food cooked and served fast. We had three shows a night and now we're increasing them to five shows a night. I think we'll put on another four or five short order cooks and we'll be able to handle any size crowd.

Good, we'll be back soon and we'd like to go over the menus and the help with you.

OK, Al.

Angelo, go back to whatever you were doing and Moe and I are going to take a look at things before we leave.

Angelo leaves, I feel better now, I thought it was going to be worse than that. Hanri really got his ass chewed out, I'm glad it wasn't me. That Al, he's a real tough cookie. You can't mess with him. He's soft spoken, but what a temper. No more messing around here for anybody.

Well, Al. I think you got everybody's attention, says Moe. You took care of things very nicely. You won't have any problems down here. Now, lets head back to the Bronx and find out about this Jersey crew.

Chapter 65

Jimmy and Christina land at Dulles Airport in Washington D.C. and they go and get their luggage. Lets get a cab and go to a hotel and check in. How about if we go to a hotel near Arlington. This way we're near both Washington and Arlington. They hail a cab and she tells the driver to take them to the Hilton in Arlington. The driver puts their luggage in the trunk and they head for Arlington. It's a nice ride and it doesn't take to long to get there. Jimmy gives the driver the fare and a tip. The bellhop comes out and gets the luggage. They follow him into the hotel and to the front desk.

Welcome to the Arlington Hilton. How long will you be staying with us?

At least two days.

They finish checking in and Jimmy asks, can we rent a car here at the hotel?

Yes, sir. there's a car rental booth right around this counter. The clerk rings for a bellhop and he hands him the key and tells him to take Jimmy and Christina up to Room 1432.

The bellhop puts the luggage on his cart. Where would you like me to put the luggage.

In the bedroom.

Would you care for anything else?

No, not right now and Jimmy hands him a tip.

Lets put our things away and go get some lunch.

OK, Jimmy. That sounds good, I'm getting hungry.

Jimmy, there's a nice little restaurant close by.

OK, lets go.

They go out the door and walk to the restaurant hand in hand.

Jimmy is thinking, she's a really nice person, she never changed. Still that sweet little girl personality that I remember. Well, maybe things will work out for the two of us.

Here we are, Jimmy. Patty's Irish Pub. They go in and there's a nice crowd here and Irish music is playing.

The waiter asks, would you like a table or a booth?

How about a booth?

They slide in on either side facing each other.

My name is Shamus. What'll it be, folks?

A couple of mugs of beers.

How do you like this place, Jimmy?

Wow, I like it.

They have the greatest Shepard's Pie. Would you like to have that?

Yeah, I think I'd like that.

Shamus, the waiter comes back with the two mugs of beer. Did you decide on what you would like to eat?

Yes, we would like to have the Shepard's Pie.

Good choice. I'll be right back. He leaves and they toast each other.

Quite a place, seems like everybody is having a nice time.

Yes, I come here every so often after work with some of the people from my office.

When do you have to go back to work?

Tomorrow.

OK, we'll pick up a newspaper and I'll check it out and see if there's anything interesting. We can pick up a car when we go back to the hotel and I'll drive you home later.

No, Jimmy. I want to stay with you tonight. I'll go to work straight from here.

OK, then. I'll drive you to work in the morning.

Oh, that would be nice. I hope that something good will turn up for you.

This seems like a nice place to settle down. What do you think, Christina?

Oh, I think that would be wonderful, I'm sure you would like it here.

Shamus comes back with the Shepard Pies. Here you are folks. Is there anything else that I can get you?

Yes, Shamus, two more mugs of beer.

The two of them start to dig in.

Yuuum, remarks Jimmy. This is great.

I'm glad you like it.

I really love being with Christina. I'm starting to fall for her all over again. This time is different, we can do something about it. We were just kids back then on the Jersey Shore. I really fell for her, but when the summer was over, that was the end of our summer romance. Nothing could ever have come of that back then. It's funny how life is. There I was in Cleveland, trying to figure out what my next move was going to be, and who comes walking straight into my life, the girl that I fell in love with as a kid a long time ago on the Jersey Shore. I know now, this was no accident. God had this planned. He sure works in strange ways.

Shamus shows up with the two mugs of beer. How are you doing? Did you enjoy the Shepard Pie?

Oh, yes. We did, it was delicious.

That was one of the best meals that I ever had, we have to come here again. They finish up and pay the check and Jimmy goes over to Shamus and puts a five dollar bill into his hand and they say goodbye to him.

Jimmy and Christina leave and walk hand in hand back to the hotel.

Gee, Christina. I love being with you.

And I love being with you too, Jimmy.

He gives her a big hug and kisses her on the cheek.

They get to the hotel and pick up a newspaper and then go to the car rental booth and Jimmy rents a mid sized car.

Chapter 66

Chris is waiting to meet Dennis at the German Stadium.

How's business? He asks Fritz, the owner.

Not so good. Things are starting to slow down. People used to come here for picnics and dances and to go swimming. That's all in the past now, this was one of the best family places in all the Bronx. Now I have developers coming around here all the time wanting to buy the place. Lucky for me that the place is all paid for or I would lose it. Aw, nothing lasts forever. Maybe one day, I'll take one of those guys up on their offer and sell it.

Really, you'd sell this place.

Yeah, I'm thinking of it. Maybe I'll retire and go to Florida and open a small German restaurant. Well, we'll see.

Dennis walks in and Chris says hello to him.

Dennis, this is Fritz, he's the owner, and Fritz, this is my friend Dennis. They both say hello to each other.

Two beers, Fritz.

They sit down and Chris says, here's to a nice day.

Chris. I spoke to my friends that are guarding Edward and they'll go for it.

Good, says Chris. What night is good?

Tonight or tomorrow night. They go on at midnight. He's on the 35th floor in room 3541. There's a door to the bedroom and they'll leave it open so your guys can come in and take care of business. The door is behind the chair where Edward will be sitting watching TV. My friends will be out in the other room and the door between the rooms will be closed. When your guys are finished. They just go to that door between the two rooms and say, all done. Close the door and leave the way they came in and lock the door.

OK, Dennis. Here's ten thousand and the day after I'll bring the other 40 and meet you here.

OK, Chris. They both get up and say goodbye to Fritz.

Chris goes to his office and gets in touch with Sal and Tony. He asks them to come to his office right away.

Sal arrives first and Chris tells him he just left Dennis. Tony comes in and Chris tells the two of them all about his meeting with Dennis. I gave him ten thousand up front and I'll give him the rest the day after it's done.

Good, now I'll get in touch with Moe.

Hi, this is Tony. Do you have a minute?

Sure.

I'd like to see you.

OK, do you want to come up here to the Paddock?

Yeah, I'll be there in about 20 minutes.

OK, see you then.

Tony tells Chris and Sal that he'll run up and see Moe. On second thought, you'd better come with me Chris. You got all the details and I don't want to screw things up. OK, Sal. You go ahead and take care of our business and Chris and I will see Moe. We'll be in touch with you later.

They all leave and Chris and Tony get into Tony's car and go to see Moe at the Club Paddock.

Well, it seems to be a good plan that you and Dennis worked out. We'll run it past Moe and see what he thinks. Here we are. They both go in and there's Moe waiting for them.

Hi you doing, guys?

Good, and you Moe?

Great. Lets go into the back and we can talk. They all have a seat and Moe asks, what's happening?

Chris just saw his friend the detective. He got the guys that are guarding this guy Edward to go along with this thing and they're on board.

OK, tell me the rest.

Chris tells Moe everything that he and Dennis worked out and the only thing left now is when can we do it, tonight or tomorrow night.

I'll make a call and we'll see.

Moe picks up the phone and calls Timmy.

It's Moe. Can you come over here right away?

Sure, I'll be there in about 20 minutes.

Alright, Timmy is on his way. Would you like a drink?

OK, a beer for me, and me too, says Chris.

Tony tells Moe, I was over to Conrad's the other night and he asked me if I could help him out of a jam he got himself into.

Yeah, what kind of a jam?

It seems that John over in Queens is leaning on him and squeezing him and he's going into the hole.

Tony, stay away from this one. John is moving in on him and taking it. Nothing can be done about this. Conrad could have avoided this if he had paid tribute to John, so that's it. Remember he's not under anyone's protection. So, it was open season on him. Forget it, Tony. Don't get yourself involved.

OK, Moe.

Timmy knocks on the office door.

Come in.

Timmy, this is Tony and Chris.

Glad to meet you.

Tony and Chris shake Timmy's hand and say hello.

Moe tells Tony and Chris, go ahead and tell Timmy about everything.

They tell Timmy all about Edward and where he's at. Can you take care of it tonight?

Sure.

He's in Room 3541 at the Concourse Plaza Hotel. These guys come on duty at midnight.

My partner and I will be there at exactly one o'clock.

OK, Timmy, everything will be ready. We'll see you tomorrow.

I'll be going now, says Timmy. See you tomorrow.

Well, guys. He's the best. Be here tomorrow with the 30 thousand.

OK, Moe. Can I use the phone for a minute?

Sure, go right ahead.

Hi, Dennis. This is Chris. It's on for tonight at one.

OK, Chris. I'll talk to you tomorrow.

Chapter 67

DA Gallo walks into his office and he's feeling great. He loves the feeling of being on top of the world and doing what no other District Attorney in the Bronx ever did. As soon as I get all that evidence from Edward, I'll have this case against Stanley Shaffer nailed down. I'll get Stanley in here and squeeze him until he gives me the names of everybody that he ever took a dime from. I'll threaten him with twenty years in jail unless he gives me those people. I'll offer him a plea bargain and he'll be sweating like a stuck pig. The newspapers will call me the champion of the people and I'll be elected to any position that I run for. I'll be unstoppable. I'll be the next Governor of the State of New York. I think I'll visit Edward today and turn up the heat on him.

He calls his secretary on the intercom and tells her to send Hickey into my office. Hickey comes running into DA Gallo's office. He's one of DA Gallo's Assistant District Attorneys.

Bob, get your notebook and come with me.

Yes, Sir, he runs back to his desk and gets his notebook and briefcase and then returns to DA Gallo's office. All set, Sir.

Follow me. Bob. They get on the elevator and get off and walk across the street to the Concourse Plaza Hotel. Thirty fifth floor. They get off the elevator and go to room 3541. DA Gallo knocks on the door and the Detective on duty looks through the peep hole and sees DA Gallo.

Hello, Mr. Gallo.

Hi, Detective. Is everything alright?

Everything is fine.

Where's Edward?

He's in the bedroom watching TV.

Follow me, Bob.

How are you doing, Edward?

OK.

Bob. Sit down behind me and take out your notebook.

Yes, Sir.

Are you ready to give me the evidence?

I told you, I'll give it to you in two more days.

Edward, why don't you give me the evidence today instead of waiting for two more days? Get it over with, stop thinking about it, you have no choice but to give it to me. Remember, we made a deal.

Yeah, that's right, you'll get it in two days.

Be reasonable, give me the evidence today and you'll be able to sleep better, you won't have to think about it any more.

Look, Mr. Gallo, you'll get all that evidence in two days. I'll testify in court and all charges against me will be dropped and I'll be let loose. Is that correct?

Yes, that's correct, Edward.

Well, I haven't seen any papers to that effect signed by you. I want that agreement signed by you and witnessed by that guy sitting behind you by tomorrow.

What are you trying to do? My word is good, you can trust me.

Bring me those papers by tomorrow and I want you to sign them right in front of me and then I want that guy behind you to witness them in front of me.

Edward, you can't threaten me.

Well, if you don't, you're not getting anything from me, and I don't give a shit what you think or do.

Now, lets not fly off the handle, Edward. I'll get those papers to you by tomorrow and you can give me that evidence in two days. There's been a slight misunderstanding between us.

Bob, find out what Edward would like to have for dinner? Perhaps a nice big juicy steak with sauteed mushrooms and a nice bottle of red wine and anything else he wants. While you do that, I have to talk to the detective. Excuse me, I'll be back in a minute.

He tells the two detectives, make sure you give Edward anything that he wants. I want him to be in a good frame of mind for tomorrow.

OK, Mr. Gallo.

DA Gallo goes back to Edward's room and tells him that he has to go now and that he'll be back tomorrow and we'll get that agreement signed.

Bob, did you get that dinner order from Edward?

Yes, Sir.

Well, Edward. Enjoy your dinner and we'll see you tomorrow. Oh, and Bob, pick up Edward's order and deliver it to him.

Edward, what time would you like to have your dinner?

Seven would be fine.

OK, have a nice evening and DA Gallo and Bob leave.

They go to the elevator and press the button. They get off and walk across the street to the Bronx County Court House.

I nearly blew it. This guy is pretty smart, he had me boxed in and I had to let him have his way or I was losing my golden goose. I have to talk to Bob and tell him not to let any of this out, otherwise I'll be the laughing stock of the Bronx County Court House and it'll hit the newspapers like a ton of bricks. I can see the headlines now. Drug Kingpin snaps his fingers and has The Bronx County District Attorney take his order for a steak dinner with sauteed mushrooms and a bottle of red wine.

Chapter 68

Moe is on the phone with Timmy, go get Gingy and come over to the Paddock.

OK, Moe. We'll be over in about a half hour.

We have to be very careful with this one. It's a hot potato, we can't afford to have anything go wrong. When Timmy and Gingy get here, we'll go over everything and make sure there's no holes in this thing.

Timmy and Gingy show up. Lets go back to the office. They all sit down. Let's go over the whole thing and make sure we didn't skip over anything. Now, are the two of you packing?

Yeah.

Do you have wide brim hats with you.

Yep.

Alright, take these rubber gloves with you and put them on before you go into the hotel. You're going up to the 35th floor and it's room 3541, it's a two room suite. Don't go in the first door, it's the next door and that's the bedroom door. It'll be unlocked and the guy will be sitting in a chair watching TV. The cops guarding him will be in the other room and the door between the two rooms will be closed. Go in quietly and put a gun to his head. Tell him to keep quiet and nothing will happen. Blindfold him with this, Moe hands Timmy an oversize napkin. Make sure that he don't have anything on him, pat him down real good. Gingy, go to the window and open it and then go back and help Timmy. Have him stand up and turn him around once. He won't know what direction he facing. Then say to him, come on and don't make a noise. He'll be so scared, he won't know where you're taking him. Walk him over to the window and take off the blindfold and throw him out the window. Leave the window open and go to the door between the rooms and tap on it and say, all done. Go to the door that you came in and turn the latch to lock it and leave. Take the elevator down and walk out. I'll be waiting for you across the street.

Timmy, what do you think?

Seems OK to me.

And you, Gingy?

Sounds good to me too.

OK, it's about midnight, we might as well get going. They check to make sure that they have everything and get into Moe's car.

There shouldn't be a elevator operator on duty right now but if there is, get off at different floors and walk up to the 35th floor.

Moe parks across the street from the Concourse Plaza Hotel. Lets just wait a few minutes.

Gee, this was one of the best hotels in all of New York City. The Yankee Stadium is just a few blocks from here. This was the best hot spot in the Bronx and when the Yankees were at home, they would stay here. Boy, those were the days. My old man had a club not to far from here and it was jumping seven nights a week. Oh, well. Everything changes.

OK, time to get the show on the road. I'll be sitting right here. Don't forget to put the rubber gloves on.

Timmy and Gingy get out and walk across the street and into the Concourse Plaza Hotel. There's no elevator operator on duty and they both get on the elevator and press the button for the 35th floor. It starts moving and stops at the 35th floor. They get off and walk to room 3541.

Over here, Gingy. This is the door. They adjust their hats and quietly open the door and go in.

There's Edward sitting in the chair watching TV. Timmy and Gingy walk up behind him and Timmy puts the gun to Edward's head and tells him, keep quiet or I'll blow your head off.

What's this?

Shut up and stay still.

Gingy covers Edward's eyes with the blindfold and Timmy tells him to stand up.

He spins Edward around and motions to Gingy to open the window.

Gingy opens the window and then goes back over to Timmy and Edward.

Come with us and don't made a sound and they walk Edward over to the window.

OK, take it off.

Gingy whips off the blindfold and they both grab hold of Edward and toss him out the window.

Edward is screaming as he's falling to his death.

Timmy goes to the door between the rooms and taps on the door and says, it's done.

Then the two of them walk over to the door that they came in, turn the latch and leave. They get on the elevator and push the button for the lobby. They get off and walk across the street and get into the car.

Did everything go alright?

Yep, it's done.

Up in room 3541, one of the detectives says to the other.

Did you hear someone scream?

I'm not sure, lets see if everything is OK with Edward.

Yeah, but wait a few minutes, this is a good movie. Lets see the end first.

Chapter 69

Everyone at the Bronx County Courthouse is buzzing about the suicide that happened last night over at the Concourse Plaza Hotel. There's a rumor going around that the guy who jumped out the window was a witness for the Bronx District Attorney and he was in protective custody.

Up on the second floor, the Bronx District Attorney's Office has gone nuts, they're all running around like chickens without their heads. DA Gallo comes in and they all quiet down. You could hear a pin drop and then all of a sudden, DA Gallo starts screaming.

HOW DID THIS HAPPEN? I know this was no suicide. I just saw Edward yesterday and he was OK. Somebody tossed him out that window. How did anyone besides us know that he was in protective custody at the Concourse Plaza? They knew exactly where he was in the hotel. Someone in this office let it leak out about him. When I find out who was responsible, they will spend the rest of their life in jail, I'll make sure of that.

That's the end of our case against Stanley Shaffer and the end of our careers. All of our dreams are over. No more cleaning up crime in the Bronx. I'll be lucky to get elected as dog catcher. Suicide, my ass. Wait till the newspapers get a hold of this. I can see the headlines now. DA Gallo's prized witness Flew the Coop. DA Gallo continues to rant and rave.

Hickey, get those two detectives in here that were on duty with him last night.

Yes, Sir.

Hickey runs out the door. Where are those two detectives that were on duty guarding our witness?

They're home.

Call and tell them to come here right away.

Hickey tells DA Gallo that the two detectives are coming over right away.

When they get here, send them into my office.

Hickey comes running into DA Gallo's office. The newspaper and TV reporters are here and want to see you. Tell them I'll get in touch with them later on.

Hickey goes out and tells the reporters that the DA is very busy and can't see them right now.

They start yelling that they want him to come out here right now. If he doesn't, we'll tie up this whole Courthouse till he does.

Hickey runs back to DA Gallo's office and tells him.

Oh, brother. I better go and see them or they'll roast me.

OK, Bob. Lets go out and see them.

OK, fellas. Calm down.

What happened to your Drug Kingpin? Did he commit suicide?

The police are investigating and we should be able to answer all your questions later on today or tomorrow. But for now, I have nothing else to report.

All the reporters start to grumble.

Now fellas, please clear the Courthouse so that we can do our jobs.

DA Gallo and Assistant DA Hickey go back to the office.

Bob, what do you think happened?

I really don't know. He was under a lot of pressure. When I brought his dinner to him yesterday, he started talking to me. He said he was afraid that if he was set free, the people that he was dealing with would kill him as soon as he hit the street. He felt that he was trapped between us, the drug dealers and the people that he was dealing with at the Bronx Borough President's Office. He was really shook up. Maybe he really jumped out the window and committed suicide.

Well, the Medical Examiner should be getting in touch with us pretty soon. Bob, I was thinking. We could turn this around and it could make us look like hero's. This could work out to our advantage. We can dump this whole thing on the drug dealers. Think of it, let the public know that this is really a very dangerous situation up here in the Bronx with all these drug dealers. We can create a leak to the press, saying that there is evidence that the Drug Rings had Edward thrown out the window because he was our star witness and he was going to testify against them. We can forget about Stanley Shaffer and focus on the Drug Dealers. Start rounding up all the low level dealers on every street corner in the Bronx. Then we'll start bringing in some of the higher level Drug Dealers and let them know that we want them to give us some of the top guys or we'll put them all out of business. We can let the press know that Edward was a big time drug distributor and was dealing with all these Drug Dealers. Think of some outrageous amount of money that he was making and that he was doing this right under the nose of the Bronx Borough President's Office. Let's drop all charges against Stanley Shaffer. We'll call it insufficient evidence. It'll go away in a few weeks and we can start in on our Crusade against drugs. This can turn out to be bigger than the case against Stanley Shaffer.

There's a knock on the door. The two detectives are here. Show them in.

Have a seat. Now, Detective Cavillo and Detective Cullen, tell me what happened last night?

We were sitting in the other room guarding Edward and all of a sudden we thought we heard a scream. We went in to see if everything was alright with Edward. He wasn't there and the window was open. We looked out and there was a body on the sidewalk. We called in to the Precinct and the police got there in a few minutes. They checked the body, he was dead, and they determined it was Edward.

Did anything unusual happen that evening?

Nope, just that Assistant DA Hickey came in with Edward's dinner.

Anything else?

No.

OK, you can go, thank you both.

As they're leaving, the Medical Examiner shows up.

Come in, Doctor. Have a seat. Well, Doctor. What have you got to report?

There was no bruises, trauma, bullets wounds, stab wounds or poison. The body was in reasonable condition. No signs of sickness or disease. He had just eaten steak and mushrooms and he had some alcohol in his system. There was no struggle in the hotel room and it looks like he committed suicide.

OK, Doctor. Thank you very much.

Well, Bob. Looks like he jumped.

Chapter 70

Moe and Al meet at the Zerega club to go over the business at the Spanish Steps and things up in Yonkers and Mount Vernon.

The books look pretty good to me. What do you think, Al?

So far, so good. I'm still a little concerned about that incident that happened at the Spanish Steps.

Yeah, me too. Nothing else has happened since then, but we better keep our eyes open. We'll wait and see if anything else happens. If there's anymore trouble, we'll take care of it and send a message. Let Angelo and Henri know if anyone of those guys show up at the Spanish Steps again, take them down to the basement and put them in one of the freezers until we get there.

OK, Moe. I'll call Angelo right away. Al goes to the phone and calls Angelo. OK, I told him what to do if there's anymore trouble.

How's things up in Yonkers and Mount Vernon?

One of our guys thinks that he's being short changed on the count. I've been keeping an eye on that store and the count has been dropping for the past week.

Hmm, we might have a problem there. Keep a check on that place for the next week. If it continues, we'll nip it in the bud before it gets out of hand. Don't let on that we're taking a hard look at that place. If something is going on, lets find out who's doing it. How many guys are working there?

Just two, one of our guys and one of the Yonkers guys.

Well, it could be one of them or it could be the both of them. Anyway, let it play out. How's the rest of our action?

The numbers and the sports are very healthy down here.

Great, Corporal and Ernie will be very happy with that news.

Chris is on his way to the Zerega Club to see Moe.

I'm really getting involved in this business. I never thought that it would ever get this deep. Well, I'd better be careful from now on. All this is getting pretty heavy. Things happened so fast that I wasn't even thinking about what was going on. The idea of making all this fast money got a hold of me. Here I am, delivering money to Moe for having that guy thrown out the window. I'm in up to my eyeballs, no turning back now. He parks his car in front of the Zerega and knocks on the door and Arnie opens it.

How you doing, Chris?

Good, and you Moe?

Great, and they hug each other.

Chris says hello to Al and they shake hands.

Excuse us for a moment Al. Come on into the back room Chris. They go into the back and have a seat at the table.

Chris takes the money out of his jacket and hands it to Moe.

Thirty thousand, right?

Yep, thirty thousand, Moe.

Is everything alright now?

Yeah, everything is fine, no more problems.

Good, now lets go out front and have a drink. What'll you have, Chris?

A beer.

How about you, Al?

Coffee for me.

Well, here's to a nice day for all of us. They drink up.

I got to be going now, I have some business to take care of.

Nice seeing you, Al.

Thanks for everything Moe and Chris leaves.

Chris is thinking, I'll get in touch with Tony and Sal and go over everything with them and then I'll see Dennis and give him the forty thousand. Everyone will be paid up. You never know when we might need their services again.

Chapter 71

The phone rings and Miriam Shaffer answers it.

Hello, Mrs. Shaffer, this is Bill Campbell.

Hi, Bill. Wait a minute and I'll get Stanley. It's Bill Campbell.

He gets up off the sofa and follows Miriam into the kitchen and she hands him the phone.

I just got back from the Bronx County Courthouse and guess what?

What is it?

DA Gallo's star witness is dead.

What?

Yeah, he's dead. He committed suicide.

Oh, that's terrible.

You'll be seeing all about it on TV pretty soon. He jumped out the window at the Concourse Plaza Hotel where they were keeping him in protective custody. All charges have been dropped against you. Isn't that great?

I can't believe it. Are you sure that the District Attorney really dropped all the charges against me?

Yes, all charges have been dropped against you. There's no more case. Edward is dead and so is the case. No evidence, no witness and no case. The DA doesn't believe that he committed suicide. He's now saying that the Drug Dealers threw him out the window because he was going to testify against them. He's trying to salvage his own ass. There's no evidence that he was thrown out the window. There were two cops guarding him and the Medical Examiner declared it a suicide. Well, Stanley, why don't you meet me at the

Chinese Restaurant on Johnson Avenue and we'll have some lunch?

OK, Bill. I'll see you there in about thirty minutes.

OK, Stanley. See you.

Stanley turns to Miriam, it's over.

What's over?

The witness, Edward, he committed suicide. All charges against me have been dropped.

They dropped the case. Oh, my. You mean there's no more problems?

That's right. All those problems are gone. I'm going to meet Bill now. He invited me to lunch at the Chinese Restaurant in Riverdale. I'll be back later on and I'll tell you all about it. Stanley kisses his wife Miriam and leaves.

I wonder who threw Edward out the window? I really trusted Edward, I never would have believed he would turn on me. It just goes to show me, you can never trust anyone. I always thought he was such a stand up guy. He sure fooled me. He should never have gotten involved with that dope business. We were making it hand over fist. I'd better be careful who I do business with from now on. That DA Gallo will be watching me like a hawk. I'll just clean up a few things with Sal and drop everything else. Miriam and I will take a nice vacation and I'll take over as Vice President for Cabletime right after the election.

Bill is already sitting at the table and he gets up and says hello to Stanley.

Hi, Bill. They shake hands and sit down.

The waiter comes over and says hello to Stanley and Bill. Would you care for a drink gentlemen?

A bottle of beer for me, and a beer for me too.

Well, Stanley. Here's to you.

And to you, Bill. What a stoke of good luck. It's hard to believe that Edward committed suicide.

Well, It sure worked out good for you, that's what counts. DA Gallo is really burned up. He doesn't believe that Edward jumped out the window. He's going to be looking at everything and everybody that had anything to do with Edward or you and the Bronx Borough President's Office. Be careful, Stanley, he just saw his whole career flushed down the toilet. If he can, he'll start all sorts of trouble. He can't go after you and he can't make any accusations about anyone. He would just make himself look like a jerk. Edward is dead and the Medical Examiner declared it a suicide and there were two cops with him when he jumped. All he can do is play up the narcotics angle and try to keep it in the newspapers that he's cleaning up crime in the Bronx. He'll make some arrests and keep his name in the newspapers and hope that he's re-elected. Everything will be forgotten and you'll be hard at work as Vice President for Cabletime.

The waiter comes back. Are you ready to order, Gentlemen?

Yes, we are and they give their order to the waiter.

You know Bill, I never dreamed anything like this would ever happen. When DA Gallo and the cops came and arrested me, I nearly crapped in my pants. I saw my whole life come apart. Everything that I worked so hard for disappeared in a few seconds. My wife and family humiliated and all our friends and neighbors in total shock that this was happening. I'm so lucky. I get a second chance in life instead of ten years in jail. Here I am having Chinese food with one of my best friends. It's like I just woke up from the worst nightmare that I ever had.

The waiter returns with their orders. Is there anything else I can get you?

Yes, two more beers.

Chapter 72

Quint is just getting dressed to go see John over at the Queens Boulevard Club. John wants to take over Conrad's Cloud Room and I think he wants to make me the manager. He was pretty well pleased when I went over there and had Conrad sign the contracts to supply everything for the Cloud Room. I know he thinks that I'm a good earner. I had all those bars and strip clubs sign up and he's making plenty. I could really increase business at the Cloud Room. I could call it Conrad's Cloud Room for Gentlemen. It'll sound like only guys with money will be going there. The women will be drawn to it like bees to honey and the guys will go there when they see all those women swarming to the Cloud Room. I'll jack up the prices and the Cloud Room will be a gold mine. Well, I'll get going now instead of day dreaming. Quint gets into his car and drives to John's club.

Casper knocks on the office door. Quint's here. Tell him to come in.

Sit down. I want you to go over to Conrad's Cloud Room tonight after closing and tell Conrad that we want the money he owes us. I'm not waiting any longer. If he doesn't pay all of it, I want him to sign the club over to us right away.

How much does he owe?

Over eighty five thousand.

Wow, he must have bought a lot of stuff.

Yeah, he did. This is no charity organization.

What if he doesn't.

I want Casper and Doug to go with you and I'll send a few other guys along. Take Conrad out to the parking lot and use him for some target practice.

What do you want us to do with his body?

Leave it there so that it can be a message to everyone that if they owe us money, they better pay on time.

And if he signs the papers?

Take him outside and use him for target practice.

What?

What's the matter with you? Are you hard of hearing? You heard me. Get back here at two o'clock in the morning and pick up Casper and Doug and the other guys. Don't forget your piece.

OK, John. I'll be back at two o'clock.

Quint leaves and gets into his car and heads for home. Boy, I knew he was a pretty tough guy, but I never knew this side of him before. He doesn't show any feelings at all. It seems like he's made of stone.

Moe and Al are on their way to the Spanish Steps. I think there's going to be trouble down at the Spanish Steps tonight.

Al asks, what makes you think that?

I've been overhearing some things at the Paddock and they ain't good. For instance, one of the families over in Jersey is going to start trouble at the Spanish Steps and try to take over. They think that Corporal is getting to old for this and that Ernie doesn't have the balls to do anything if they start something. They're going to test Ernie and see if they can get away with it. So, lets see if there's anything going on. I have Timmy and Gingy coming down to the Spanish Steps later on.

They park in front of the Spanish Steps and Moe tells the doorman, here's the keys and park over in the garage and then they go in and go to the Office.

Al, tell Angelo and Henri to come in here for a minute.

Al finds Angelo and asks him, where is Henri?

I'll go find him.

OK, the both of you come to the Office when you find him. Moe and I will be waiting.

Henri, quick. Come with me to the Office. Moe and Al are here.

They knock on the Office door and go in. Moe is sitting behind the desk and Al is sitting in the armchair.

Have a seat. They both sit down.

We know the both of you are pretty busy, but this won't take long. The word is out that the same guys from Jersey are going to start some trouble here tonight.

Angelo, how many bouncers do you have working tonight?

We got six here tonight.

Can you bring in about another four?

Yeah, I'll call them right now.

OK. Moe, I was able to get four of them. They're coming in right now.

Good, that makes ten. Here's what's going to happen.

Hanri, if you spot anything give the high sign to the bouncers or to Angelo or us and we'll take care of it. Tell your bouncers, when trouble starts, get the trouble makers and take them down to the basement and tie them up and lock them in the freezers.

Al, lets go down to the basement and get the ropes and chairs ready. It's about nine o'clock now, so you guys go out there and do your jobs.

Everyone goes out and gets ready for action.

Timmy and Gingy arrive.

Follow me guys, he leads the way and they follow him to the basement. The party should be starting soon. We're expecting a little trouble from one of the families in Jersey. They're going to test Ernie to see if they can make him back down.

When they come in they're going to start trouble. We're going to take them down to the basement and tie them up in chairs and put them in the freezers. Before we put them in the freezers, we douse them with water and let them cool their heels for awhile.

After the Steps close, we'll bring them out one by one and find out who sent them over here. When we're finished, we pile them into the van that's parked outside by the loading dock and then dump them into the Hudson River. That should send a message to those guys in Jersey.

It's nearly one o'clock and the place is packed. Things seem to be going along pretty good.

All of a sudden, a fight breaks out in the back. The bouncers rush into action and surround them. They grab six guys that started the fight and hustle them out of the room and down a flight of stairs into the basement and pat them all down. The bouncers hand over six guns to Al.

Well, well, look at these guns. Don't you guys know that it's against the law to carry guns around. OK, sit them down on those chairs and tie them up.

The six of them are yelling. You can't do this to us. Let us out of here. When we get out of here, your going to get it, you'll be sorry.

Now gag them up. OK, guys. Fill those buckets up with water. Good, now pour the water over them. The six of them are soaking wet and their eyes are wide open and filled with fear.

Open those two freezers and put three of them in each freezer. You can see the look of terror on their faces as they're being put into the freezers. When they're all in the freezers, the doors are slammed shut and the lights are turned off.

One of them is thinking. How did I get myself into this fix? I'm going to die in here.

After everyone leaves the Spanish Steps and the place is locked up, Moe, Al, Timmy and Gingy go down to the basement and open up one of the freezers.

These guys look blue and nearly frozen to death.

Moe points, take that one out and close the door, take the gag off him.

Who sent you? Tell me or I'll kill you right now.

The guy is trying to talk but his teeth are chattering and he's shaking like a leaf.

Moe slaps him across the face, tell me.

Frank Gaspary sent us.

OK, take him over there. Bring out another one.

They bring out the next one and take the gag off him.

This guy is shaking so much he can hardly talk.

Who sent you here? Tell me or I'll kill you right now.

Moe slaps him across the face. Tell me.

Frank Gaspary.

Bring me the next one. Take the gag off.

This guy is dead.

Bring the rest of them out.

They open the freezer door and bring out the rest of them.

Take the gags off them. Who sent you guys here?

They all look like they are going to die from the cold any minute and they finally are able to say Frank Gaspary.

OK, untie them and take them up to the loading dock on the side of the building and put them into the van. They're so frozen they can't move and they're tossed in one on top of the other like cord wood.

OK, Gingy, you drive the van and Al, you go with Gingy.

We'll drive up to Innwood and dump them into the river. Follow me right up Broadway.

Timmy, put this silencer on the gun. Before we dump them in the river, put a bullet into each one's head.

They turn off Broadway and head for the Hudson River.

Moe parks and takes a look. Nobody around. OK, get them out of the van and bring them down here.

They get them down on the pier and Timmy puts a bullet into each one's head. When Timmy gets finished they toss the bodies into the river and get back into the car and van and go back to the Spanish Steps.

Those bodies should arrive in Jersey in about a week or so after floating down the Hudson. The Jersey guys will be wondering about what happened to their friends tomorrow. When they find out, they'll be shitting in their pants and this guy Frank Gaspary will be leaving town.

They park the van next to the loading dock and park the car in front of the Spanish Steps.

Lets go inside and have a little drink before we go home.

Chapter 73

Quint shows up at John's club at about two in the morning. He opens the door and goes in. Casper and Doug are waiting there for him.

Quint, come in. Are you ready to go over to Conrad's?

Yeah, I'm ready. Where's the other guys?

They should be here any minute. Now, when you get there, don't let him try to sweet talk you. I want the money and I want him dead. You understand? Just don't play around too long and don't take anything off the body. I want to send a message to everybody else not to get any ideas.

I want you to run the place. We'll go over all that tomorrow. Come over here about two o'clock in the afternoon. Keep the place closed for a couple of days and then open it like nothing ever happened.

Casper knocks on the door, the rest of the guys are here.

Casper. Bring them in here and you and Doug come in here too.

This is Quint and he's in charge. You're all going over to Conrad's Cloud Room. Quint's running the show and just do what he tells you.

Quint, just make sure that everybody is gone before you take care of business. Check all the restrooms and make sure there's no one in any of them and make sure there's no cars in the parking lot. You guys all know why you're going there. Any questions? OK, line up and get your money.

They all line up one by one and John pays each one of them one thousand dollars.

Doug, check each one and make sure they have their piece.

OK, we're ready.

Quint, get everyone into the cars. Casper, you follow Quint and when you're all finished, come back here and get your own cars and leave.

OK, lets get going.

They all follow Quint and get into the cars.

Casper follows Quint in his car and they head for the Cloud Room.

Conrad is saying good night to all the employees. The last of the cars leave the parking lot. It's very still and there's a half moon out tonight. There's an eerie silence and the parking lot is bathed in bluish moonlight.

Quint and Casper are parked out on the street. After waiting about five minutes, Quint tells the guys in his car, lets do it. He gets out and waves to Casper to follow him.

They go to the back door of the Cloud Room and Quint takes out a key and opens the door They all go in and Quint closes the door and locks it. He signals the rest of them to follow him.

He opens the office door quietly and goes in with the rest of them right behind him.

Conrad jumps up when he sees all the guys with Quint.

What's going on? He's terrified and feels sick to his stomach.

Casper, pat him down and see if he's got anything on him.

He's clean.

Conrad, I told you not to get behind in your payments to John. He wants all the money that you owe him and he wants it right now.

Conrad answers, you know I don't have the money.

How much do you have there on the desk?

I didn't count it yet.

Gimme it, I'll count it.

Quint starts counting. There's only twenty three thousand here. Where's the rest of the money?

There's about three thousand in the safe.

Open it.

Conrad opens the safe and Quint pushes him aside.

He grabs the money and counts it. There's only two thousand here. Is there any more money around here?

No, that's it.

Gee, it's not your lucky day, is it? OK, Conrad. Sit down.

He sits down and thinks, they're going to kill me.

Quint puts a sheet of paper on the desk in front of Conrad and then hands him a pen.

Now write. I, Conrad Williams, hereby sell and transfer title to Conrad's Cloud Room for the sum of Ten Thousand Dollars to John Zagallo. Now, sign it.

I signed it but it's not worth shit. I'll go to my lawyer and have them all arrested and thrown in jail. They think they're hot shit. These dumb jerks. I'll just go along with all this bullshit and they'll leave thinking that they own the Cloud Room. No sense getting my self killed.

That wasn't so bad, was it, Conrad?

John is really a nice guy, he's giving you a chance to pay what you owe and then he'll give the bill of sale back to you. You gotta understand, John's a businessman. It's nothing personal, it's only business.

Doug, bring us a bottle so that Conrad and I can have a drink.

Conrad is still shaking but he drinks the whiskey.

Well, time for everyone to go home. Get your jacket, Conrad. We'll walk you to your car. We don't want anything happening to you. This is a rough neighborhood at night.

These guys would have killed me if I didn't sign that paper. Good thing that I didn't give them a hard time.

They all walk outside and Quint tells Conrad, you better start running to you car. It looks like it's going to start raining.

Conrad looks up. It's not going to rain.

HA, HA. I made you look up, but I think you'd better start running anyway.

Quint pulls out a gun and Conrad starts running for his life.

Alright, time for a little target practice.

The others start shooting. They're yelling, run the other way.

The only way out is behind them. He's running in circles trying to save his life.

Casper and Doug are laughing and then they all start laughing at Conrad.

Quint is having the time of his life and yells out, what a bunch of lousy shots you are, you couldn't hit the broad side of a barn.

Conrad is screaming, please don't shoot me. I signed the papers and gave you all the money I had. Please give me a chance.

Quint yells. OK, stop playing around and get serious. They all shoot Conrad and he falls to the ground, dead.

Casper and Doug walk over to Conrad's body and shoot him in the head.

Quint says, well guys. We've had enough fun for one night.

Chapter 74

Jimmy goes to the phone and calls Liz.

It's me, Jimmy.

How are you, Jimmy?

OK, Liz. I only have a few minutes.

Where are you, Jimmy?

Up north. Liz, did you get that letter that I sent you?

Yes, thank you.

Good. What's happening up there?

My brother told me that a lot of people got killed up in Yonkers and that the guys you worked for now control everything in Yonkers and Mount Vernon.

Yeah, anything else?

Yes, a friend of yours named Sammy got murdered and they cut his head off and stuck it up on an iron picket in front of the Bronx Zoo.

What? When did that happen?

A couple of weeks ago? Jimmy, I'm afraid for you. Those guys are looking for you.

OK, don't mention anything about me calling you. If anybody asks, you haven't seen or heard from me since we broke up in Florida. Take care of yourself. I don't know when I'll be able to get in touch with you again. Liz, thanks again for everything, I'll never forget you. Goodbye.

Gee, Jimmy thinks. I really screwed up. I better be careful from here on. Maybe I could find a plastic surgeon and get a new face. I got my new Drivers License and Social Security Card but I gotta change my looks. I'll find a little business and they'll never find me.

Chris stops by his office and asks Andy if there's any messages.

Yeah, a Miss Collins called and left a number for you to call her. I left it on your desk.

He goes into his office and closes the door.

Hi, it's Chris.

Thanks for calling me back.

Is everything OK, asks Chris?

Well, not really, could you come over to Queens, I need to talk to you.

Yeah, sure.

Meet me at the Astoria Diner right over the Triboro Bridge, do you know where it is?

Yeah, I know where it is.

Can you meet me there in a half an hour.?

Sure, I'll leave right now.

Andy, I'll be in touch with you. He gets into his car and drives to the Astoria Diner. I wonder what's going on with her? Tony mentioned that she was having all sorts of problems. Well, I'll see what's going on with her. He pulls into the Astoria Diner parking lot and goes in. There's Amy sitting in a back booth. He slides in next to her and they kiss each other.

Chris, I'm sorry to call you like this but I have to ask you a few things.

That's OK, tell me what's going on?

She tells him everything about her husband, her kids and about losing her job.

Gee, I'm sorry to hear about all these things.

I was hoping that you might be able to help me out.

Why, sure, Amy. Chris reaches into his pocket and pulls out a roll of bills. He counts out five hundred dollars. Here, Amy, take this.

She puts it into her purse and gives him a big kiss. Thanks, Chris. I knew that I could count on you.

Now, don't mention this to Tony, he tells her.

You know that I wouldn't do a thing like that. When will I see you?

How about we meet each other Monday or Tuesday?

OK. you can call me at that number, I'm staying at my mother's place for awhile.

OK. I've got to get going now. See you soon, Amy.

Chris leaves and starts driving back to the Bronx. Man, it's hard to break away from her. She is trouble, I should know better. But once you get a taste of something like that, it's just about impossible to break the habit.

Amy is finishing her coffee. I got Chris on the hook and I'll see him every week. Between him and Tony, they should be good for about fifteen hundred a week. Now, I better call Joey and have him meet me. I don't want him thinking that I forgot him.

Chapter 75

The whole family is over for dinner and Tony Junior is going to announce that he and his girl are engaged and they are getting married in two weeks. The reason that they are getting married so soon is that he is going into the Army in two months. His girl, Angela, is a sweet little thing and she comes from a good family.

Tony, is everything OK?

Yeah, everything is fine. When are they going to start coming, he asks?

They should be showing up any minute now.

The doorbell rings and Tony goes to open it. It's Angela's mother and father.

Hi, come in. I'm Tony and this is my wife, Marie.

Hello, I'm Angelo and this is my wife Magdalena.

Here, let me take your coats. Please, come in.

Marie takes Magdalena's hand and leads her into the living room.

Oh, what a beautiful home.

Oh, thank you. Please sit down.

The door bell rings again. Excuse me while I go see who that is.

Marie and Tony go to the door. It's Tony Junior and his girl, Angela.

Hi, Mom and Dad. Tony Junior kisses his Mom and Dad.

Hi, Angela. Marie and Tony hug and kiss her. Come in. Give me your coats. Your Mom and Dad are in the living room.

Here come the rest of the family. They all come in and give Tony their coats and hats.

Marie, take everyone into the living room. They're all saying hello and talking and gathering in the living room.

Marie has arranged to have a few maids to help her out. There's a bar set up at the end of the living room so that the guests can have a drink. The maids serve appetizers and everyone goes to the bar for drinks. The families and friends are all getting to know each other and chatting away.

Marie announces that dinner is ready and would everyone please follow her into the dining room and find their place.

When everyone is seated, Tony asks them to join him in saying grace.

The maids start serving the soups and salads. Next they start serving the main course. When they're finished, the maids serve dessert and coffee.

Tony taps his glass with his spoon. May I have your attention, please. This gathering of our two families is to announce the engagement and marriage of Angela and my son Anthony. I'd like to offer a toast to both of them and may they have a blessed and wonderful marriage all their lives.

They all break out in applause and cheers for the two of them.

Anthony Junior gets up and addresses everyone. Thanks for coming over this evening. It was a wonderful dinner and thanks, Mom and Dad, for welcoming Angela into our family.

Next, Angelo Marino gets up. Thank you, Marie and Tony, for inviting my wife and I and our family to this beautiful family dinner. Anthony, we want to welcome you into our family. Our daughter Angela, has been a joy and a blessing to us, now it's time for her to go with the man in marriage that she loves so much. May the good Lord bless and keep you both all the days of your life.

The place breaks out in cheers and everyone is clapping. Everybody is hugging and kissing each other. Marie and Magdalena are crying like babies and hugging each other. They are so happy that their son and daughter are going to be married. Tony and Angelo are hugging each other.

You have a wonderful son and I know that he will be a good husband.

Tony says, you have such a beautiful daughter and Anthony loves her. I know that the two of them will be happy and have a good life.

That was a wonderful dinner you and your wife prepared. We'll be going now and again, thank you very much.

Mr. and Mrs. Marino leave and all of the family and friends leave also.

Well, son. Angela and her family are very nice and your Mother and I love you and Angela. Your Mother is getting everything ready for the reception, so I think that she and Angela should do it together.

Good idea, Dad. I'll tell Angela. I know she'll be happy planning everything with Mom. Well, Dad. I'll take Angela home now and thanks for everything. So long, Mom. We'll be leaving now.

Angela, we love you. Get home safely. Goodnight, Anthony. I love you.

Chapter 76

Hi, Amy. It's Chris. I was just thinking about you. How are you?

I'm doing good.

How about you and I get together today.

OK, that sounds good. I'll meet you over at the Sheridan Hotel in about an hour.

Chris is thinking. I do miss Amy, she is different than all those women that I've been with. I know that she's using me but I have the money now to play around a little bit. I just have to be careful that Tony doesn't catch on. That would be the end of our friendship. Well, it should be a nice day, just hanging out with her and eating and drinking and having all the sex that I want. Man, she can go day and night. She must have monkey glands. I'll just check in with Andy and see if everything is OK.

Hey, Andy. Anything doing?

Just Sal, he said that he took care of everything and Tony will be busy with his wife getting things ready for his son's wedding.

OK, Andy. If anything comes up, call Kenny. He'll take care of anything that comes up. I'll be in touch.

Lets see, I'll stop by the liquor store and get a few bottles. I think we'll have Chinese food, she'd like that. Like my father always said. Treat a whore like a lady and a lady like a whore. I'd better get going, I don't want to be late. He gets in his car and heads for Queens.

Tony should be pretty busy for the next couple of weeks with the plans for his sons wedding. With all these things going on at the same time, we'll all be so wealthy that we won't ever want for anything.

Hmm, it might be time for Eileen and me to get a bigger house. We have to keep up with Tony and Sal. I'll ask Tony if he could build it for us. That should make Eileen pretty happy. She's a good woman and a good mother. I don't want her involved with any of this. It's too bad that I'm such a woman chaser. I guess that I got it from my father. He'd hump anything he had a chance to. Well, I'd better be very careful. I just have to remember, don't shit where you eat. Chris spots a liquor store and he stops and goes in. Give me a bottle of that red wine and a bottle of Baileys.

That will be $42.32. He hands the clerk a fifty and the clerk gives him his change.

OK, I guess she's there already. He parks the car and goes into the lounge and there she is, sitting at the bar. Boy, she's something. What a knockout.

Hey, Chris. she gives him a great big kiss on the mouth. Lets go over to that table.

Gee, you look great, Amy.

Thanks, Chris. You always say such nice things to me.

The waiter comes over and takes their order.

How's everything with you, Amy?

Not to bad, everything has quieted down for the moment.

How about you, Chris?

Aw, that little problem we had is all gone and Tony and Sal and I just closed on some great business deals.

Oh, I'm so happy for you guys. I wish some good luck would come my way.

The waiter comes back with their drinks.

Well, here's to us and a nice day together. They toast each other.

It's so nice being with you, I missed you so much.

Yeah, I've been so busy, I hardly have a moment to myself. Hey, Amy. They got a big indoor swimming pool here. How about we go swimming?

I don't have a bathing suit.

Well, lets go get some swimming suits.

OK, that sounds great. Chris pays the check.

Lets go get a room first. Tell the clerk that we want a king size bed, she giggles.

We would like a room with a king size bed.

OK, sir.

She really starts giggling.

Will that be cash or credit card?

American Express.

Thank you, sir. Room number 473. Will there be anything else? Yeah, is there anyplace where we can get some swimming suits?

There's a gift shop right here in the hotel.

Great, we'll pick up the room key after we get the swimming suits.

The gift shop is to your left, sir.

Chris and Amy go hand in hand like two young lovers to get their bathing suits. Chris picks out a pair of bathing trunks and Amy picks out a teeny weeny little poker dot bikini.

Look what I found, a little poker dot bikini, I always wanted a teeny weeny poker dot bikini. Can I have it, Chris?

Why sure you can have it.

Oh, thank you. She goes to the mirror and holds it in front of herself. Oh, I can't wait to put it on. Hurry up, lets go to the swimming pool.

Chris pays for the swimming suits and they stop by the front desk and pick up the room key. They get on the elevator and he hit's the button for the forth floor. They get off and find room 473 and he unlocks the door.

Oh, what a nice room. Hurry up and lets put on our swimming suits. She goes to the bathroom and puts on her bikini and comes out.

He already has his bathing suit on and he looks at her. He's wide eyed. Wow, she looks like she just stepped off the cover of a Playboy magazine. What a vision, a tiny red and white polka dot bikini, flaming red hair and red patented high heels shoes. We'd better take some towels with us.

OK, lets go. They start walking to the elevator and they pass a guy just getting off. He stops in his tracks and just stares at her.

They get on the elevator and it stops at the lobby floor and they start walking towards the swimming pool. She has the towel slung over her left shoulder and she has this little wiggle in her walk. Everyone is looking at her as she is prancing through the lobby. All the guys can't believe their eyes and are spellbound by her. She's really putting on a show and she loves it.

They get to the pool and she drops her towel on a beach chair and kicks her high heels off.

Come on Chris, jump into the water. She takes a running dive into the water and he follows her.

When he comes to the surface, she starts splashing him. He starts splashing her and they are like two little kids having a great time. They swim the length of the pool a few times and he stops all out of breath. She swims a little longer and then joins him at the shallow end of the pool.

She kisses him and then drags him back out to the deep end of the pool and pulls him under.

He comes up and starts sputtering. She is laughing and having a good time. They stay in the water a little bit longer and then get out and lay down on the beach chairs.

The pool attendant comes over and asks if they would care for a drink.

She asks for a vodka martini and he orders a beer.

I haven't had such a good time in quite a while, I love being with you. Remember, you promised that you would always keep on seeing me.

Lets order some Chinese food. I'm starting to get hungry.

Let me dry you off and then we can go upstairs. He starts drying her off and then running the towel through her hair.

Umn, feels good. Now, let me dry you off. She dries him off real rough and he thinks to himself, she's pretty strong for a women.

This time, she covers herself with the towel as they walk through the lobby. They get on the elevator and go to the forth floor. Chris opens the door and they go in.

I'm going to take a shower.

OK, I'm going to order the Chinese food. Would you care for anything special, Amy?

I'll have the same as you, but get me two egg rolls.

OK, he calls the Chinese Restaurant and orders the food and tells them to deliver it to the Sheridan Hotel, room 473.

She comes out of the bathroom and has a sheer night gown on. Do you like it?

Yeah. I'll fix us a drink while you take a shower. He finishes and comes out with a towel wrapped around his waist.

She hands him a drink. Here's to us, Chris.

She stands right in front of him and he gets up from the chair and kisses her and he's really feeling romantic and his temperature is rising.

BAM, BAM, BAM. There's a loud knock on the door, it sounds like someone is going to knock the door down.

Amy jumps off the bed and runs for the bathroom and locks herself in. Oh, no. It has to be Brian. She's terrified and consumed with fear. He's going to kill me this time.

Chris yells, who's there? I can't understand what he's saying.

Hold on, I'll be right there. Chris puts his pants and shirt on and opens the door. He looks out and then he looks down.

There's a little Chinese guy with a long pig tail and he's about three feet tall standing there with a paper bag .

He's holding his hand out. Twena fi della.

What?

Twena fi della.

What?

Wha, yo no speaky enlay.

Chris pulls out his wallet and hands him thirty dollars.

Tan yo peas.

You can come out now.

Amy comes out. That guy scared the life out of me. I thought it was my husband, the way he was knocking so hard and so loud.

Chris is ready to pass out, he has to hold onto a chair. I thought I was going to have a heart attack. All that loud pounding on the door, I thought we were going to get killed. I need a drink after that.

Chapter 77

Tony's wife, Marie is with Eileen and her daughter, Francine. They're setting up the Ballroom at The German Stadium and they're asking Hans, the manager, some questions about the seating arrangements.

Lady's, there's plenty of room for all your guests.

How about the band?

We can accommodate a band of up to fifteen musicians.

How big is the dance floor?

Your standing on it now.

Wow, this is it? It's really big.

You see those markers. Each marker is for one hundred people. This way when they are setting up the tables there's no guesswork about how the ballroom should be set up. Now, if you let me know how many people are going to be attending, I'll have the tables setup. We can have the serving tables set up and out of the way. Would you like to see the kitchen?

Yes, we would. He opens up the doors and they go in.

Wow, this is some kitchen.

Yes, it sure is. We can handle any size affair or wedding.

Francine says, you could feed an army with no trouble at all.

We'll have all the help that you'll need. Now, if you need anything, just let me know?

Oh, you've been such a great help, Hans, thank you.

So, if you'll excuse me, I have to take care of a few things.

Francine remarks, this is such a huge place. Your son and his wife will have a great wedding reception. If I ever get married, I want to have my wedding reception right here.

Then you better hurry up and get married soon because they're going to turn it into a country club.

They are? What a shame. It's such a beautiful place.

Amy is thinking to herself. Tony's son is getting married and he's going to be busy for the next couple of weeks. And I'm not going to be invited to that wedding. Tony should have thought of something and had one of his friends take me to that reception. I would have been the best looking and best dressed women in the whole place. But, I'll wait and show them all, then it'll be my turn.

Tony's going to keep his promise and marry me. I'll make sure that he keeps his promise. And Chris is going to take care of me whenever I snap my fingers. It's going to be so perfect. I'll have everything that I ever wanted.

Who ever first said, I can have my cake and eat it too, was so right. Now, I'll just keep Joey happy until I'm ready and then I'm all set. Good thing he's a little slow or otherwise I'd never be able to pull this off.

Chris, Tony and Sal are on their way to Pelham to check things out. There's my Project Superintendent. Sal stops the car and they get out.

Hey, Tony, how's things?

Fine. We just stopped over to see how things were coming along.

We're right on schedule, we have the plumbers and the electricians finishing up. We'll be all finished in about three months.

Tony says, we'll have Stanley Shaffer over here to formerly open the Hospital and take credit for another community improvement. We'll invite the whole community to the opening and have all the civic leaders here. Lets go over to the boat where we can have a little privacy.

OK, Shawn. It looks great. Keep up the good work. As soon as we're finished here we'll get to work on the other two projects in Queens.

They get into the car and head to Ray's Boatyard. They park right next to the boat and go on board.

Hi, Captain. We'll be in the Salon for awhile. Tony opens the door and they go in. Any games on?

Yeah, the Yankees and Red Sox are playing.

Tony turns the TV on and he gets some beers and hands them to Chris and Sal. Well, here's mud in your eye.

Well, guys. What did you think about that little meeting we just had with Corporal?

I don't know, says Sal, something must be bugging him. He's a funny guy, sometimes it seems like he's talking in circles, but he's really talking to somebody without coming right out and saying it. When he said to us that ten percent of everything that we make was going directly to Vito, that was a statement that Vito was moving up pretty fast. He wanted to see if there was any reaction about his authority from any of us.

Remember, he made sure that all the bosses were there. After we left, he had some of the Bosses from Brooklyn come over and see him. He was laying down the law to all of us and letting every one know that he's still the undisputed Boss of this family and he's ready to defend that position. He told everybody that he was planning on retiring to see if anyone would make a move on him, inside or outside. Those two things that happened, the first from Yonkers and Mount Vernon and the second from New Jersey were ready made for him. He showed the world that nobody can cross him. He's as strong as he ever was and maybe even stronger.

He waited for Ernie to get out of the can before he made his moves. Ernie is his right hand man and he's trusted by Corporal. Ernie will wait forever until Corporal gives the word that he will be the Boss. Even after that, Ernie will always defer to him. Corporal will be the real Boss until he dies. He'll never give up being the Boss. I think that sometimes he can read our minds.

Tony says, I don't think he likes the idea that I'm running around with Amy even though he never mentions it. Did he ever say anything to you guys about it?

No. Not me. Both Chris and Sal answer.

Well, just don't piss him off about anything. Maybe my son's wedding will put him in a better frame of mind. He always liked my kids and he always looked forward to seeing them. Yeah, he's that way. He loves kids. Maybe because he and Sally never had kids. Well, I know that he and Sally will really enjoy going to Tony's wedding and reception.

Wow, the Yankee's are losing to the Red Sox again. Here, have another beer. This is turning into a good game.

Chapter 78

I don't know about any of these business's that I've seen so far.

Don't get discouraged, Jimmy.

Yeah, I trying not to.

I have to tell you something. I've been on the run ever since I met you.

What do you mean, you've been on the run?

Well, It's a long story and you deserve to know the truth. I got into some trouble in New York and now the people that I used to work for are looking for me.

What kind of trouble?

I was clipping money from them and they found out.

Can't you just go see them and tell them your sorry and try to pay them back?

It's not that simple.

These people are the Mafia and I stole from them. Anybody that steals from them winds up dead. There's no apologies accepted from them.

Is there anybody that you can speak to?

No, that's why I'm trying to find something to earn a living. I've got enough money to last for awhile, but without a source of income, it's not going to last to long.

Why can't you just get a job until something comes up?

Here in Washington? It's not likely. I'm afraid that someone will recognize me.

Remember that day in Cleveland when we went to the race track?

Yes, what about it?

I was spotted by a guy from New York that knows me.

How was that possible?

I dunno, I didn't see the guy at all. He must have seen us at the race track. The way I found out was when we were checking out of the hotel the desk clerk told me that a guy asked him what room we were staying in. He didn't tell him and when he found out he wasn't staying at the hotel, he told him to leave or he would have him thrown out of the hotel. He also told me that guy stayed outside the hotel most of the night. He probably was waiting to see where we'd go. It's a good thing for me that it was raining or he would have followed us when we left in the morning. I just can't go anyplace where these guys usually hang out.

Are you sure that guy was following us?

Yeah, I know him. The desk clerk described him to a T. He's one of Corporal's soldiers. I'm certain that he called New York and told them and that's why he was waiting there so long.

Who's Corporal?

He's the Godfather, the one that I worked for.

You mean that you're in the Mafia?

Yeah, I guess you could say that.

You never mentioned that to me.

Yeah, I know. It's something that I could never talk about outside the family.

You mean that you told your mother about you being in the Mafia?

No, it's not that kind of family, that's what the Mafia calls the people that belong to organizations like Corporal's group. I belong to Corporal's family and he's the head of it. He's the Boss, he is the Godfather.

I would never have thought that you were a gangster.

And I'm going under the name of John Martin. I don't want you to get mixed up in any of this.

Oh, Jimmy. What can we do? I'm so worried about you.

I'm not sure yet. Lets give this a little more time, hopefully, something will come up. I just have to very careful. Look, I gotta get in touch with my mother. I'll go to a phone booth and give her a call in a little while.

OK, Jimmy. I'll go with you.

They go to a hotel about two miles away and go in. He finds an empty phone booth and she sits down on a sofa while he calls his mother. The phone rings.

Hello, Mom. This is Jimmy.

What a surprise, how are you?

I'm OK. How you doing, Mom?

I'm doing alright.

I'm sorry I didn't call you sooner.

Some people have been looking for you. They told me that you didn't show up for work. Liz stopped by and told me that you had a problem on your job and that you had to leave for a little while. She gave me some money and told me not to say anything about you to whoever comes here asking about you.

Yeah, that was nice of her to do that.

Are you in any sort of trouble?

Aw, just a little misunderstanding, I'll straighten it out.

I have to go into the hospital in a few weeks to get a checkup.

Why? What's the matter?

Nothing much, my doctor just wants to run some test's on me.

What hospital are you going to?

Montifiore Hospital.

When?

He's going to let me know.

OK, I'll call you back in a few days. Find out when you're going into the hospital?

Where can I get in touch with you?

I'm traveling right now, I'll let you know when I get settled down.

OK, Jimmy. Take care of yourself and thanks for calling.

How's your mother, Jimmy?

She has to go into the hospital to get some tests done on her. I have to go there when she goes into the hospital.

But what about those people that are looking for you?

It'll be alright, nobody will know that I'm going to be there.

Are you sure you should go?

I just gotta go, she'll feel better if I'm there with her.

Lets go get a bite to eat and then we can talk a little bit. They go over to a small restaurant and they both have soup and sandwiches.

Why don't you look in the Wall Street Journal? Sometimes they have great business opportunities. You might just be looking in the wrong place.

Yeah, you might be right. When we're finished, lets pick up the Wall Street Journal.

On their way out they pick up a copy of the Wall Street Journal and go back to their apartment and look at the business's for sale section.

There's a lot for sale all over the country. Here's one, Apartment house for sale. Thirty six apartments, six story building. Fully rented. For more information call 555 999 8888. Lets call and see what's it's all about.

Jimmy calls, we're not here, leave a message. He leaves a short message and hangs up and turns on the TV and finds a good movie.

How about a beer?

Yeah, thanks.

She opens the bottle and hands it to him.

Don't worry, Jimmy. I have a feeling everything is going to work out and thanks for telling me all about everything. You can trust me never to say anything. She goes over to him and gives him a kiss.

The next morning, Christina takes a shower and gets herself ready to go to work. I'll call you later on. If you go out, I'll leave a message on the answering machine. Love you and she leaves.

Jimmy takes a shower and shave and gets dressed. He opens the yellow pages and finds the numbers he's looking for and writes the phone numbers and the address's on a piece of paper.

He leaves and goes down to the street. There's a cab parked right in front of the building. He give the address to the cab driver and off they go. It takes about twenty minutes to get there. Jimmy pays him and gets out of the cab.

Georgetown Gun and Firearms. He opens the door and goes into the store.

How you doing? What are you looking for?

Let me see a .38 revolver.

The store clerk opens a glass case and takes out a .38. Here you are and he hands it to Jimmy.

Nice weight. Jimmy opens it up, and then closes it. How much?

This one is three hundred and fifty dollars plus tax.

OK, and gimme a box of shells.

Could I see your driver's license.

Sure, Jimmy hands him John Martin's driver's license. The man looks at Jimmy and then at the drivers license. He starts writing down the information from the drivers license and then hands it back to Jimmy.

Let me see that shoulder holster. The clerk hands it to him. Jimmy tries it on and sticks the revolver into it. OK, I'll take it. He hands it back to the clerk.

That'll be four hundred and thirty three dollars and seventy two cents.

Jimmy hands the clerk four hundred and thirty four dollars.

The clerk rings the money up and gives Jimmy twenty eight cents back and then he wraps everything up and gives it to Jimmy.

Nice doing business with you. Come back again.

Jimmy leaves and walks to the corner and hails a cab.

Where to?

He tells him and it takes about fifteen minutes to get there. They pull up in front of Maxey's Target Range. He pays the cabbie and he goes in.

Hi, I'd like a range for about fifteen minutes.

We rent the ranges out for a minimum of thirty minutes.

OK, that's fine. How much is that?

Twenty five dollars. If you need any shells, we got them.

OK, I'll let you know.

You'll be on range twenty one.

Jimmy goes in and hooks up his target and sends it down. He takes his gun out and takes aim and starts shooting. Not bad. He unloads the empty shell casings and reloads the gun and sends the target down again. He aims and starts shooting till he empties the gun. When he's finishes he pulls the target back again.

This is fun, right on the money. I'm getting better at this. I think I'll do this again. He sends the target down and starts shooting again. He pulls the target back, this time, he has a couple of bull's eyes. I'm getting to be a real sharp shooter. This is a real nice gun. He puts the gun on safety and then he loads up his revolver and puts his gun into the shoulder holster. OK, now I'm ready. No more kidding around. Anybody comes looking for me, they'll get it right between the eyes.

Chapter 79

Marie and the girls are all finished with the invitations and they're ready to be mailed out.

Hans comes over and asks, do you have the seating arrangements?

Yes, here they are, Hans.

OK, I'll get the tables set up and then we can get the name cards made up.

Hans, here's the menu.

He looks it over. Good, I'll order the food and beverages and we'll be all set.

Sally, what do you think of the seating arrangements?

She looks at it, I think it's fine.

Marie asks Eileen and Francine what they think?

Everything looks great.

Ladies, you did a wonderful job.

Hans, if it wasn't for you, we would have had a tough time putting everything together.

Well ladies, we make a good team.

Now, if you'll excuse me, I have some things to take care of.

Lou parks outside the Zerega and goes in.

Tiny, is Corporal and Ernie here?

Yeah, they're in the back.

Lou goes in and hugs and kisses Corporal and hugs Ernie.

How's things? Lou.

Things are coming along great. The Mayor and his Deputes are lining up some more big projects. They asked me what I thought of Tony's Company becoming the lead Contractor on some of these projects. I said I'd let them know by tomorrow. These projects will make us millions, Corporal.

OK, what do you think, Lou?

As far as I'm concerned, I think he's the best and he's one of us.

OK, Ernie, call Tony and ask him to come over.

What else is happening?

It looks like the Mayor and his Deputes are going to make a lot of big changes in the City and they're giving us the biggest slice of that pie. We support him and make sure that he gets reelected and we got it made for as long as he's in office. Lou opens his briefcase and hands Corporal a big manila envelope.

Corporal opens it and looks inside. Hmm, it's pretty fat.

Ernie, hold onto this. Thanks, Lou. You're doing a good job.

Tony comes in and says hello to everybody and hugs and kisses Corporal.

Lou, tell Tony what you told me.

Lou tells Tony about the big projects the Mayor and his Deputes are planning. I was asked what I thought of your Company becoming the lead Contractor on most of them.

Yeah, we can handle that.

Then you got it.

Thanks, Corporal.

Lou put this whole thing together.

Thanks, Lou.

That deserves a toast to Lou. Tiny, bring in a bottle of Champagne.

OK, lets all toast Lou. He's been the best earner that this family ever had. Lou, here's to you.

Tony, make sure that the Mayor and his guys are happy with everything you build for them.

Amy calls Joey and tells him to meet her at the Diner. Joey drives there and sees Amy sitting in a back booth.

Hi, Joey.

Hi ya doin, Amy?

Would you like to have something?

Yeah, just coffee.

Coffee for the two of us.

Joey, I want to take the kids to my mother on Monday night.

Why at night?

My husband will be working.

OK, what time do you want me to be there?

One o'clock in the morning.

Why so late?

He works the night shift.

OK, I'll be there. Monday night, one o'clock in the morning.

Here's some money. Just remember, park the car and I'll come out.

Alright, I'll see you. I gotta take care of a couple of things.

Well, everything is all set. I sure hope nothing goes wrong.

Chapter 80

It's a mad house here, says Tony.

Take it easy. Everything is fine. Just get dressed and relax. Have a little bite to eat and turn on the TV. There must be a good baseball game on.

Yeah, your right, Marie. I'm sorry. He picks up the phone and calls Chris.

Hey, Chris. How you doin?

Good. What's new?

This place has gone insane, people running all over the place. All this yelling and screaming, it's enough to drive anybody out of their mind.

Aw, take it easy, remember it's your son's wedding day. You want me to come over?

Naw, thanks for asking though.

Eileen and Francine are getting them selves ready and Eddie is going over to get his girlfriend. So, I'll see you at the church.

OK, see ya. He makes himself a sandwich and gets a bottle of beer. Lets see who's playing today. He turns on the TV and he starts thinking about his son Tony and Angela. I hope everything turns out good for them. He's always been a good kid and I pray that they will have a blessed life together.

The door opens and his son Tony comes in.

Hey, Dad. Could I have a few minutes with you?

Sure, sit down. Is everything alright?

Yeah everything's fine. I just wanted to thank you for this great wedding that you and Mom are making for us. You are the best Mom and Dad that anyone could ever have.

Thanks Tony. I appreciate that.

Well, I'll finish getting ready.

Marie comes in and asks, are you ready, Tony?

Yeah, I'm ready. Lets go. They get into the limousine waiting outside.

Oh, Tony. I'm so excited. Our little Tony, getting married.

He's not a little boy any more, he's a grown man.

Oh, Tony. You know what I mean. Remember the day when we got married. I'll never forget it, we had the reception down at that little Italian Restaurant on Mulberry Street. That was the happiest day of my whole life. And now, we're off to Tony's wedding.

They arrive at the church and sit in the first pew.

Tony is up at the alter waiting nervously. The organ starts playing and Angela and her father enter the church and start walking down the aisle. Tony looks at her, she's so beautiful. He can't get over it. We're getting married. It's like a beautiful dream and he doesn't want to wake up. Before he knows it the priest is saying, I now pronounce you, Man and Wife. You may now kiss the bride.

He wakes up from his day dream. It's not a dream, it's real. We're really married. They start walking up the aisle and the organ is playing and everyone is waving and wishing them good luck. When they get outside, rice is being thrown and pictures are being taken. They get inside the waiting limousine and are driven off to the reception. The others follow in their limousines and cars.

The wedding guests start going into the building and Hans is directing all the guests to their tables.

Tony and Angela are escorted to their table and then their families and the wedding party are seated.

The band starts playing and then the waiters and waitresses start serving the food and drinks.

Outside, Vito is handling the security. Everyone is checked to make sure there's no gate crashers. The cops have the street blocked off and no one can get in without an invitation.

Moe has the entertainment all lined up. Frankie Campione is here and Abbat and Costemo came in from Hollywood. Carlos Cugat and his Latin Band from The Spanish Steps are playing and everyone is up and dancing.

The food and drinks are great and Hans has everything moving along nicely.

Corporal and his wife, Ernie and his wife, John and Sonny and the big Bosses are all here enjoying themselves. The Bishop and The Mayor and his Deputes and Lou are present and really having a good time. Al and Moe and Abe are also there It looks like all of New York City's Royalty is here. Tony and Chris and Sal are having the time of their lives.

It's starting to get dark outside so Hans goes to Corporal.

It's getting dark.

OK, whenever your ready, start the fireworks show.

Hans gets up on the stage and announces that we are going to have a little fireworks show and would everyone step outside and enjoy it.

When everyone is outside, he gives the signal to start the show. The sky lights up over the water and the sound of the fireworks is deafening. It's like the Forth of July at the Statue of Liberty. It's breathtaking and lasts for for about fifteen minutes and then it's over.

Everyone is in a state of awe. They've never seen anything like this in their lives.

The guests start to go back inside and the band starts playing the Stars and Stripes Forever.

Wow, this brings everybody to their feet and then they start marching around the hall followed by all the guests. The band comes down from the stage and starts marching with them. The bride and groom start marching. Hans gets a big American Flag and hands it to a member of the wedding party. The band plays, the bugles play and the big bass drums go BOOM, BOOM BOOM.

Corporal and his friends join the marchers and so do the Mayor and the Bishop and all the rest of the guests, even the kitchen help and the cooks and waiters and waitresses come out and join them. They march around the hall a few times and then Frankie Campione and Carlos Cugat start singing God Bless America. This really brings the house down and there's not one dry eye in the place. This is the greatest wedding reception that I ever went to, says Tony.

Now folks, I want to introduce you to the Bride and Groom. Mr. and Mrs. Anthony Greco. The band starts playing and Tony and Angela get up and dance. Everyone starts to clap and then all the guests start to dance.

Oh, Tony, that was wonderful. Marie starts crying.

What are you crying about?

I can't help it, I'm so happy. Oh, Tony. You've made me the happiest woman in the whole world.

Chris is dancing with his wife Eileen and she says, what a wedding reception this is. Whose idea was that to have the fireworks?

That was Corporal's idea.

Well, lets go up and give Angela our envelope.

Yeah, people will be leaving soon. We don't want to get caught up in a traffic jam.

Chapter 81

The phone rings and Joey answers.

It's Amy, don't forget, be there at one o'clock.

Yeah, yeah. I'll be there, what's the matter with you? I told you, I'll be there.

Joey, I'm sorry. I'm a little nervous. I just want to get the kids to my sister. My husband wants to take them away from me.

Yeah, stop worrying, I'll be there.

Oh, Joey. Thanks, I'll never forget you, I'll always be grateful to you.

What a pain in the ass, I gotta stop doin favors for people.

Amy tells the kids, sit down and have your supper. The kids sit down and start eating.

Mommy, are we going to see Daddy soon?

Yeah, you'll see him soon.

He promised to take us to the Zoo and get us ice cream.

OK, finish up your food and I'll give you your baths. They finish their supper and she gives them their baths.

Now, put your pajamas on and lets get to bed.

But, Mommy. It's too early and we want to watch TV.

I said get into bed. No TV tonight.

I don't want to go to bed yet, it's to early.

I don't care, you're going to bed right now.

But why can't we watch TV for a little while?

Eddie, go to bed right now. Eddie goes into the bedroom and Amy closes the door.

Come with me, you little brat.

Amy is furious and drags Missy into her bedroom and closes the door. I want to talk to you, you've been giving me a hard time lately and you better start doing what I tell you. Now, you go to your room and get into bed.

Every time we have to go to bed early, bad men come here and go to bed with you and you do bad things with them. I'm afraid and I'm not going to bed early.

Amy slaps Missy across the face.

Missy starts to cry, I going to tell Daddy.

You little bitch, I'll fix you. She grabs her and rips off her pajama top and wraps it around her little neck and pulls it tighter and tighter until little Missy is lifeless.

Amy lays Missy down on the bed and goes to the children's bedroom and looks in. Eddie is sound asleep.

OK. I'll just put her into her own bed and when Joey gets here, we'll take Eddie and Missy out of here and get rid of them.

She has a cup of coffee and waits for Joey to get here. It's one o'clock, she looks out the kitchen window, there's Joey.

She opens the window and waves to him to come in.

Joey comes in and she asks him to take the screen off the window in the kids room and leave it right outside the window. Then she wakes Eddie up.

Joey, take her and put her in the car. He picks up the little girl and carries her out, he doesn't know that she's dead.

Come on, Eddie. He's half asleep and she takes him by the hand and they follow Joey to the car. Get in the back seat, Eddie.

Go over by Roosevelt Avenue first. I've got to drop something off.

Stop here. Now stay here, she tells little Eddie, I'll be right back. She opens the front door and picks Missy up and takes her into a dark alley and lays her down on the ground. She comes back and gets into the back seat.

OK, go over by Conrad's Cloud Room.

She opens up her handbag and takes out a plastic bag and puts it over Eddie's head. He struggles but she holds him down until he's dead.

Hey, what the hell are you doing back there? Joey slams on the brakes.

She takes the plastic bag off Eddie's head.

You just killed the kid. You told me we were going to your sister's place.

Shut up and give me a hand with him.

Joey opens the car door and takes Eddie's body out.

Bring him over here and put him down in the bushes. Now, lets get out of here.

What did you do to those kids? They're dead.

Joey, you better not say anything or I'll say that you killed them.

What?

You heard me. Here's some money, keep your mouth shut and don't you ever say anything about this to anyone.

Take me back home. I'll be in touch with you and don't call me.

Joey drives her back home and he leaves.

I can't believe what happened. She killed her two little kids. That bitch, I'd better get out of here. I have to get this car cleaned up, inside and outside. She's liable to tell the cops that I did it. Holy shit, how the hell did I ever get mixed up with that lunatic.

Amy gets back home and decides to wait until six o'clock in the morning to call the cops.

I'd better wipe that window screen down before the cops get here. When she's done she comes back in and turns on the TV.

It's done. That jerk Joey will never say anything about this. Now, all I have to do is call the cops and tell them that somebody broke in and kidnapped the kids while I was sleeping. I know the cops are going to hassle me to death and accuse me of killing the kids. I'll just act like I'm hysterical and about to go to pieces. I'll yell, who would do a thing like this? I'll scream, please help me find my children. When they find them I'll faint. That should convince them that I had nothing to do with their kidnapping.

They'll find out that I was running around with Tony. So what, I saw a lot of guys, I was a bar maid and a cocktail waitress. I was just trying to help out.

Well, It's just about that time, I'll call the cops now and tell them that the kids are gone.

She calls the police, the desk sergeant answers. Hello, my name is Amy Collins.

My children are missing, she sounds hysterical. The window is open and someone must have taken them.

Where do you live?

She gives him her address.

We'll be there in a few minutes.

A police car arrives and she runs outside to the cops.

My two babies are missing, someone took them.

Calm down, lets go inside and you can tell us what happened.

They sit down at the kitchen table and one of the cops starts writing in his notebook. Tell me what happened.

I got up to give them breakfast and I went into their room and they were gone. I looked all over the house but they were gone. The window was open and the window screen was laying outside on the ground. Oh, please find my babies. Who would do a thing like this?

Where's the phone?

He calls the precinct. This is Mc Carthy, put me through to the Detective Squad.

Murphy here, what is it Mac?

You better get over here, He gives him the address. There's two kids missing, the mother said someone broke in and took them.

We'll be right over. They get there and Detective Murphy speaks to Patrolman Mc Carthy.

She's the mother and he tells Detective Murphy what she told him.

Did you look around?

Yeah, there's no signs of a struggle and the window in the kids room is open. There's a window screen laying outside the open window.

OK, don't touch anything. Lets take her down to the precinct and talk to her. In the meantime, alert all cars about the two missing children. Get the cop on the beat over here. Don't let anyone in here until our guys get here and go over everything.

The detectives tell Amy to get her coat on and come with them.

Where are you taking me?

We're going to the Precinct. We have to ask you some questions.

She puts her coat on and goes with them. They go into the Detectives Office and sit down.

Would you like to have some coffee or a glass of water?

No, I just want my babies.

We have all the cops in the City looking for them.

They start questioning her, where's your husband?

We're separated.

Where's he now?

He's working.

Did you call him?

No, not yet, I called you first.

A cop comes into the room and talks to Detective Murphy.

OK, put on your coat and come with us.

Where are we going?

I'll tell you when we get there. They put her into the back seat of the squad car. The police car is speeding with its siren on. It stops and they open the door and ask her to get out.

Detective Murphy takes her by the arm and walks her over to the alley way. There's a little body laying on the ground.

Take a look. Is this your little girl?

She looks at Missy and lets out a scream.

Oh, no, no. She faints and the detective catches her.

Put her into the Squad car and take her back to the Precinct. Did anyone notify the Medical Examiner?

Yeah, he's on the way.

OK, you guys, stay with the body until he gets here. I wonder where the little boy is?

A Squad car pulls up at the Precinct and Brian Collins steps out.

My name is Brian Collins. I heard that my wife was here.

Come this way, Mister Collins.

This is Detective Murphy.

Sit down, Mr. Collins. I have some bad news for you. You're daughter was found dead.

What?

Brian looks like he's going to drop. Detective Murphy grabs him by the arm and sits him back down. Your wife is in the other room. She's taking it pretty hard.

Where were you all night?

I was working out at La Guardia. I'm a mechanic and I work the night shift.

What time do you start work?

Midnight.

And what time do you get off?

Nine in the morning. What happened to my daughter?

We don't know yet. Your wife called us this morning and told us that your children were missing.

Where's my son?

We're looking for him.

Oh, my God. What's happening?

Take it easy.

How can I take it easy? Do you guys have any idea where he is?

Not yet. Every cop in the city is looking for him.

Can I talk to my wife?

Sure, come on. He opens the door.

Mrs. Collins, your husband is here.

Brian goes over to her and wraps his arms around her.

Oh, Brian. Someone took our two babies. Missy is dead and the cops haven't found Eddie yet. What are we going to do?

The police are doing everything that they can.

Mr. Collins, we can take your wife over to her mother.

Yeah, that's a good idea.

Detective Murphy calls in one of the patrolmen and tells him to take Mrs. Collins to her mother's place.

OK, Mrs. Collins. Patrolman Lukas will drive you to your mothers place. When we find your son, we'll let you know.

Brian, what should I do?

Go to your mother. I'll call you later. I'll stay here and see if I can help. He hugs her and gives her a kiss on the cheek.

She leaves and goes with the cop.

Mr. Collins, sit down, please. Tell me what you can.

He tells Detective Murphy about himself and the troubles that they've had in their marriage and he answers all the questions that Detective Murphy asks him.

Finally, he's asked. Do you have any idea who would do this?

No, I don't.

Chapter 82

Amy gets to her mother's house.

Oh, Amy. My poor child. Come in.

Mom, Missy is dead and the cops are looking for Eddie.

Oh, my God.

I want to lie down for awhile, I have such a headache.

Come with me, now lie down on my bed. Try and go to sleep. Her mother covers her with a blanket and leaves the bedroom.

Well, I think that everyone is convinced that someone broke in and kidnapped the kids. What a headache I got. I'll just have to wait and see what happens. All hell is going to break loose when they find Eddie. I'll call Chris later on and tell him about Missy and to handle her funeral. I've got to get some sleep.

The newspapers get a hold of the story and the headlines read. Two children kidnapped. The story goes on to read. Two children kidnapped from their home, one is found dead in a rat infested alley way, the other is still missing. A massive search is under way. The police are investigating.

Kenny reads the newspaper about the two children but does not connect it to Chris. Later on in the day, he gets a call from Chris.

How's things, Kenny?

Everything is fine.

Any messages?

Naw, no messages.

In the meantime, the detectives are combing the area around Amy's apartment house and asking neighbors if they saw anything unusual. They're going through Amy's apartment and looking for clues. They take the garbage and the sheets from the beds and look in all the dressers and cabinets in the apartment. They go through the clothes in the closets and everything in the bathroom.

Detective Murphy is wondering. There's something wrong here. Something's not right.

One of the detectives comes in and talks to Detective Murphy. I have a lady outside that lives in the building. She said that she saw Mrs. Collins and a man taking the children to a car at about one o'clock in the morning.

Where is she?

She's right outside.

Detective Murphy goes outside with him. This is the lady that I spoke to.

I'm Detective Murphy. I was told that you saw Mrs. Collins and a man taking her children to a car about one o'clock this morning.

Yes, that's right.

Can I have your name?

Yes, Theresa Fusco.

And where do you live?

Right there, she points to her window. It's on the second floor overlooking the courtyard.

Could you come with me to the Precinct? I'd like to ask you a few more questions.

OK, I have to go upstairs and get my purse.

Fine, I'll be right here.

She returns in a few minutes and they get into the Police car and go to the Station House. He helps her out and they go into the Homicide Detectives office.

Have a seat Mrs. Fusco. How about some coffee or a glass of water?

No, thanks.

Now, Mrs. Fusco. I'm going to turn on this tape recorder and record everything that is being said. This is Detective Kenneth Murphy interviewing Mrs. Theresa Fusco and he gives the date and time and location. Now, tell me what you saw this morning.

I couldn't sleep so I was just sitting by the kitchen window. I saw Mrs. Collins and a man taking her children to a car and then they drove away.

Describe everything that you saw to me.

The man was carrying a little girl and Mrs. Collins was holding Eddie by the hand and walking with him to the car. The man put the little girl in the front seat and Mrs. Collins put the little boy in the back seat with her and then they drove off.

What did the car look like?

It was a four door car and it was black.

Did you hear them say anything?

Yes, the man seemed to be arguing with her.

Do you wear glasses?

Yes, only for reading.

Is there anything else that you remember?

No, that's about it.

Thank you, Mrs. Fusco. You've been a great help. If we need anything else, we'll be in touch with you.

Your welcome, I hope that you find that little boy.

He calls one of the patrolmen and tells him to drive Mrs. Fusco home.

Detective Murphy calls the DA. You better come over here right away. You'll want to hear this.

Chapter 83

District Attorney Drew arrives at the Station House and goes into the Homicide Detectives Office. Is Detective Murphy here? I'm DA Drew.

Yeah, I'll get him for you.

Hey, Murphy. The DA is here.

Thanks. He goes into the office and says hello to DA Drew and they shake hands.

Have a seat. I just interviewed a neighbor of Amy Collins and I'd like you to listen to this tape recording of the interview.

Detective Murphy plays it for him.

Well, this changes the whole story that Amy Collins told you.

Yeah, lets dig into her past a little before we bring her in again. If we bring her in now, she'll get a lawyer and he'll tell her to say nothing. Let her think that we believe her story. Now, find out all about her. Let's start with her husband. Don't tell any of these reporters around here anything. Let's see who she gets in touch with first. Put a tap on her phone and follow her day and night. Have you heard anything about the boy?

Nothing yet.

OK, make a copy of this tape and send it over to me. Let's keep in touch.

In the meantime, Amy calls Chris's Funeral Home and tells Kenny about her daughter, Missy. Her body is at the Medical Examiners.

Kenny takes the information and tells her to come over to the Funeral Home and then they'll finish the arrangements.

Would you tell Chris, he's a friend of mine and I'd like to speak to him.

Where have I heard her name before? Oh, yeah. She left messages here before for Chris. Yeah, now I remember, she's a friend of Tony's.

He goes over to the outside desk. Hey, Andy. Do you still have yesterdays newspaper.

Yeah, here it is.

Kenny goes into the office and sits down. There it is, two children kidnapped and there's her name. Amy Collins.

Holy smokes, That was her. I better get in touch with Chris.

Kenny tells him about Amy's daughter and she wants to speak to you.

Go ahead and take care of all the arrangements. Don't tell her anything else. I'll call you back later on.

OK, Chris. I'll talk to you later.

Amy is feeling pretty confident now. I think those cops bought the story. I'll call Joey in a couple of days and get him calmed down.

She goes out to the kitchen and has some coffee with her mother. They start talking about Missy and her mother is wondering about Eddie and how come nobody has heard anything about him.

I'm going out for a little while to get some fresh air. She gets all dolled up and gets into her car. She doesn't know that the cops are following her.

From now on, I'll use the public pay phones. I hope that Chris calls soon, I want to get all these things out of the way.

Aw, I think that I'll go visit some of my girlfriends.

Chapter 84

Over at the Zeraga, Ernie is having a cup of coffee and reading the newspaper. He gets on the phone and calls Corporal.

Hey, Corporal. This is Ernie. Did you take a look at the newspaper yet?

No, what's up?

Tony's girlfriend is all over the newspapers. Her kids were kidnapped and one of them was found murdered and the other is missing.

What?

Yeah, Corporal. The cops are investigating.

Call Tony now and find out if he's heard about this? It could be trouble for all of us. We don't want the cops snooping around here. I'll be down there in a little while. Send Vito over here to pick me up.

OK, Corporal.

Detective Murphy is going through an overnight bag found under her bed. Boy, look at this stuff. Pictures of her and this guy Tony Graco and a lot of the wise guys that he hangs out with.

Hay, Knecht. Do you know who this guy is with Tony Greco and Mrs. Collins?

Yeah, that's Chris Caruso, he's a Funeral Director.

Oh, yeah. Now I recognize him. OK, lets make a list of everything in this bag and make copies of all these papers and pictures.

Detective Murphy calls DA Drew.

I have a bag here that has all these goodies in it. It's Mrs. Collins overnight bag.

Good, now we're getting somewhere. Any news about the little boy?

No, not yet. Murphy asks DA Drew, did you get the Medical Examiner's report yet?

Yeah, death by strangulation. Do you still have a tail on Mrs. Collins?

Yeah.

OK. Just keep things the way they are and lets see what else turns up.

Chris tells Tony and Sal about Amy's kids.

How did you find out?

She called Kenny and told him, and then he called me after he spoke to her. She asked for me and he told her that I'd get in touch with her. I told Kenny to take care of all the arrangements and I'd call her later on.

Wow, that is a shocker.

Tony, if you go to the funeral, everyone will be asking what your connection is with her. Let's wait until we hear more about all this.

Yeah, you're right, Sal. Poor thing, who would do a thing like this?

I'd better stay away from the office for awhile. I wonder what's going on?

Chris is worried. Tony doesn't know anything about me and Amy. I'll just keep quiet and out of sight for awhile. I'll call my friend Dennis to find out about everything that's going on.

Sal is in deep thought about this and everything else that's happened. I'm involved. All these killings that go on, I'm part of it. I better start distancing myself from all this.

Tony tells Sal, don't be worrying about Amy and her kids, that's not our problem.

Chapter 85

Chris, pick up the phone, it's Dennis.

Hey, Dennis. How's things?

Not so good.

What do you mean?

Chris, this is going to hit the newspapers pretty soon. The Queens DA's Office is going to charge Amy Collins with murder and you and Tony's name's came up.

What do you mean?

Look, Chris. They haven't charged her yet, but they searched her apartment and pictures of you and Tony were in her overnight bag.

Oh, man. What do you think I should do?

Right now, don't do anything. If they find her son and he's dead, the shit is really going to hit the fan. They're going to jump all over Tony. I'll try talking to some of the guys out in the Queens DA's Office to pass on you. I know I can talk to the guys in the Bronx.

Chris tells him, she called my office and we're taking care of her daughter's funeral.

Well, try and get her daughter buried as soon as possible. The DA's office didn't release any more information yet. If they find her son and he's dead, don't have anything to do with his funeral.

Chris, how tight are you with Tony?

Real tight.

OK, you might as well tell him what's going on. I'll keep in touch with you.

Yeah, thanks Dennis.

Sal asks, what's the matter Chris, you look like you saw a ghost?

That was Dennis.

What did he want?

Chris tells him what Dennis told him.

Holy shit. We better tell Tony right now.

Yeah, your right.

Tony, this is Chris. Can we talk for a minute.

Sure, I'll be right back, don't go away.

I just got a phone call from Dennis, he tells him what Dennis told him.

I can't believe she'd do a thing like this.

Tony, you got to calm down.

I gotta call my lawyer.

Tony, take it easy, he's gonna tell you the same thing. You had nothing to do with this. For the time being, stay away from her.

Yeah, I gotta think.

Kenny, this is Chris. Did you get the kids body?

Yeah, the body is laid out and Mrs. Collins is here and she keeps asking for you.

When's the burial?

Tomorrow.

Good, tell Mrs. Collins that you've been trying to get me, but the phone service is very bad where I'm at. Is everything else alright?

Some detectives were here this morning asking for you. I told them that you were away on a business trip. One of them left his card and I told him that I would give you the message when you called in.

Let me have his name and phone number.

Kenny gives it to him.

OK, Kenny. I'll call you later on or tomorrow.

Dennis, this is Chris.

Yeah, what's happening?

I called my office this morning and the office manager told me that two detectives were there looking to talk to me.

OK, did he get their names.

Chris gives him the name and phone number.

OK, I know these guys, I'll get in touch with them and call you back.

Chris tells Tony and Sal that he just got through speaking with Dennis. He knows most of the detectives in the Queens and the Bronx DA's Offices. He's gonna call back after he talks with them.

Back at the Funeral Home, Amy's family arrives and they all go into the chapel and start crying.

She goes out to the lobby and lights up a cigarette. Tony should be here, she says to herself, that selfish son of a bitch. I gotta go through this all by myself. I wish he were here.

Chapter 86

Sal wanders off by himself. He's really worried and confused by the chain of events that's happened. This is not what I bargained for. When I first met Chris and Tony it all seemed very exciting. Meeting all those wise guys and hanging out with them. Business deals coming our way. I should have gotten out when that property came up for sale over at Pelham Parkway and we nearly had that guy killed to get it. Since then, that seems to be happening all the time. I haven't killed anyone yet but I know they're going to tell me to kill somebody sooner or later. That's the only way you can prove yourself to the family. No one can get out once they're in. I just don't know what to do right now. All this with Tony and Amy Collins is leading to no good. Chris is supposed to be Tony's best friend and in the meantime he's humping Tony's girlfriend. If Tony ever finds out he'll have him killed. If I could figure a way to get away from all this, I'd be gone in a heartbeat. I'd better never let anyone know about what I'm thinking of or I'll be dead before you know it. Aw, let me get a drink and try to forget all this bullshit for the time being.

Detective Murphy gets a call from one of the Patrol cars.

Yeah, what is it?

Better get over here, we just found the boy over by the Grand Central Parkway south of that Conrad's Cloud Room.

I'm leaving now. Murphy and his partner, Detective Knecht head over there. There's lights all over the place from the Patrol cars. There they are. Park it here and follow me.

Hey, Murphy. Over here.

The poor kid, it looks like rats got to him and his body is decomposed.

Did the Medical Examiner get here yet?

He's on his way.

OK, lets take a look and see if there's any evidence laying around. Hey, Knecht. Come over here.

Take one of the patrolmen with you and pick up Amy Collins and bring her here. She's at a bar over in Whitestone.

The Medical Examiner arrives and takes a look. The body is pretty well chewed up. Are you guys finished taking pictures?

Yeah, we're all finished.

We're not finished yet, they're bringing the mother here to identify the body.

So, what do you think Murphy?

I don't know yet. We should know more after you autopsy the body.

Detective Knecht pulls up and gets out of the Patrol car.

Murphy, I got her in the car.

OK, you and one of the patrolman bring her over here.

Take the cover off the body. Is this the body of your son?

She looks at the body with half his face eaten off by rats and insects running all over the body and crawling out of his mouth and nose.

She's screaming and yelling and trying to turn and run away.

Bring her back here. Murphy repeats. Is this the body of your son?

Yes, Yes, she's screaming, now let me out of here. She's hysterical.

OK, Knecht. Take her back to where you found her. We're finished. You can wrap the body up and take it to the Medical Examiner's Office.

Murphy, you're heartless, says the M.E.

Not as heartless as she is.

Chapter 87

Sal, let me talk to Chris. It's Dennis. He hands the phone to Chris.

The cats out of the bag. They found the boy. He's dead. The newspaper reporters will have the story in a few hours. You'd better let Tony know. They'll be all over his ass. Now, Chris. I spoke to the guys out in Queens and the Bronx. They're giving you a pass, but it's going to cost you.

Now, here's the rest. Tony's girlfriend is going to be arrested and booked on murder charges. They're going to have him come in for questioning and they might arrest him depending on what they come up with. There's two hungry DA's looking to hang a lot of people on this one. When he goes in for questioning, he'd better have his lawyer with him.

OK, Dennis, thanks, call me if anything else comes up.

The shit just hit the fan. He tells Sal about Amy and what's happening. We better let Tony know what's going on.

Sal calls Tony. Chris just got off the phone with his friend, Dennis. Bad news. He tells him about the call.

Oh, shit. The little boy too. Everything is going to be in the papers. I'd better get in touch with my lawyer. Oh, man. Marie will see all this in the papers. She'll go to pieces. I'd better get in touch with my sons and let them know what to expect. I'll ask them to stay with their mother until this goes away.

Chris says, I've got to call Kenny right away.

Am I glad that you're still there. Kenny, the cops found Mrs. Collins son. Start the funeral early in the morning. Are you gong to the church with the little girl?

No, we're going straight to the Cemetery.

OK, Kenny. Call Mrs. Collins and tell her that we have to start early because all the newspaper reporters will be at the Funeral Home. And also if she wants us to handle her son's Funeral we'll have to go straight to the Cemetery because of the newspapers.

OK, Chris. I'll take care of it.

And tell her not to worry. Everything's been taken care of. I should be back by the end of the week.

Corporal and Ernie are at the club and Vito brings in the newspapers. Here's the evening editions of the News and Mirror.

Holy shit. Look at this, look at these headlines. TWO CHILDREN FOUND MURDERED, MOTHER TO BE ARRANGED FOR MURDER.

Corporal is really angry. That woman is nothing but trouble. Get Tony and Chris and Sal up here. If any cops come around here, tell them that we haven't seen them since Tony Junior's wedding. Tell all the guys to stay away form here for awhile. Have all the collections go to Abe and Al. And have Moe come by here the first thing in the morning and let him know what's going on.

Down at the Precinct, Detective Murphy is on the phone with District Attorney Drew.

OK, Murphy. The autopsy on the boy was inconclusive. But here's what we're going to do. I want you to go to her house and bring her in for questioning tonight. Don't arrest her right now, wait until her daughter is buried. Then arrest her and we'll put her in The Women's House of Detention until someone comes along and bails her out. Start building our case against her and lets see who else we can snag.

Chapter 88

Tony, what do you want to do?

I'm not sure if I should go home or stay in a hotel.

How about staying at my place?

Thanks, Sal. That sounds like a good idea. I'll call my lawyer and have him come over to your place.

Hey, Chris. Why don't you call Dennis and find out what else is going on.

Yeah, good idea. Chris parks outside Sal's house and they go in.

Tony calls his lawyer and asks him to come over to Sal's place. He gives him the address and directions.

Chris takes the phone and calls Dennis.

Hey, Dennis. How's things?

Here's what happening. Amy Collins was arrested and is in the Women's House of Detention. Bail will be set tomorrow. Your friend Tony has been mentioned as a suspect in the murder of the kids. They know all about him and Amy Collins and they're looking to question him. The newspapers are making this into a big case. They're going to run with this for all it's worth. He better get a hold of his lawyer before he shows his face anywhere. Now, Chris. I'm going to see the Bronx Homicide guys and tell them that you'll drop off that package.

How much?

Five G's to start with.

Where should I bring it to?

Take it to the 50th Precinct Homicide Office and give it Detective Harold Robbins. Call me when you deliver the package.

Over at the District Attorneys Office, Murphy and DA Drew are looking over the evidence and Murphy asks.

How much do you think they'll set bail at?

It all depends on who's putting up the bail money and who the lawyer is.

Murphy says, I'll bet you it's Tony Greco that's going to be footing the bill.

Yeah, it should be interesting to find out how much he knows about this. How's Amy Collins doing down in the lockup?

From what I heard, says DA Drew, she's taking everything very calmly now. She made her two phone calls.

Who'd she call, asks Murphy?

First, Anthony Greco, she left a message and then she called Chris Caruso, she was told he was away on a business trip. Well, we know that Greco was running around with her, and what about this guy Caruso, asks DA Drew.

He's a Funeral Director and he buried her kids.

Is that all he was to her? Lets check him out some more.

Your right, responds Murphy. I'll get in touch with the detectives at the District Attorneys Office in the Bronx and they can find out if he was one of her boyfriends.

Yeah, I'd like to hear all about his night life too.

Sal is really worried. All this because of that little tramp and these two jerks. And they're my partners, I'm in big trouble. I wonder if they know anymore than they're telling me.

Chapter 89

What a mess, Sal Is thinking to himself. Chris ran over to the cops and gave them Five Thousand dollars to keep this quiet about him and out of the newspapers. If it every got out about him being involved in this mess, he'd be out of the Funeral Business by tomorrow. Wait until Tony gets home, the shits gonna fly. His wife and his whole family are gonna be on top of him. I wouldn't wanna be in his shoes. His lawyer should be here any minute now. There's the doorbell, it's probably Tony's lawyer.

Hi, I'm Ron. Tony's Attorney.

Tony, Ron is here.

Hi, Ron. Have a seat.

Tony. Lets get right down to business. Tell me what's happening? Forget about the newspapers. Tell me your story from the beginning.

Well, I met this cocktail waitress named Amy Collins and I started having an affair with her.

How long ago did you meet her?

About a year ago.

Did you ever talk about your personal life with her?

Yeah, some.

How about your family and business?

Yeah, I did.

Did you ever discuss things with her that could be harmful to you? Yeah.

Such as?

Well, I'd rather not tell you.

You might as well, because if this gets into court, she might use it against you to get out of this jam.

Tony looks at Sal. You're not going to like what I have to say.

Tony, I rather hear it from you than read it in the newspapers.

OK, I was trying to impress her. I told her about some of the things that went on with the people that we know.

What exactly did you tell her that could be so important?

I told her about a guy that we arranged to have killed.

Did you tell her about other things?

Yeah, I told her about what these people are involved in.

Did you mention any names?

Yeah, I mentioned a lot of names.

Does she know any of those people?

Yeah, quite a few.

Did you have anything to do with the killing of those kids?

No.

Did you help her in anyway to get rid of her kids?

No.

Did you know or did you have any idea that she was going to do this?

No, I swear to God, I didn't know about any of these things.

OK, I understand that's she's been arrested and she's down at the Women's House of Detention. I'll make a few calls and find out when they're going to set bail. Now, Tony, in order to keep her mouth shut, you're going to have to post bail for her. And you're going to have to get her an Attorney.

OK, can you recommend anyone?

Yes, I'll call him right now and give him the information.

Ron makes his call. OK, he'll take care of the bail hearing and let us know how much it'll be. Now, I'll call the District Attorney's Office and let them know that you just got back and I'll make an appointment for us to go see him.

OK, we'll go see him this afternoon. Don't go home yet, wait until we finish with the D.A. Now, Lets go over what you're going to tell him.

Sal asks, would you like some coffee and anything to eat?

Yeah, some bagels and donuts, thanks, Sal.

While all this is going through Sal's mind, he's thinking, it's a good thing that he got his lawyer here. It doesn't look that bad right now. The big thing that he has to face now is going home. I hope that everything works out for his wife and family. Wow, I can't believe that he would go shooting his mouth off and tell Amy Collins all about Edward being tossed out the window. If that gets out, I'll be in hot water too.

Chapter 90

Amy Collins is brought to court for the bail hearing. Arthur Coffee goes into the Judge's Chambers before the court is in session.

Hey, Arthur. What brings you out here?

I'm here for the bail hearing on Amy Collins.

Hmm, I going to set bail at say, 50,000 dollars. Who's putting up the bail?

Anthony Greco.

Oh, yeah. I know him, he's that big state contractor.

Yeah, that's him.

Arthur, don't forget that testimonial dinner that's being given for me.

Oh, I didn't forget. I have two tables for myself and my family and friends.

OK, Arthur. I'll be seeing you at the dinner.

He goes out into the courtroom and over to Amy Collins.

Mrs. Collins. My name is Arthur Coffee, I'm your Attorney. I'm here for the bail hearing.

Hi, Mr. Coffee.

Now, when they call your name, we'll just go up and stand in front of the judge. Don't say anything. As soon as the hearing is over I'll go out and take care of the paper work and then I'll take you home.

Amy Collins.

That's us.

The District Attorney reads the charges against her.

The judge says, I set bail at 50,000.

Next.

The court officer comes over to her.

Just go with him and don't say anything unless I'm present.

That didn't take too long, did it? Lets go and I'll take you to your mother's house. Tony will be in touch with you in a few days. Take this money and try to stay away from your old friends and the clubs. The cops will be following you everywhere you go and your mother's phone will probably be tapped. Here we are, I'll see you soon.

Arthur Coffee calls Tony's Lawyer. Hi, this is Arthur Coffee. Is Ron there?

Hi, Arthur. How did everything go?

Very good, the judge set bail at 50,000.

Wow, that's all. That's great. Did you take her home?

Yeah, I dropped her off at her mothers place.

Drop by my office tomorrow so we can both go over a few things.

OK. I'll see you.

Tony, Amy is out on bail. You might as well go home and see your family.

Yeah, you're right. Could you drive me home, Sal.

Sure, lets go. They get into the car and Sal drives him home. Here we are.

Thanks, Sal. I be in touch with you tomorrow.

Tony walks over and opens the door. Everybody starts screaming, it's unbelievable.

Sal puts the car in gear. I'm getting out of there before anybody sees me. Poor, Tony. This is probably the worst day of his life. I'd better get in touch with Corporal and let him know what's going on. I'll go to my office and see what else is happening. He goes in, nobody here, just as well. He checks his messages, nothing important but here's one from Ernie. I'd better call him right away.

Hi, Tiny. this is Sal. Could I talk to Ernie?

Hey, Sal. Corporal wants to see you, Tony and Chris in the morning.

OK, Ernie. We'll be there.

I'll call Chris and give him the message. Forget about Tony, he's got enough trouble.

Chris, this is Sal. I just checked in with Ernie. Corporal wants to see us in the morning?

OK, I'll meet you there about ten. Anything else?

Yeah, Tony's lawyer took care of that other thing and how about that package?

It's done.

Man O man, what a day. I'll grab a bite to eat and hit the sack.

Chapter 91

Sal and Chris both arrive at the Zerega at about the same time. Tiny lets them in.

The bosses are waiting. They both go over and hug and kiss Corporal and then hug Ernie and Vito.

Where's Tony, asks Corporal?

He's got some big problems at his home right now. I don't think he'll be making it over here today.

Corporal really looks mad.

Sit down. We can't afford this kind of bullshit. Listen and listen carefully. It brings a lot of unwanted attention. It's bad for business. When you guys came into the family you took an oath that you would never let your dirty laundry smear the family and that you would be loyal and never dishonor this family. Well, two of you are responsible for bringing the cops and newspapers close to our front door. They're starting to look real close at our family. I want the three of you to get this mess cleaned up. How could you get involved with this tramp that murdered her two children. You guys are a disgrace to this family. And I going to tell you, I don't ever want to hear of that woman being on Arthur Avenue again. If I do, you'll all wish that you were never born. I don't want any of this crap to interfere with our business or operations.

Now, Chris. tell me your side of the story.

There's nothing to tell, I made some mistakes and it'll never happen again.

Sal, I know that you had nothing to do with that woman, but these are your friends and Business Associates. Didn't you see what was going on? You should have warned them

that she was trouble. I want to remind the both of you one
more time, this is a serious business that we're involved with.
We can't tolerate any more mistakes like this again. You put
all of us in harms way. Now, I want to hear how you plan to
clean this up.

We're taking care of the people over in the Queens and
Bronx District Attorneys Offices, answers Sal. Tony has his
lawyers handling the Amy Collins case. As far as the family
goes, it is not involved.

OK, Sal, for the time being I don't want any business handled here at the Zerega. All collections go to Abe and Al.

Chris, go home now and take care of your family. Take
them out for dinner. As a matter of fact take them to the
Allerton Steak House. Let everyone know that there's no trouble in the family. Keep me posted about Tony's family. And
Sal, I want you to keep an eye on things and don't let this thing
interfere with our business.

They both go to Corporal and hug and kiss him and then
hug the bosses and leave.

Chris, lets go have a drink at Gino's.

Yeah, that's a good idea, I'll follow you.

They go in and sit at the bar and order a drink.

Chris, I thought the both of us were dead. Corporal is really
pissed off. I don't think I've ever seen him this mad, says Sal.
The bosses were just waiting for Corporal to give them the go
ahead and they would have killed us on the spot. Let me tell
you, if we weren't bringing in the money, we'd all be dead by
now. I hope that everything will be OK for Tony and his
family.

Sal gets a phone call from Tony. Sal, Marie just collapsed
and we had to take her to the hospital. She's in the emergency
ward right now, wait a minute, hold on, the doctor just came
out. Sal, I'm gonna have to call you back. She had a heart
attack and they're taking her up to the Intensive Care Unit.

Poor Marie. I hope she'll be alright. Sal calls Chris and
tells him about Marie.

Oh, that's awful. What hospital did they take her to?

Einstein Medical Center. Tony had to run, he said that he would call me back as soon as he finds out about her. Chris, do you think all this with Amy caused this to happen to Marie.

I dunno. I just hope she'll be alright.

OK, Chris. I'll call you back as soon as I hear from Tony.

Chris goes into the living room and tells Eileen about Marie.

Oh, my God. Poor Marie and her boys. What can we do?

Right now, nothing, we have to hope and pray to God that she'll be alright.

Chris is thinking, if Eileen ever found out that I was involved with Amy, she would kill me. I better hope that she keeps her mouth shut. She knows everything. I had to go shoot off my mouth to impress her and I told her everything about Corporal and the family. If they ever find out, my life isn't worth a plug nickel.

A thought occurs to Sal. Detective Murphy and District Attorney Drew are preparing the charges to send to the Grand Jury. They'll send them back by tomorrow. They might have enough to charge her with murder and get a conviction. When she finds out she's going to be tried for murder, she'll probably try to cut a deal to save her own skin. No matter what, They'll get a conviction. Now, they'll keep up the pressure on everyone that she had anything to do with.

The phone rings. Sal, she's dead. Marie's dead. Sal, she's gone. They couldn't save her. Sal, the last thing she said to me was. I forgive you and I love you, Tony.

Sal, I caused all this. I'll never forgive myself for this. How will I live without her? My sons must hate me. Oh, Sal. I don't know that to do.

Tony, I'll come over and get you.

Thanks, Sal. But not yet. I want to stay with Marie and my sons for awhile. I'll call you later.

Chris, it's Sal. Marie died.

What?

Yeah, she passed away, it was so sudden. Tony is there with her and his sons. When he called me back, I couldn't believe what he was telling me. He's in a state of shock right now. I asked him if he would like to have me come over and get him.

Yeah, that was nice of you.

He wants to stay there for awhile and he said he'll call me back.

Chris goes into the living room and tells Eileen, Marie just passed away.

Oh, my God. I can't believe what you just said. Oh, no. This can't be. Eileen breaks out into tears.

The phone rings. Chris, It's Kenny. Tony Jr. just called and told me that his mother just passed away. He wants you to call him.

Chris feels sick to his stomach, his mind is starting to run wild. What the heck is happening? I better get control of myself.

Chapter 92

I think I'll go by the Zerega and say hello and see what's going on.

Hey, Sal. How you doin?

Pretty good, Ernie. How about yourself?

Good, how's Tony taking everything?

He's all broken up about Marie.

Yeah, my wife and I are going over to pay our respects later. You know, Corporal's wife Sally and Marie were very tight. This is affecting everyone.

Sit down here, Sal. We know that you had nothing to do with this tramp Amy. You gotta understand, we don't care what any of you guys do with your private lives, but a thing like this can never be allowed to happen again. From now on you're gonna have to keep an eye on both of them. If you see or hear anything that's not kosher with them, you hafta tell Corporal and me. I'm making you responsible for them. All of you are good earners, but if anybody does something to bring this family down, they'll pay the price. After the funeral is over, I want Tony to come in here for a talk.

OK, Ernie. I'll take care of it. I just stopped in to say hello, I'll be leaving now, I've got to take care of some business.

Sal leaves and goes to his office. Along the way, a thought comes to him, Ernie was warning me that someone could be killed. There won't be a next time. As he said, they'll pay the price. That sent a chill up my spine. He goes into his office. Any messages?

Yes, a few. I put them on your desk. He goes in and sits down. There's one from Chris.

Hey, Chris. It's Sal.

Chris tells him, I just got a call from Dennis. The shit really hit the fan. Tony has to appear in court as a material witness. They're going to put him through the wringer. But, he's going to be able to keep the lid on us.

Chris, come over to my office and we can talk.

OK, I'll be there in a few minutes.

What does he mean, they're gonna keep the lid on us? I had nothing to do with that bitch. There's a knock on his door.

Come in. Boy, that was fast. Sit down and tell me what else Dennis had to say?

Dennis said, Tony has some very good lawyers and he's gonna walk away from all of this, but not before they really drag him through the mud. They won't be able to connect him to the murder of the kids, but it's gonna be pretty ugly.

Sal asks, what's this about Dennis saying he's going to keep the lid on us?

Sal, I told you about me running around with Amy.

Yeah, and I told you that it was a bad idea.

Yeah, you were right, I should have listened to you. I didn't tell you the other thing. I was with her one night and I had a little to much to drink. I was bragging to her about Corporal and how we're connected. I told her about Stanley Shaffer and how we got rid of the witness.

Holy shit, you told her about that?

Yeah, I thought nothing of it at the time.

Do you know what you've done to us. If that ever gets out, we're dead. We can't go to anybody about this. That bitch has us wrapped around her little finger. You can't tell Tony that you were nailing her. That would be the end of our business deals with him. We're in some fix. You better get the word to her that if she keeps quite about us we'll help her out. In the meantime, take care of Dennis and his guys.

Yeah, he wants me to bring them another five thousand today.

Well, you'd better get on your way with the money for them. Let me think about this for awhile and after you drop off the money, come back here and we'll figure out our next move.

Chris leaves and Sal is thinking, I'm in this up to my eyes. We'd better come up with something to get us out of this.

Chapter 93

Weeks go by and things are starting to settle down. Tony's wife is buried and the newspapers are starting to zero in on Amy. It seems like they think that she is just a frustrated housewife that lost it and she killed her kids in a moment of rage. The lawyers that Tony got for her are really doing a good job. They're practically getting the public to feel sorry for her and putting all the blame on her husband for her frustration and temporary insanity. The judge is leaning towards her and rendering decisions in her favor. The District Attorney is going nuts, he can't get her to turn on anybody and she won't admit to anything. She keeps on saying that someone kidnapped her children and the DA can't get anybody to say anything.

Sal knows the truth. Tony and me were at my house one night after his wife was buried, the both of us were talking and drinking.

Sal, I gotta tell somebody and you're the only one that I really trust. Amy told me who helped her. It was Joey and he was there when she killed her son and that he helped her to get rid of their bodies. I went to Moe and asked him to have his guys kill Joey and dump his body over in Jersey. That was the end of the only person that was witness to what happened that night. I made a big mistake with her.

Amy and me were drinking and fooling around one night and she was asking me some questions about the people that I do business with. Well, I told her a few things that I shouldn't have. One of those things was about the witness against Stanley Shaffer and how we had him thrown out the window of the Concourse Plaza Hotel and who did it.

Sal can't believe what he's hearing. The both of them, Tony and Chris don't know about each other telling her the same story. That's hot shit. What a pair of numbskulls. She's pretty slick. She'll get away with murder and hold that shit over their heads for the rest of their lives. It's hard to believe that she pulled this off. She's a low life bitch and the most cold blooded killer that I ever came across in my whole life.

Tony went on to tell me, I once told her that if she wasn't married and didn't have kids and if I wasn't married, I would marry her. I was only trying to get her as a steady piece of ass. She really believed that. She's out of her mind and dangerous. Now she's got this hanging over my head. I don't know what to do about this. I spoke to her lawyer and he told me she's going to be convicted on circumstantial evidence and that she'll receive about seven years. She'll do about four years and then they'll let her go.

After this whole thing is over, she's got it in her mind that we're going to get married. What am I gonna do?

Right now, I don't have a clue. Try and take it easy, this trial is going to go on for awhile. Keep on taking care of her. She's not going to dump on anyone. I'm sure her lawyer told her the same thing that you told me. She's no fool and she knows that she has you by the balls. So, live with it. For the time being, just don't rock the boat.

I gotta go now, thanks for listening to me, Sal. Please don't ever repeat what I told you.

You know me. I would never dream of anything like that, I swear on my mother's grave.

Thanks, Sal. I know that I can trust you. Tony leaves.

Whoa, Tony really dropped the whole thing on me. I must look like the Father Confessor. What a tangled mess Tony and Chris got themselves into. Tony better be careful, he might be the next one on her hit list.

Chapter 94

Chris, there's no one around here so we can talk. Sal tells him, you had better change your life around, and I'm telling you this for your own good. If you ever mention what I'm telling you now, I'll deny it. Corporal and Ernie are watching you. If you step out of line, they'll get rid of you. Tony doesn't know anything about you and Amy. If he ever finds out, he's liable to do something to you. This is going to go on forever, so you better think twice before you do something that you might regret. Remember your family, don't do anything that might hurt them.

Yeah, your right, replies Chris, thanks for telling me. I'll never mention our talk to anyone. Tony said that he might stop by and see how everything is coming along.

Have you seen Dennis lately?

Yeah, Sal. He and his friends are bleeding me to death. Now it's five thousand every two weeks, but it's better than having the newspapers splashing it all over the front pages. I guess it'll go on until Amy goes to jail. Corporal wants all the guys that are married to go to the Allerton Steak House on Mother's Day.

Sal says, well that leaves me out, I'm not married.

Amy is out on bail and I hope Tony stays away from her, if he don't, there's going to be a lot of trouble. The cops will be following her day and night until she goes back to court for sentencing.

Sal's thinking to himself about Corporal and the family, he's got them all coming back to the club. Business as usual. Ernie is telling everyone that Corporal wants all the married guys to show up at the Allerton Steak House for Mother's Day and he wants everybody to see there's no more trouble and that we are one big happy family again. Corporal is one smart guy, instead of staying angry with what happened, he's showing everyone that we're back on track and moving on.

Dennis is with his buddies at the DA Office. We should let up on Chris, this whole thing is just about dead and she's going to jail, so I think that this should be the last payday.

A few of them object, but the majority say, we got enough. Lets not bleed the guy to death.

Chris delivers the package to Dennis, and he tells him. Chris, this is the last package.

Thanks, Dennis. I'll never forget how you and your friends helped me out.

Just stay out of trouble, Chris.

Corporal and Sally are getting ready to go over to The Allerton Steak House for Mother's Day. Sally is all dolled up and Corporal is dressed nicely. Vito is waiting downstairs for them. They come out the front door and Vito says hello to Sally and Corporal.

Hi, Vito. He helps Corporal into the car.

They arrive at the Allerton Steak House and go in. All the family and their wives are there. The bosses are there with their wives and Corporal and Sally sit down at the table with them.

The waiters start serving dinner and everyone is having a good time and a small band is playing some old Italian favorites.

All of a sudden the whole place becomes silent. The band and the singer stop playing and singing. All eyes are on the bar and no one in the place can believe what they see.

Tony and Amy Collins just walked in.

A roar goes up and the women are going wild and some of the guys are pulling out their guns and rushing towards Tony and Amy and they're intent on killing both of them.

Ernie yells, STOP, STOP.

He rushes up to Tony and Amy. Are you nuts, get her out of here quick and stay out of here.

Tony and Amy run for their life's and get into his car and drive away.

The whole place is in an uproar and all the woman in the place are screaming and yelling, KILL THEM.

Ernie gets up on the bandstand and tries to calm everyone down. He tells the band to start playing. Slowly, the crowd settles down.

Ernie tells the waiters to bring Champagne for everyone. He tells the guests that there was a big mistake and Tony was invited in error. Please enjoy the rest of your dinners and have a good time and he proposes a toast to all the Wonderful Wives and Mother's at this enjoyable event.

Corporal says nothing about Tony. He tells Sally, here's to my beautiful wife. Salute.

Ernie is thinking to himself, I should kill that son of a bitch and his whore.

The day comes to a close and everyone goes over and kisses and hugs Corporal. All the ladies go to Sally and hug and kiss her too.

Ernie, you handled everything nicely.

Ernie calls Tony, get over here quick.

You mean right now?

Yeah, right now.

Tony gets into his car and drives over to the Zerega as fast as he can.

Ernie, Vito, Moe and Abe are there.

Sit down.

Tony sits down and doesn't utter a word.

Ernie asks him, what the hell is wrong with you, you wanna get killed? Why did you bring that bitch there today?

Tony answers, I didn't know that you guys were having a big party.

What? Today is Mother's Day. Corporal has a big dinner every Mother's Day at The Allerton Steak House. You should know that.

I forgot it was Mother's Day and nobody told me about the dinner.

Ernie is glaring at him. I can't believe that happened. Corporal is really pissed off. I'll talk to him about this. I'm gonna give you a piece of advice. Stay away from that tramp.

Sal is thinking about what happened on Mother's Day. Tony told me the whole story, it's a wonder that the both of them weren't killed by them.

Amy finally gets sentenced and is sent to an upstate prison for women and Tony visits her every chance he gets. He has no choice, she has the goods on him and he has to keep her happy or he's up the creek.

Years later, she finally gets out of prison and she asks Tony. Are you going to keep your promise?

He starts hemming and hawing, I can't do that right away, we have to wait awhile.

Tony goes to see Corporal. He tells him the whole story and how she's pestering him to marry her. I could never do that, she'd drive me crazy every day of my life.

Corporal thinks about it for a moment. Tony, I told you this a long time ago. The family comes first. So for the continued security of this family. My decision is, you're gonna have to marry her.

No. Please Corporal, not that. There must be another way.

Tony, she has to much on you and the family. If something happened to her, I'm certain that she has letters ready to be sent to the cops about you and the whole family. You're the one that caused this to happen, now you have to pay the price. Marry her and get it over with.

Sal thinks, what a price to pay. He'll have to sit there every day with her while she holds this hammer over his head. He blew it, he had everything a guy could want and now all he has is her.

Chapter 95

Hey, Mom. This is Jimmy.

It's great to hear from you. How are you?

I'm fine, Mom. How you doing?

I'm alright. I'm going to the hospital in a few days for my checkup.

What seems to be wrong?

The doctor thinks there's something wrong with my heart. He told me not to worry. He just wants to do all these tests to make sure everything is alright.

Mom, I'm coming up there. Just don't tell anybody that I'm going there. What day are you going to the hospital?

I'm going there on Thursday.

OK, Mom. I know that you'll be a little busy that day. What day will they be doing the tests?

On Friday.

OK, Mom. I'll be there on Saturday.

Oh, Jimmy. That will be wonderful, I can't wait until I see you.

I'll see you then, Mom.

Take care of yourself, Jimmy. I love you.

And I love you, Mom.

Jimmy starts getting ready to go to New York. He calls a hotel in New Jersey and makes reservations for Friday. Next he calls a car rental agency and reserves a car for Thursday. I'll just pack a bag and break the gun down into a few pieces and pack it away real good.

He and Christina go out for supper and he tells her that he's going to see his mother and he'll be gone for a few days and not to worry.

Jimmy, do you think this is the right time to go to New York?

I gotta go, it's my mother and I know that she needs me right now.

I understand, Jimmy. Do you want me to come with you?

It's nice of you to ask, but everything will be alright. I'll get to New Jersey on Thursday night and then I'll go over to New York on Saturday. I'll wear one of those hooded jackets and look like everyone else. It's real cold up there right now and everybody wears those hooded jackets.

OK, Jimmy. Please be very careful and don't take any chances. When you come back and after your mother gets out of the hospital, why don't you bring her down here?

We can get some sort of business that will keep you out of those peoples sight. Just start a new life, you have everything that you need to do it.

You're right, Christina. When I get back, how about we get married and settle down?

Oh, Jimmy. I'll marry you. Just get back here safe and sound.

OK. When I get back we'll get married when ever you say.

Christina throws her arms around him. I love you, I'll be the best wife in the whole world to you.

They call it a night and head for home.

The both of them rise early and Christina gets ready for work and Jimmy makes breakfast for the both of them.

What are you going to do today, Jimmy?

I got a few things that I have to take care of before I go to New York.

OK, Jimmy, I'll see you when I get home. Love you.

And I love you, Christina.

She leaves and Jimmy takes a shower and gets dressed. He goes outside and hails a cab. Take me to the Georgetown Gun and Firearms.

I'd like to use a range for awhile.

That'll be 25 dollars and you'll be on range five.

He sends the target down and takes aim at it. He fires the gun a few times. Hmmm, not bad, nice pattern. Lets see if I can do just as well on a quick draw. He puts the target back on the line and draws his gun real fast and shoots. Nice, good enough to take anybody down. He keeps practicing for awhile until he gets used to the gun.

Pretty good. Now, I'll just clean the gun and buy some more rounds. He brings his target up to the counter and gets a cleaning kit and a box of rounds.

That'll be forty-five dollars.

Jimmy gives him a fifty dollar bill and the attendant gives him five dollars change.

Can I sit over there and clean my gun?

Sure, Mr. Martin. Go right ahead.

Jimmy breaks the gun down and cleans it real good. Then he puts it back together and puts it into his shoulder holster.

I handled that gun pretty good. Now I'm ready to go to New York. I think I'll just walk a little bit just to feel how it is to have this gun on me.

It's a nice brisk day and after walking for about 30 minutes he hails a cab and tells the driver to take him home.

When Christina gets home, he kisses her and tells her that he is going to leave early in the morning. Lets eat in tonight. How about we have a Pizza?

Yeah, she says, that would be nice.

After they eat, they watch some TV and then they hit the sack.

The clock rings. It's 6 o'clock and Jimmy gets up and hops into the shower and then gives himself a quick shave.

Christina is up and she makes breakfast for the two of them and they sit down at the table and eat.

Thanks for making breakfast, Christina. When I get to Jersey I'll give you a call. I'll get going now.

Jimmy, promise me that you'll be careful and get back here as soon as you can.

I will. I love you, Christina.

I love you too, Jimmy.

Jimmy goes downstairs and hails a cab.

Take me to the airport. I'm picking up a car. Off they go, they get there in about 25 minutes.

Jimmy gets his bag and goes inside the car rental office.

Good morning. How can I help you?

I have a reservation for a car.

Name? John Martin.

OK. May I see your license and credit card?

Alright, here's your license and credit card and papers. The car will be here in a minute. Have a nice trip and fill the gas tank before you turn it in.

Jimmy walks to the door and here comes the car. He walks over to the car and the attendant gives him the keys and Jimmy hands him a few dollars and puts his bag into the trunk.

He puts the car in gear and takes off for route 95. Traffic is starting to build up. Once I get out of Washington, the traffic should die down. He gets to the Jersey Turnpike in about four hours. A couple of more hours and I'll be in Fort Lee and I'll check into the motel.

Nearly in Fort Lee. That wasn't a bad trip. I'll go to the motel and check in and then I'll get a bite to eat.

He checks in and follows the bellboy to his room.

Thanks, here's something for you, Jimmy hands him a few dollars.

He opens his bag and gets his gun and then he goes over to the desk and assembles the gun and puts it into his shoulder holster. Then he stands in front of the mirror and says to himself, you'd never know that I was packing. Now, I'll get something to eat and pick up a newspaper. After having a bite to eat and picking up a few newspapers, he goes back to the motel.

I think I'll grab a nap and then take a look at the papers. When he wakes up it's about eight o'clock. I'd better call Christina, I don't want to have her get worried.

Hello, Christina. I'm in Jersey.

Hi, Jimmy. How was the trip?

It was a nice trip.

How's everything, Christina?

Good, no problems. I'm just here thinking about you.

Don't worry. Everything will be fine. After I see my mother I'll start back. I'll call you tomorrow. Sleep well, I love you.

And I love you.

Jimmy looks over the newspapers. Nothing of interest. He turns on the TV and finds a cowboy movie and settles in to enjoy the movie.

The phone rings. It's six thirty.

Jimmy gets up and showers and shaves. He finishes and gets dressed. Now I'll get something to eat and go over to the hospital.

After breakfast, he calls the hospital and asks what room his mother is in.

She's in 507 and visiting hours are from nine till nine.

I'll get over there about eleven. This way I won't bump in to anybody.

It's funny how fate is. Corporal is going to Montifiore Hospital this morning for a check up. He's going to be put in a room on the fifth floor, Room 515 and his wife and Vito and Ernie are going to be with him when he checks in.

Nobody suspects that there's going to be a hit on Corporal. The family from New Jersey want to get even with him for taking out some of their guys and anyway, they think this is a good time to get rid of him. Ernie is going to be the new Boss and they think that they can get rid of him too.

Nobody knows that Corporal is headed for the hospital, so they think. It leaked out somehow, and now that bunch in Jersey see their opportunity to gain control of the Bronx and Manhattan. The trap is about to be sprung.

Jimmy gets to the hospital and parks his car in the hospital parking lot. He goes to the fifth floor and waits at the nurse's station while his mother is still with the doctor in her room.

Corporal gets off the elevator on the fifth floor with his wife Sally along with Ernie and Vito.

At the same time four guys from the Jersey family get off a different elevator down the hall.

They spot Corporal and pull out their guns and start running towards him.

Jimmy is standing right there watching all this start to happen. He whips out his gun and runs over and stands in front of Corporal to protect him and he starts firing at them.

The guys from the Jersey family are firing away at Corporal and Jimmy.

Ernie and Vito are shooting away at the guys from Jersey and they both are hit, but they continue firing until they run out of ammunition

The guys from Jersey all got hit and they are either dead or bleeding to death.

Corporal is alright, they never hit him because of Jimmy protecting him.

Sally is screaming and there's so much panic. Everyone is yelling and screaming and running for their life.

Jimmy is wounded and down on the floor. Blood is running from his side.

Jimmy, what are you doing here? You saved my life.

Vito and Ernie come running over. It's Jimmy, He saved Corporal's life.

Ernie looks at Jimmy. I can't believe this. Where did he come from?

Jimmy, where are you hurt?

My chest.

The doctors run over. They examine him. Quick, get him into surgery right away.

Jimmy says, please have my mother come here, she's in room 507.

Ernie runs to her room. Come with me quick, your son had an accident and he's asking for you.

She goes with Ernie and sees Jimmy laying on the floor bleeding.

Jimmy, Jimmy. Oh, my God. What did they do to you?

Oh, Mom. I'm sorry for all the trouble I caused you. Please forgive me.

Three hospital attendants pick Jimmy up and take him to surgery.

Ernie is holding on to Jimmy's mother.

Corporal tells Jimmy's mother. He saved my life. He came out of nowhere.

Jimmy's mom tells him, he was coming to see me.

You don't recognize me, do you? It was a long time ago. After you came out of the Army, you and I met and went together for awhile. I never told you that Jimmy is your son. I left you because I didn't want our son to become like you.

You're Josephine. Now I remember. Corporal is in shock.

Oh, God. Jimmy is my son. Please forgive me and please don't let my son die.

Jimmy's mother is helped over to the surgery waiting room by Ernie.

After about six hours, Jimmy is brought out and taken to the ICU.

The doctor comes over and tells them. It'll be a little while before he comes to.

Corporal is still in a state of shock. The doctors want to get him into his room.

No, I want to stay here with Jimmy.

Vito and Ernie have been taken care of and patched up.

Finally, Jimmy comes out of his sleep.

Mom, it's good to see you.

Oh, Jimmy. I love you. She holds his hand and they talk for a little while.

The doctor comes in and asks everyone to leave.

I'll be right outside, says Jimmy's Mom

They all go outside and the doctor tells them. He's in serious condition. We're doing everything we can to save his life. It doesn't look to good.

Oh, please doctor, don't let him die.

The doctor tells her, we'll do everything we can to save your son's life.

Sally is talking to Corporal. Please, honey, don't blame yourself. You didn't know about Jimmy. We have to pray for him.

After a few hours, the doctor comes out.

You'd better go in, he going fast.

Mom, I leaving now, I want you to know that I love you and don't cry for me. Please kiss me goodbye and I'll be waiting for you up in heaven.

Oh, Jimmy. I love you and she kisses him.

Oh, no. My Jimmy is gone.

Corporal and the rest of them go over and kiss Jimmy on his cheek.

Tears are running down Corporal's cheeks.

It's all my fault. I went into this business and this was my reward. Oh, dear God. Can you ever forgive me.

www.ingramcontent.com/pod-product-compliance
Lightning Source LLC
Chambersburg PA
CBHW051747040426

42446CB00007B/253